LULU'S PROVENÇAL TABLE

Also by Richard Olney

Simple French Food
French Menu Cookbook
Yquem
Romanée-Conti
Ten Vineyard Lunches
Provence the Beautiful Cookbook
Principal Consultant, *The Good Cook* (27 volumes)

Lulu's Provençal Table

The Exuberant Food and Wine
from Domaine Tempier Vineyard

Richard Olney

Foreword by Alice Waters
Photographs by Gail Skoff

HarperCollins*Publishers*

HarperCollins books may be purchased for educational, business, or sales promotional use. For information please write: Special Markets Department, HarperCollins Publishers, Inc., 10 East 53rd Street, New York, NY 10022.

FIRST EDITION

Designed by Patricia Curtan

LIBRARY OF CONGRESS CATALOGING-IN-PUBLICATION DATA

Olney, Richard
    Lulu's provençal table : the exuberant food and wine from Domaine Tempier Vineyard / by Richard Olney ; foreword by Alice Waters ; photographs by Gail Skoff.
        p. cm.
    Includes index.
    ISBN 0-06-016922-2
    1. Cookery, French—Provençal style. 2. Domaine Tempier.
I. Title
TX719.2.P75046 1994
641.59449—dc20   93-39155

94 95 96 97 98 RRD 10 9 8 7 6 5 4 3 2 1

Acknowledgments

My gratitude is due, above all, to Madame Lucien Peyraud—Lulu—who, for well over a year, willingly sacrificed weekly afternoons to visit me and to chat about the food that she has cooked for family and friends and the life that she has led with them for fifty years and more, to Lucien Peyraud, the impassioned and adorable patriarch of Bandol wine, and to all the Peyraud family, most especially Jean-Marie and his wife, Catherine, François and his wife, Paule, and Laurence Peyraud. Fleurine, Marion, Colette, and Véronique have all contributed, as well as numerous grandchildren, Zavier, Jérome, Valérie, and Florence, among others.

Alice Waters, whose enthusiasms tolerate no checks and whose love for the Peyraud family, of Lulu's table, and the wines of Domaine Tempier knows no bounds, deserves credit for having insisted that I write the book and for having placed me in the hands of her agent, Susan Lescher. Kermit Lynch, who imports something more than a third of Domaine Tempier's production into the United States and who, with his wife, Gail Skoff, and their children, spends half the year amid the vines of Bandol, joined his enthusiasm to Alice's to create a formidable barrage.

I am grateful to Gail Skoff, with whom I worked closely in the choice of subjects and of final photographs, for her suppleness and for the lovely clarity of her work, and to Patricia Curtan for the beauty of the book design.

Finally, I owe a great thank-you to my editor, Susan Friedland, for putting up with my unorthodox, pre-computer-age methods of writing and for her admirable restraint in the use of the "blue pencil."

The sign, depicting the Tempier bottle label, at the entrance to the domaine.

CONTENTS

The tree-lined entrance to the domaine.

FOREWORD
by Alice Waters

I MET the Peyrauds, the proprietors of Domaine Tempier, for the first time in the mid-seventies. I was introduced by Richard Olney, a mentor, who by then had been a neighbor and a friend of the family for years, and who had been a welcome guest at Domaine Tempier long before that. I felt as if I had walked into a Marcel Pagnol film come to life. Lucien and Lulu's warmhearted enthusiasm for life, their love for the pleasures of the table, their deep connection to the beautiful earth of the South of France—these were things I had seen at the movies. But this was for real. I felt immediately as if I had come home to a second family.

I'm not sure what they saw in me. I could barely speak passable French, and I had no credentials as a restaurateur or wine expert, but they embraced me and seated me at Lucien's right hand, opposite Lulu. I remember the whole family was there and that Lucien, as he has done ever since, fed me the very best bits. (If there are sea urchins, for example, he will butter a piece of bread and make me a little sandwich piled with their roe.) I tried to stutter in French my thanks and feelings of unworthiness, and Lulu leaned sympathetically toward me and said, "Don't worry. I understand everything."

Ever since, every time I have arrived at Domaine Tempier, the entire Peyraud family has understood everything and has made me feel totally at ease. There was the summer we showed up on the first day that a fierce mistral had started to blow. How had Lulu foreseen the change in the weather and before the boats all had to be tied up, managed to get together the fish for the bouillabaisse I had been dreaming of? There was the sweltering afternoon in the summer of '93 when my husband, ten-year-old daughter, and I arrived exhausted, to be revived after a few hours of privacy and napping by an open air supper of soupe au pistou, fresh figs and cheese, and an apricot and green almond compote. The first glass of rosé (and second and third) could not have been more refreshing if it had been the coolest mountain spring water. Always we are treated like long-lost children home for a visit, and always we are immersed in the same hospitality and the luxurious feeling of being at home. Lulu assures me that my French is very much improved. Lucien offers a wise toast at table that reminds us of the transcendental virtue of wine and food and friendship united. Jean-Marie, the son who vinifies the Domaine's incomparable wines, predictably waxes poetic about the gratifyingly high degree of alcohol in this year's vintage. And Lucien, just as predictably, reminds us that wine is nothing without balance and finesse.

The wines of Domaine Tempier were on the wine list at Chez Panisse long before I met their makers. Gerald Asher was the first to import them, and he has written eloquently about Bandol and the Peyrauds. Robert Parker, the wine writer and critic, has called Bandol "the most privileged of Provence's appellations," and ranks Tempier as its sole "outstanding" producer. However, it is thanks to my friend the wine importer Kermit Lynch that the red and rosé wines of Domaine Tempier are now probably more famous and more beloved in America than in France. Because of his passion for the flavors and sensations of Bandol, Kermit now makes his home there half the year. Because of his enthusiastic promotion of Bandol and the influence of its flavors, a new generation of talented wine makers in California has planted many new vineyards of Mourvèdre (the grape that is the essence of Bandol) and are also happily harvesting fruit from recently rediscovered venerable plantings of Mataro (the state's legal name for Mourvèdre). I think this is as exciting a change in direction for California wine making as the shift to Cabernet and Chardonnay was a generation ago, and not only because these wines go so well with the kind of simple, garlicky food I love to cook at Chez Panisse.

How wonderful to have Lulu and her daughter-in-law Paule as our guests in Berkeley a few years ago, and how gratifying and heartwarming to see her greeted by wine makers and wine lovers with great outpourings of affection and recognition. We served a week of Provençal dinners in their honor with menus inspired by the cuisine of Domaine Tempier. At every dinner, Lulu graciously accepted the homage aimed her way. And every afternoon, she and Paule could not be talked out of helping us peel garlic, bone sardines, and shell peas and fava beans.

Lulu's indefatigable spirit in the kitchen and her recipes transcribed here so lovingly and accurately by Richard Olney represent to me the apotheosis of what is often called in France *"la cuisine de bonne femme."* Lulu always seems to know precisely what to do, effortlessly, without ever overdoing it. It amazes me how she is always present at the table, whether she's cooking for a party of twenty or a party of three. I remember one late evening when Lulu had not expected us for supper but nevertheless insisted on cooking us a little something. She had a basket of wild mushrooms that she proceeded to quickly brush off and then sauté with garlic and lots of herbs. Although she seemed to be cooking them almost unconsciously, chatting away with us over a welcoming glass of rosé, they were probably the most flavorful wild mushrooms I have ever eaten. Her food is often earthy, always delicious, and always appropriate to the moment.

In part it has to do with the impeccable ingredients she chooses. She goes to the fish market in town just as the boats are coming in and the fishermen dump their catch onto outdoor tables under a canopy of plane trees. The fish are still jumping around and the crabs are trying to crawl back to the sea. Lulu never knows what she's going to make until she's been to the market. There may not be much choice, but if she finds the right fish she might stuff it with the fish liver, herbs, bread crumbs, and fennel and bake it in the oven. The extra-virgin olive oil she uses comes from the olives that grow at the Domaine, the herbs and fennel from the garden behind the house or growing wild on the hillsides. There may be green almonds from the property or figs from Jean-Marie and Catherine's house; the squash blossoms may come from the neighbor's little farm stand at the bottom of the hill. If the guests are very lucky, François will have been diving for sea urchins. Lulu searches for what is alive, knowing that that is *always* what tastes best. This is her particular sensibility about food—a sensitivity that seems to come to her instinctively.

The Peyraud family's example has been helping us find our balance at Chez Panisse for years. Like them, we try to live close to the earth and treat it with respect; always look first to the garden and the vineyard for inspiration; rejoice in our families and friends; and let the food and wine speak for themselves at the table.

Lunch table on the terrace, seen from beyond shuttered doors.

Domaine Tempier
The Vineyard and the Peyrauds

Domaine Tempier is a vineyard and an ancient dwelling, nestled in the hillsides outside the neighboring fishing ports of Bandol and Sanary, some ten miles from Toulon and thirty miles from Marseilles. The oldest part of the house, in which, today, are installed the officcs and tasting rooms, dates from before the French Revolution. The living quarters were built in 1834 by the Rounard family, whose daughter, Léonie, received the domaine as part of her dowry at the time of her marriage to François Tempier. Léonie and François Tempier were the great-grandparents of Madame Lucien Peyraud, born Lucie Tempier and known to Lucien, to five daughters, two sons, fourteen grandchildren, several great-grandchildren, and to adepts of wine and food the world round, as Lulu.

Domaine Tempier is also the Peyraud family, impassioned, exuberant, indefatigable, dedicated to the belief that the meaning of life lies in love and friendship and that these qualities are best expressed at table. Perhaps love and friendship can never be quite the same in the absence of the cicada's chant, of fresh sweet garlic and voluptuous olive oil, of summer-ripe tomatoes and the dense, spicy, wild fruit of the wines of Domaine Tempier, which reflect the scents of the Provençal hillsides and joyously embrace Lulu's high-spirited cuisine. For Lulu, cuisine is a language, the expression of love; for Lucien, wine is the expression of love. In Provence, cuisine and wine are as inseparable as Lulu and Lucien.

Lucien Peyraud and his twin, Louis, were born December 16, 1912, in Saint-Etienne. Their parents dealt in silks and ribbons. Neither twin wanted ribbons—Louis evolved toward industrial engineering; Lucien's passion was agriculture, which rapidly became centered on viticulture. After two years at the Ecole Supérieure d'Agriculture in Aix-en-Provence, Lucien spent the early 1930s doing apprenticeships in vineyards and fruit orchards in the region around Aix and by a stint of obligatory military service. In 1935, in Sanary, where his parents rented a summer villa, Lucien encountered, on a diving board, a lovely seventeen-year-old wisp of a girl, Lucie Tempier. The effect was explosive.

Lucie Tempier was born December 11, 1917, in Marseilles. Her father, Alphonse Tempier, owned a leather-importing firm that had been in the family since before the Revolution, but his great love was painting and his idol was the Aixois painter, Cézanne. The Tempiers spent Sundays and summer holidays in Sanary, in the family villa, which Alphonse Tempier had built before the First World War, at the summit of the colline de Notre Dame-de-Pitié, next to the sixteenth-century chapel of the same name, with a sheer view of the port and a sweeping view of the surrounding mountains. Inspired by her father, whom she adored, Lulu was studying art at the Ecole des Beaux-Arts in Aix-en-Provence when she and Lucien met. They were married October 17, 1936, in the chapel of Notre Dame-de-Pitié. In the family album, beneath the photo of the radiant couple leaving the chapel, the date is inscribed in Lulu's hand, followed by a great exclamation point.

Wedding pictures and mementos from the family album.

Lulu and Lucien at Domaine Tempier in the spring of 1936.

Lucien, Lulu, and Lucien's twin, Louis, 1936.

Lucien was out of work. He settled for a job with an irascible proprietor of fig and cherry orchards in Solliès-Pont, a village in the Gapeau valley, not far from Toulon. He recalls with distaste the large, black, tasteless figs, picked under-ripe to be shipped off to London and Paris ("Poor city-folk—nothing like wrinkled gray figs with pearls of honey escaping, picked ripe from the trees!"). The first child, Fleurine, was born March 1, 1938 (all the children were born in Marseilles, where Lulu spent a month after each delivery with her parents). Three years of fig culture were more than enough; at the beginning of 1939, Lucien agreed to momentarily abandon agriculture and to join his father-in-law in the leather-importing firm. Jean-Marie was born April 12. On September 3, France declared war on Germany and Lucien was mobilized.

July 10, 1940, marked the end of the Third Republic and the installation of the Vichy government. Lucien was demobilized July 14. At the same time, Alphonse Tempier offered Lucien and Lulu the Domaine Tempier. François was born July 26, 1940.

Lulu's father had inherited the domaine from his grandmother, Léonie, at her death in 1917. The wine was sold in bulk, in Marseilles for the most part, until the depression of the 1930s, when everything began to collapse. Alphonse Tempier, whose occupations in Marseilles obliged him to farm out the domaine, had all but seven of the twenty-three acres of vineyard torn up and replanted to peach trees. The farmer, who preferred vines to fruit trees, moved to a neighboring property. Like most rural properties at that time, there was no electricity, water was brought up from a well by a hand pump, and of course, there was no telephone. Lucien bought a cow to provide milk for the children and a horse to pull a plow and to transport peaches to the market. Food was scarce. Lulu says, "It seemed like the only thing there was plenty of was Jerusalem artichokes. Lucien used to bring home cartloads of them to feed the cow and he would say, 'Choose the best for the family,

Lulu.' After the war, no one wanted ever again to taste a Jerusalem artichoke."

Despite deprivation and uncertainty about the future, excitement was in the air around Bandol when Lucien and Lulu settled in with the family at Domaine Tempier. André Roethlisberger was the Swiss proprietor of Château Milhière, near Sanary. His wines, at that time, were the best in the region (the property has since disappeared, victim of shabby housing developments). He had studied the history of Bandol wine and was determined to raise the overall quality to that of the past. His goal was for BANDOL to be recognized as an "Appellation d'Origine Contrôlée" (AOC) by the Institut National des Appellations d'Origine (INAO), an official organization created in 1935 that imposes complex, quality-related strictures on all French wines or brandies granted AOC status. In 1939, André Roethlisberger had created, with the few other proprietors who believed—or wanted to believe—in his dream, a syndicate for the improvement and promotion of Bandol wine (it was usually referred to as the Syndicat des Anciens Vins de Bandol because its official name, Le Syndicat des Producteurs des Vins Fins de la Région Historique des Vins de Bandol, was too much of a mouthful to pronounce). This was wonderful bait for Lucien. He bit hard and has never since loosened his grip; he became André Roethlisberger's confidant, colleague, and successor.

THE WINE OF BANDOL

Today, as in centuries past, the wines called "Bandol" come mostly from a cluster of communities surrounding Bandol, the port from which they were once shipped. Bandol also occupies center stage in the natural amphitheater that describes the Bandol microclimate— a basin of terraced hillsides facing the sea and surrounded by a belt

Alphonse Tempier, Lulu's father, in 1968 at the age of eighty-nine.

The domaine in 1943.

of mountains. The vines receive a maximum of sun and, at the same time, are protected from spring frosts and excessive summer heat, both by the proximity of the sea and by the mountainous barrier. The soil is arid, stony, and chalky, with a high clay content, more or less sandy—hopeless for other crops but typical of the soils that produce great wine.

During the eighteenth and nineteenth centuries, the deeply colored red wines of Bandol were celebrated for their solid structure, their finesse, and their ability to age. They were served at the table of Louis XV. A sea voyage was thought to improve them and many, which were shipped to the Antilles, were shipped back to France, rounded out by the long trip. Until shortly before the Revolution, when the port of Bandol was deepened, ships had to anchor in the harbor beyond, where kegs of wine were floated out to them. Following the Napoleonic wars, Bandol became an important cooperage center and some twelve hundred merchant ships were carrying more than six million liters of wine each year to the Caribbean, North America, Italy, and other French ports.

In 1864, phylloxera, the insidious vine root louse, mortal enemy to the many varieties of the European wine grape, arrived in the south of France on cuttings of American wild grape vines. It spread rapidly, attacking the vineyards of Provence before reaching throughout France and to vineyards around the world (it had, until then, been contained in North America, east of the Rocky Mountains, nourished by wild grape vines whose roots were immune to its effects). By 1872, the Bandol vineyards had been completely destroyed.

Immune hybrids were created; the wine was bad. Finally, the only solution was to graft European wine-grape cuttings onto root stocks developed from American wild grapes and adaptable to European vineyard soils. Bandol vineyards had been planted largely to the Mourvèdre grape, a late ripener and a low producer. For more than a century, wine authorities had been proclaiming the superiority of Mourvèdre over all other grape varieties in the vineyards of Provence and, most particularly, in those of Bandol. And yet, when it came to reconstituting the vineyards, growers chose, for the most part, to plant high production varieties of indifferent quality. Bandol's antique celebrity vanished. By the late 1930s, although the local population had begun to be proud of the wines of Château Milhière and Sanary's artists' colony (Moïse and Renée Kisling, the Aldous Huxleys, and Sybille Bedford, among others) were ravished by them, elsewhere in France Bandol was unknown.

On November 11, 1941, the INAO decreed that, henceforth, the wines of Bandol would be classed AOC: Appellation BANDOL Contrôlée. It was a great moment for André Roethlisberger, Lucien Peyraud, and a few others. The area of production was limited to appropriate soils and orientations within eight community boundaries: Bandol, Sanary, La Cadière, Le Castellet (including Le Plan du Castellet, where Domaine Tempier is located), Le Beausset, Evenos, Ollioules, and Saint-Cyr. The principal grape varieties for white wine are Ugni blanc and Clairette; for red and rosé wines, Mourvèdre, Grenache, and Cinsault. Production is limited to a maximum of forty hectoliters per hectare (about 520 gallons per acre). A surprisingly timid clause imposes a minimum of 10 percent Mourvèdre among the red varietals. Thanks to Lucien's persistence, it was raised to 20 percent, then to 30 percent. Today, red Bandol wine must contain a minimum of 50 percent Mourvèdre, the vines for red Bandol must be at least eight years old, and those for Bandol rosé or white at least four years old. Red Bandol must be raised in wood for a minimum of eighteen months; Bandol rosé and white may be bottled after six months and need no longer be raised in wood.

In 1942, Lucien acquired, with the benevolent aid of his father-in-law, fifteen acres of remarkable vineyard site within the *lieu-dit*

9

(place-name), la Migoua, situated in the steep hills of Le Beausset-Vieux, outside Le Beausset. Most of the vines, too old to produce, were torn up and replaced with Mourvèdre. On November 11, the Germans occupied the "Free Zone" of France. The following day, they arrived at the domaine in search of houses to requisition. They were dissuaded by the lack of water and electricity (and, Lulu believes, by the presence of three small children and a pregnant mother). On November 26, the French navy was scuttled in the port of Toulon and the countryside was full of sailors, fleeing for fear of being taken prisoners of war. Lulu arrived home with a half-dozen sailors and, half an hour later, Lucien arrived with as many more. "The house was transformed into a dormitory," recalls Lulu, "but of course we couldn't keep them for long because the Germans were always turning up unexpectedly."

Marion was born May 1, 1943. In October, Lucien bottled his first wine—five thousand bottles of vin rosé, "Domaine Tempier, Appellation BANDOL Contrôlée, 1942." The distinctive and lovely label, with its little woodcut of an antique frigate, framed with fleurs de lis, a sentimental souvenir of Bandol's sea voyages when France had kings, was designed by Alphonse Tempier. In November, the Allies bombed Toulon. In the eight months to follow, they continued to bomb Toulon, Marseilles, and many of the villages in the Bandol area—Sanary, La Cadière, Saint-Cyr. Free French and American troops invaded Provence August 15, 1944. Paris was liberated August 25, de Gaulle's provisional government of the French Republic was announced on September 6, and picking at Domaine Tempier began on September 18.

On March 3, 1945, Lucien was elected president of the Syndicat des Producteurs des Vins d'Appellation d'Origine Contrôlée Bandol (reelected every three years until his retirement in 1982—thirty-seven years of battle for the glory of Bandol).

On May 8, the Germans surrendered. The war was over.

Lucien and Lulu with (left to right) François, Jean-Marie, Fleurine, and Marion, 1943

Colette was born October 20, 1945. Electricity was installed and, in 1946, an open pickup truck was purchased for wine deliveries. It served also to drive the children to the beach. Lulu remembers being terrified one day, while driving with the children, to see her six-year-old, François, peering at her upside down through the windshield—it had seemed to him a good idea to crawl up on top of the moving truck.

In 1947, the telephone was installed.

Lucien was appointed to the national board of the INAO July 19, 1947. Laurence was born December 20 (there was an eight-year pause before the youngest child, Véronique, was born, January 22, 1956).

In 1949, when Lulu's father was seventy, her parents retired to the villa in Sanary (her brother took over the leather-importing firm). Her mother died in 1962, her father in 1969. Today, her brother has retired to the villa in Sanary and is replaced by his two sons, the seventh generation of Tempier leather importers.

In 1951, Lucien made his first red Bandol, thanks to the purchase of La Tourtine, seventeen acres of narrowly terraced vineyard with direct southern exposure, which slopes abruptly down from the medieval hilltown of Le Castellet (a two-and-a-half-acre parcel of forty-year-old Mourvèdre vines at the bottom of La Tourtine bears its own place-name, Cabassaou; since 1979, La Migoua, La Tourtine, and later, Cabassaou have been bottled separately). The old cellar, built in 1880 by Léonie Rounard Tempier, in which the wine is vinified, has been supplemented by a cellar, built in 1968, in which are lodged row upon row of five-thousand-liter oak tuns for raising the wines, and another cellar, built in 1989, for the storage of bottled wines. In 1980, Le Petit Moulin, fifteen acres of vineyard in La Cadière, was joined to the domaine (arriving from Toulon on the autoroute, a desecration of the Bandol vineyards against the construction of which Lucien fought in vain for years, the sudden

Lucien carrying a cornue *of grapes from the vineyard to the cellar, 1959.*

Lulu and Lucien with friends.

vision of twin hill towns rising above the landscape, La Cadière to the left and Le Castellet to the right, is startling—so beautiful that one can almost forgive the autoroute). Today, Domaine Tempier's vines cover seventy-five acres and produce an average of 120,000 bottles of red and rosé "Appellation BANDOL Contrôlée" wine per year. Depending on the *cuvée,* the red wines are composed of from 50 percent to 100 percent Mourvèdre; about 50 percent goes into the rosé. It is for good reason that Lucien is known as "the apostle of Mourvèdre," not only to his colleagues in France, but to those wherever wine is made.

Until their respective marriages, Fleurine and Marion worked in the offices at the domaine. Except for brief periods of military service during the early 1960s, Jean-Marie and François have been working at the domaine since 1960, Jean-Marie assisting Lucien in the cellars, with the help of a cellar master and another worker, while François, with two other men, tends the vines. Jean-Marie made his first wine in 1974 and today divides his time between the cellars and the commercial paperwork. He and his wife, Catherine, live in Le Beausset-Vieux, surrounded by the vines of La Migoua, where they have raised two daughters, Valérie, who has just finished her medical studies, and Florence, who is studying music in Lyons. Catherine, who is impassioned by the complexities of the computer system, shares office duties with the secretary, Annick Vuoso. François and Paule live in an eighteenth-century house in Le Castellet, overlooking the terraces of La Tourtine, where they have raised two sons, Xavier, who is winding up his studies in oenology at the University of Bordeaux, and Jérome, who is studying medicine in Marseilles. Paule travels all over France, placing the wines of Domaine Tempier in restaurant cellars. Laurence, in addition to her activities as language professor, is the resident ambassador for Domaine Tempier in Paris.

"I hope the reader won't imagine that I never do anything but cook," says Lulu. In fact, both she and Lucien, together and separately, have packed more activity into the past fifty years than seems humanly possible. In 1952, with six children between four and fourteen years old, Lulu discovered a passion for sailing. For thirty years, she kept a small sailboat in the port of Bandol: "At first, I took all the children with me, then Véronique was born, the others grew up, and for years, whenever I had a free moment, I sailed with Véronique, then Véronique grew up and I sailed alone. It was a marvelous escape."

After Véronique's birth, Lulu decided that she was not doing enough for the domaine. She became the itinerant agent-promoter, traveling, on an average, three days a week, by car as far as Lyons, by train to more distant parts of France, to visit restaurants and place Domaine Tempier in their cellars. Later she and Paule traveled together; now she and Paule have different itineraries. When she was not traveling, she was receiving. When Lulu receives, the table is laid in advance to feast the eyes of arriving guests. In good weather, the faded rose and ochre souvenirs reflected in the façade of the old house form a background to the long table on the terrace: wineglasses sparkle in the dappled light that filters through the leaves of vines and trees and a playful motif—garlands of wildflowers or a still-life of ratatouille vegetables—provides an accent of color; the tablecloth is white in deference to a wine's robe. Sometimes, Lulu is more chef than cook: Paule is often in the kitchen, Catherine arrives with sumptuous desserts that are foreign to Lulu's repertory, Jérome has perfected the techniques of mounting Lulu's aïolis and rouilles, François takes charge of open-fire roasts or grills, and Jean-Marie chooses and serves the wines.

First of all, however, Jean-Marie has arranged a tasting in the cellars. Because Lucien now suffers badly from rheumatism, an armchair is installed there. The wines tasted are the white (which Jean-Marie has been making only since 1987, in very small quantity,

Jean-Marie and Lucien tasting.

The cellar.

from the white grapes formerly pressed with red grapes for the rosé wine) and the rosé from the most recent vintage, plus five different *cuvées* of red from each of the two most recent vintages, not yet in bottles. Enthusiasm often overrides principle and Jean-Marie begins to open bottles of older vintages for purposes of comparison. For each *cuvée,* he announces the percentage of each grape variety, the sections of the vineyard on which the *cuvée classique* and the *cuvée spéciale* have been harvested (La Tourtine, La Migoua, and Le Cabassaou carry the message in the name), the age of the vines and the degree of alcohol (Lucien may exclaim, "Jean-Marie, it is the balance, not the alcohol, that is important!"). Lucien's observations range from the lyrical to the philosophical and technical; François searches out scent and taste associations—apricot blossoms, cherries, plums, bramble, wild herbs, licorice, truffles, undergrowth. Kermit Lynch, their American importer who, during six months of the year, lives a stone's throw from the Tempier vines, is often present, taking notes. The uninitiated listen and sip in wonderment until Lucien begins to draw them out, asking for their opinions, complimenting them on their insights or gently taking issue with brash judgments. If the promised "half-hour tasting" stretches beyond an hour, Lulu (who well knows that no tasting has ever been confined to half an hour) sends an envoy to the cellars with the message that the apéritif is served.

A wide-spreading maritime pine rises at the edge of the garden where the vines begin; beneath it an olive oil millstone tops a stone table base; garden chairs and benches surround it. The guests are greeted by an array of *amuse-gueules,* or appetizers, and chilled bottles of white and rosé Domaine Tempier—or Champagne; in winter, the apéritif is served in the old-fashioned salon hung with portraits of Tempier ancestors and dominated by a nineteenth-century painting, *The Return of the Prodigal Son.* Lulu insists on being with her

The wide-spreading maritime pine.

guests from the moment the apéritif is served; above all, no one must be aware that she is preoccupied with what is happening in the kitchen, that she may have been to Bandol at the break of dawn to meet the fishing boats, arriving with their night's catch, or that she may have spent hours in the kitchen before appearing, effervescent with good-natured conversation, apparently without a care in the world. Lulu's meals are, in fact, remarkable pieces of theater, the more so because no one is aware of the direction and timing. At table, different members of the family slip away from time to time to check the progress of a slow-cooking gratin or a baking fish. François may disappear for a few minutes and reappear with a platter of vine-leaf-wrapped and grilled red mullets, while Jean-Marie moves back and forth, serving one wine after the other—the year's rosé, the still untamed, youngest red wine, drawn from the tun in which it is aging and served, very cool, in pitchers, and a series, moving back in time, of older vintages, first decanted but kept cool until the service. The wine served with the cheeses is often one of the increasingly rare vintages from the 1960s, grown comfortably expansive with the autumnal scents of humus, truffles, and game birds. It amuses Jean-Marie to serve it blindly, prompting everyone to guess at the vintage; Lucien, who recognizes all of his *"enfants,"* may exclaim, "What's going on here? I thought there was no more '64 in the cellar!" The disingenuous answer, "Oh, Papa, it must have got mixed up in a bin of another vintage," is followed by a stage whisper to the guests: "I have to hide these old bottles from Lucien or there would be none left."

The animated discussions at table turn around the food, the wines, and their relations to one another. As euphoria gains ground, Lucien may ask everyone to stand while he solemnly intones the ritual toast to *"notre chère Méduse,"* figurehead of the Provençal wine confraternity, after which all present drain their glasses (*"Lampons!"*) and exclaim *"Alléluia! Alléluia!"* An old bottle from the family reserve of *vin cuit* often accompanies the dessert and, with coffee, the Domaine Tempier *marc*, a brandy distilled from grape pressings and aged for several years in oak, of which François makes one barrel a year, arrives. Brandy glasses are offered to the guests but the Peyrauds pour the *marc* into their warm cups after the last swallow of coffee.

Lulu keeps a menu diary with, for each menu, the date, the names of the guests, and the wines. Before composing a menu, a glance at the book permits her to avoid repetitions of dishes that her guests have been served on previous occasions. Sometimes a footnote to a menu tells a story: one menu, composed around a bouillabaisse for an American couple, received at the request of a common friend, is followed by the sad observation, "he is vegetarian . . . they don't speak French . . . they spent the night . . ." They might as well have been teetotal. At times I am enlisted as a translator and all the names are too much to cope with: another bouillabaisse menu begins, "31 January '90, 6 Americans + Richard, 6 Peyrauds . . ."

TRAVELS

In addition to Lucien's multiplying activities as president, vice president, administrator, or member of innumerable viticultural, oenological, and agricultural syndicates, societies, and academies, his role with the INAO permitted him and Lulu, throughout the 1960s and 1970s, to audit the two-week sessions organized by the Office International de la Vigne et du Vin (OIV) each year in a different country, at the time of the grape harvest. The OIV is a professional, scientific, and technological international organization, founded in 1924, counting thirty-three member countries (of which the United States is one), whose participants (oenologists, ampelographers, bi-

François offering (and clowning) at table.

ologists, etc.), in the words of the OIV, "are recognized to be the top international authorities." If neither Lucien nor Lulu was especially impressed by the elite of the international vitivinicultural intelligentsia, these trips provided a unique opportunity to contact vignerons and vineyard proprietors from other cultures in their own surroundings, confirming Lucien in his belief that if everyone in the world could only understand and love fine wine, there would be no more wars. As for Lulu, she was always fascinated by the food and, upon returning home, hastened to interpret, in her own kitchen, many of the dishes she had encountered. I asked her for a few souvenirs and she wrote them down:

"Our first trip with the OIV goes back to 1962 in the U.S.S.R. I remember lots of salads of tomatoes, cucumbers, peppers, lettuce, onions . . . practically unseasoned . . . but there was always a dish full of caviar! And little chickens, racing champions, grilled over coals, delicious, and a bowl of rice . . . lots of fruit, watermelons, figs, grapes . . . we were in Soviet Georgia. Our second trip took us to Austria and the little white Grinzing wines, drunk in open-air taverns, accompanied by Tyrolean singing. We ate thin strips of veal and pork, dipped in egg and bread crumbs, salt, pepper, paprika, sautéed in butter and presented speared on little sticks of wood . . . this was 1964; the following year found us in Portugal, where we had salt cod at practically every meal, but what salt cod! I mean to say what quality! So many marvelous ways of preparing it. With the apéritif, we had little deep-fried bites and I remember a ragout with sliced potatoes and onions, crushed garlic, chopped parsley, and seasoning, sweated in a covered casserole for an hour and a half. Naturally, we tasted many ports of different ages. In 1966, we visited Bulgaria, where I remember a ragout of sliced carp and potatoes, cooked in a broth with a good lot of paprika. In 1968 we were in Rumania, where the food was basically cucumbers, tomatoes, peppers, and paprika sauces, which accompanied fish stews. In Cyprus we ate mainly grilled fish and salads, that was in 1970. In 1971, we arrived in Argentina at the height of the grape harvest, in the month of February, and in Chile, we ate out-of-doors around an immense blaze in front of which beef ribs were roasting, held upright, speared on iron rods planted in the ground. Over raked coals to the side, chipolata and blood sausages were grilled to accompany the smoky ribs! We were also surprised to see the Argentine vignerons molding with their hands clay ovens which resembled rustic baker's ovens, heated out-of-doors, in which they put empanadas, that is to say little pâtes or ravioli, stuffed with onions, chard, and hard-boiled eggs . . . they came out burning hot and golden—ready to eat.

"In 1976, we went all alone, like real grown-ups, to California, where we ate crabs on the San Francisco waterfront like everyone else—but then we had dinner at Chez Panisse . . . and that was not like everyone else! . . . a leg of lamb and a tart that I will remember all my life long! 1978 was Greece and I will not soon forget the little restaurants at the foot of the Acropolis, where, plate in hand, one went to the kitchens to serve oneself from the huge pots in which either lamb or fish, with tomatoes, onions, garlic, bay, and other aromatic herbs, were kept simmering.

"Tijuana in 1980 . . . finally, I was able to taste turkey with chocolate, that is to say, a turkey stuffed with bread soaked in milk, mixed with butter-stewed onions, garlic, and hot chilies, cooked in the oven; the dish deglazed with white wine permits one to make a sauce with cream and cocoa to serve with the bird. In South Africa, north of Cape Town, we assisted at the grape harvest in March. I remember, above all, a great, open-air fête on the Atlantic coast at which, for three hundred people, our hosts had cooked *cigales de mer* (sea cicadas/blunt-nosed slipper lobsters) the size of large *langoustes* (spiny rock lobsters) and gave to the guests wooden planks and strong knives to fend for themselves . . . and to go back for as many more as they liked! . . . while a young woman played on the piano old music-hall chansons to dance to . . . out-of-doors! This was in 1983.

"I haven't mentioned countries like Germany, Italy, Switzerland, or Spain, which we have visited so often that it seems as if they hold no more secrets or surprises . . . but I must make one exception of Sicily, where I ate with Richard Olney off a fishing boat—clear green, crisp algae seasoned with salt and a squeeze of lemon (we also ate lovely pitch-black spaghetti, sauced with tiny cuttlefish in their ink) . . . not to mention all of the magnificent recipes for eggplant, grilled and stuffed with garlic, anchovies, and some of their secret herbs. And another trip to California with the Académie Internationale du Vin, when we were received in the high hills of Chalone Vineyard and Alice Waters grilled white tuna steaks rare for a hundred people!"

During this same period, Lulu and Lucien often assisted at the dinners and vineyard visits in France, organized by Les Amitiés Gastronomiques Internationales, and they and the wines of Domaine Tempier were always present at the annual Paulée, organized by the restaurant Taillevent in collaboration with La Revue du Vin de France. Lulu is a cofounder and a very active member of Les Dames du Vin et de la Table, a feminine association (which admits male honorary members), composed mainly of women who are vineyard proprietors or who are very active partners in the direction and promotion of family vineyards.

Lulu and Lucien celebrating their fiftieth wedding anniversary, October 17, 1986, aboard
Le Marseillois, *a restored nineteenth-century schooner, anchored in the old port of Marseilles.*

The Vigneron's Year

Seasons and Menus

Fall and Winter

SAINT MARTIN'S DAY, November 11, marks the beginning of the vigneron's year. The harvest is in, the new wine is finished and has begun its evolution in oak tuns; the rosé will be bottled in the spring following the vintage, the reds eighteen to thirty months after the vintage, depending on their evolution, which is judged regularly by tastings. The vines will lie dormant for four months. The vineyard is plowed between the rows by tractor where the terrain permits; steep slopes and narrow terraces are dug with hoe and pickax; the soil is piled up around the bases of the vinestocks. The most important and the most interesting of the winter chores is pruning. The care with which it is done determines the health of the vines and the deliberately restrained production of the season to come, the concentration of flavor, color, tannin, and sugar in the grapes, and the goodness of the wine. Domaine Tempier's style of pruning, known as *gobelet,* is traditionally Provençal. The vines are free-standing; only the young plantations are trained on stakes. All of the previous year's growth is removed except for one branch on each of the three or four arms of the vinestock; François cuts each of these branches back nearly to the base, leaving a spur with two eyes, the latent buds from which the following season's growth will spring. Previously unknown funguses, whose spores enter healthy vines through the fresh cuts left by pruning shears, have complicated the vigneron's task. All wood removed from the vines must be burned immediately, lest it carry spores that a gust of wind might carry to the pruned vines. The pruner, whose *sécateur* must be very sharp, its cut very clean, is followed by a worker who immediately seals the fresh cuts with a liquid plastic substance that hardens in contact with the air, preventing the penetration of fungus spores.

Most of the olives on the property are picked in December and transported to the local cooperative mill to be crushed and pressed into oil, which is used abundantly throughout the year in all the Peyraud kitchens. By the last half of October, the green olives have grown full-size but have not yet begun to turn color. Some are picked at this stage, each is rapped lightly with a mallet to just split the skin, and they are soaked in cold water, frequently changed, for ten days to draw out their bitterness. They are then drained, rinsed, and put into an aromatic cold brine (dried wild fennel stalks, bay leaves, a strip of dried orange peel, and a few coriander seeds added to a boiling brine composed of three ounces of coarse sea salt per quart of water), left to cool, and strained. They are called *olives écachées* (or, often, *cassées*). They are ready to eat after a week in the brine, and hold perfectly until Christmas, after which their bright green color begins to fade, but they remain good until Easter. Green olives, unbruised, regularly stirred in a thin paste of water and sifted hardwood ashes for six days, well rinsed, and soaked in repeated changes of cold water for ten days before being put into the same brine, are less bitter and will hold longer. Olives that have

Olives.

begun to turn, some still more or less green, others violet and some black, the flesh too tender to be smacked with a mallet, are pricked with pins (several pins stuck through a disk of cork) before being soaked, like the *olives écachées,* and put into the same brine. When the olives are picked very ripe at the end of December, black and tender to the touch like a ripe avocado, some beginning to wrinkle, they are put into a stoneware vessel, sprinkled heavily with salt, and tossed several times daily, the liquid drained off each day and more salt added. After several days, they are transferred to a wicker basket, salted and tossed regularly for a few more days—about a week in all—before being put into a jar with bay leaves, pepper ground over, and anointed with olive oil. They should be stirred around regularly to keep them coated in oil; the olives are not salty—most of the salt flows off with the rejected liquid.

At this time of year, Lulu willingly prepares a *civet de lièvre* (red wine hare stew with a last-minute liaison of the animal's blood). Young partridges or pheasants are barded and roasted, either in a hot oven or on a turnspit before the open fire (old ones are braised with cabbage). The bards are removed shortly before they are done. They are kept slightly pink, 18 to 20 minutes in an oven for partridge, 25 to 30 minutes for pheasant, and nearly twice as long for the one and the other before an open fire. To accompany them, Lulu serves a garlicky wild salad.

With the exception of spring morels, nearly all wild mushrooms appear in Provence after the autumn rains; November is the richest month. François, Jean-Marie, and Catherine are all avid mushroom hunters. Lactaires délicieuses are abundant. François often travels farther inland and returns with cèpes and chanterelles, a small, fragile, pale yellow and gray variety. They are all sautéed in olive oil, finished with a shower of garlicky persillade and, sometimes, with a squeeze of lemon (Lulu says, "I'm not very lemon," but lemon is always at table for Lucien who uses it generously).

Large healthy specimens are marinated with olive oil and persillade and grilled over hot coals.

When there are few guests, and the weather discourages an out-of-doors apéritif, Lulu and Lucien love to serve vin rosé at the kitchen table, accompanied by sea urchins and vioulets. Both are on the market during all the months with "r," but sea urchins are never better furnished with their voluptuous orange-red roe than in the month of November. They are opened with scissors, cutting outward from the orifice, then around, to remove a circle of shell, exposing the starlike design of corals clinging to the inside of the shell. Lucien, who is dedicated to teaching and sharing joy, delights in scooping out the tongues of roe with a coffee spoon, placing them onto small rounds of buttered rye bread and passing them to guests who often have never tasted the divine sea urchin. At other times, for the apéritif, Lulu prepares creamy scrambled eggs in a bain-marie; guests spoon the coralloid cream onto individual croutons. Vioulets are rude-looking, primitive sea-floor creatures, imprecise in shape, with a tough, leathery exterior that displays a miniature landscape of adhering sea life. They are eaten hardly anywhere except between Marseilles and Toulon, where they are adored. When cut in two, a tender, lemon-colored, orange-rimmed flesh is exposed, whose exquisite taste is a mysterious lemony essence of the sea. When present, Laurence, who, like her father, is a teacher (in Paris, she teaches English to the French and to foreigners as part of an international business-administration program), instructs guests in the correct Provençal method of loosening the vioulet's flesh from the carapace with one's thumbnail.

The new crop of tender violet artichokes appears in November. The local farmers' goat cheeses go out of season until shortly before Easter. Just before Christmas, the market is flooded with cardoons, not because they have at that moment come into season, but because tradition imposes their presence at the Christmas Eve table.

FALL AND WINTER MENUS

The wines are not mentioned in the seasonal menus because the progressions are always similar (see preceding chapter).

Tomme Arlésienne is a semifresh, soft ewe's milk cheese, a specialty of Arles and the Camargue.

Apéritif: *Olives Ecachées;* Anchovy Crusts, *Anchoïade*

Hot Chick-pea Salad, *Salade de Pois Chiches*

Roast Anglerfish, *Rôti de Lotte*
Gratin of Chard with Sorrel, *Gratin de Blettes à l'Oseille*

Saint-Nectaire, Tomme Arlésienne, Roquefort

Floating Island, *Ile Flottante*

Apéritif: Salt Cod Purée, *Brandade;* Tapenade, *Tapenade*
Chard Omelette, *Omelette de Blettes*

Fresh Pasta with Seafood, *Pâtes Fraîches aux Fruits de Mer*

Rabbit Stew, *Civet de Lapin*
Purée of Sweet Potatoes, *Purée de Patates Douces*

Green Salad, *Salade Verte*

Reblochon, Beaufort

Burst Vanilla Apples, *Pommes Eclatées à la Vanille*

A typical dry-cured sausage in Provence is less than 2 inches in diameter and about 7 inches long. It should be sliced very thin. Most butchers make their own, either from pure pork or with a mixture of pork and beef, called *saucisson de ménage*. The best are made with a combination of coarsely ground and coarsely hand-chopped meats. They always contain diced fatback and whole peppercorns and are sometimes seasoned with garlic and brandy.

Apéritif: Garlic Crusts, *Croûtons à l'Ail*
Dry-Cured Sausage, *Saucisson Sec*
Artichoke Fritters, *Beignets d'Artichauts*

Mussel and Spinach Gratin, *Gratin de Moules aux Epinards*

Leg of Venison in Red Wine, *Gigue de Chevreuil au Vin Rouge*
Scalloped Potatoes with Olives, *Pommes de Terre aux Olives*

Wild Salad, *Salade Sauvage*

Vacherin

Fresh Fruit, *Fruits Frais*

❖————————❖

Apéritif: Anchovy Puffs, *Choux aux Anchois*

Sautéed Wild Mushrooms, *Champignons Sauvages Sautés*

Provençal Braised Beef, *Daube à la Provençale*
Macaroni in Daube Juices, *Macaronade*

Radicchio and Lambs' Lettuce Salad, *Salad de Trévisse et Mâche*

Cantal, Brie, Comté

Crêpes with Apples, *Crêpes aux Pommes*

THE CHRISTMAS EVE SUPPER

Each year, twenty-five or more members of the family gather at Domaine Tempier for the Christmas Eve supper. Until 1992, the menu had always been the same. The traditional Provençal supper is always Lenten. I asked Lulu why hers is not. She said, "Well, I have to cheat a little because all of our children are invited by their in-laws for the Christmas day dinner, which is when you are really supposed to eat the capons—but the rest of the menu is traditional. Someone always brings a *bûche de noël*, which is not Provençal, but I count it as one of the thirteen desserts of Christmas—the others are dried fruits, fresh fruits, nuts, and nougat . . . and, of course, the *pompe à l'huile*, or *gibassier* (a sweet, flattened and scored, biscuitlike bread made with olive oil), which is essential. We always drink an old *vin cuit* (page 56) with the thirteen desserts and break up pieces of *gibassier* to dunk in it."

THE CHRISTMAS EVE MENU

Apéritif: Tapenade, *Tapenade*

Brandade in Puff Pastry Cases, *Brandade en Vol-au-Vent*

Roast Guinea Fowl, *Pintade Rôtie*
Cardoons in Anchovy Sauce, *Cardons à l'Anchois*

Green Salad, *Salad Verte*

Cheese Platter, *Plateau de Fromages*

The Thirteen Desserts of Christmas, *Les Treize Desserts de Noël*

Although the Christmas Eve meal is traditionally a supper, the Peyrauds prefer to celebrate it at midday. In 1992, the family was also celebrating Lucien's eightieth birthday. Twenty-nine members of the family were present, including Lucien's younger brother, his nephew, the son of his twin, Louis, who had died recently, and Lulu's oldest sister. Lulu delegated the preparation of the meal to Véronique, who replaced the capons with a twenty-pound milk lamb, spitted and roasted in front of the kitchen fireplace. The weather was glorious and oysters were eaten on the terrace with the apéritif.

SPRING

The almond trees burst into flower, some white, some pink, around mid-February, the first visible promise that spring is on the way. It is time to plant the grafted young vines before they begin to stir with new life. In early March, François and the other vignerons plow the vineyard again and hoe the mounded earth away from the bases of the vinestocks. At spring's equinox, the sap begins to rise in the vines, each latent eye, formed during the previous season, begins to swell, splitting open its protective husk, and the bud emerges. The first leaves appear at the beginning of April, first to one side of the unfurling shoot, then to the other, a tendril forming opposite each leaf. The first tendrils are sterile. In late April, at the appearance of the fourth and fifth leaves, the opposite tendrils form flower buds in the shape of miniature grape clusters. The sixth tendril and those to follow are again sterile, clutching at anything they touch to fix the rapidly lengthening branches, about three inches per day at this stage. During this period, the vines receive their first treatments to protect them from the two insidious fungus maladies, oïdium (powdery mildew) and mildiou (mildew), introduced into French vineyards in the last century. François treats against oïdium by *soufrage*—blowing sulfur powder onto the vines; and against mildew by *sulfatage*—spraying the vines with *bouillie bordelaise,* a solution of copper sulfate and slaked lime; he will have nothing to do with recently developed systemic fungicides, for he believes that they poison the soil, the vines, and the wine. For the same reason, he refuses to use weed-killers in the vineyard.

Spring pruning—the removal of unwanted growth—takes place in May, when the young shoots are still sufficiently tender to be snapped off at the base without harming the vine. Flowering occurs most often during the second week of June; approximately one hundred days later, the grapes are ready to be harvested. All vignerons are passionate about the intoxicating, acrid-sweet odor that permeates the air when the vineyard is in flower; Lucien, Jean-Marie, and François often discover memories of this scent while tasting their young wines in the cellar.

A new crop of artichokes appears on the market in March, so young that the choke is still unformed. They are eaten raw, the tender base of each leaf first dipped in olive oil or vinaigrette or, as one of the elements in a bagna cauda, the hot anchoïade sauce. Lulu trims them, slices them thin, and sautés them rapidly in olive oil, to be served as is, finished with a persillade, or transformed into a flat omelette. The first broad beans appear at the same time, to be eaten *à la croque au sel,* shelled at the table, dipped in salt, and eaten with bread and butter. Cultivated asparagus begins in March and, throughout the month of April, the hillsides are covered with tender shoots of wild asparagus, no thicker than heavy twine. Their flavor is also wild, a concentrated essence of asparagus with an exhilarating bitter edge. Only the tips are tender enough to eat—they are usually broken off, sautéed raw for a few seconds in olive oil, and incorporated into an omelette, but because whole bundles are so beautiful, Lulu often parboils bundles of a hundred or so for less than a minute, drains them on a towel, and spreads them out on a huge platter with a little olive oil poured over the tips to be served with the apéritif. Guests pick a stalk, bite off the tender tip, and discard the rest.

As Easter approaches, butchers hang on display rows of un-weaned kids, wrapped in their caul. For the Easter midday dinner, Lulu pierces the kid all over, inserts slivers of garlic into the slits, wraps it in its caul, and spit-roasts it for a couple of hours in front of the kitchen fireplace, basting often with a brush fashioned from branches of fresh thyme dipped into a mixture of pounded cayenne pepper, garlic, Provençal herbs, olive oil, and vinegar. It is salted and peppered a couple of times while roasting.

During the spring months, François likes to organize at least one out-of-doors fête for thirty people or more around a *méchoui*—one or two thirty-pound, three-month-old grass lambs roasted over a pit of wood coals (he once roasted eight lambs for 250 people but that, he admits, was madness). The first time I assisted at one of his *méchouis*, twenty or more years ago, the lamb was spitted on a makeshift construction of wooden stakes in front of a blazing fire and the spit had to be turned by hand. The meat was delicious but, finally, François was nearly as well roasted as the lamb. Since then, the techniques have been refined. A pit, about a foot and a half deep, is dug in the ground with earth mounded up all around. A fire of hardwood logs is built in the pit and fed for about three hours to create a deep bed of incandescent coals. The stakes are now tall cast-iron rods, which are planted deeply in the ground. Each rod has a series of corresponding hooks at different heights, to permit moving the spit farther from or closer to the heat source. The spit is a heavy, hollow stainless steel tube ten feet long, which can accommodate two lambs. At intervals, there are holes through which crossbars can be affixed and an apparatus worthy of Rube Goldberg, consisting of an old washing machine motor and a series of wheels and belts, keeps the spit turning slowly.

From each lamb, any loose fat and all the internal organs are removed, except the kidneys, which are left in place. The lamb is seasoned inside with salt and pepper and spitted, the legs drawn out behind and wired tightly to a crossbar at the heel joints; the forelegs are slit at the "armpits," to facilitate drawing them forward, and the shank ends are wired to a crossbar. The intestinal cavity is filled with bundles of fresh herbs, predominantly thyme (which is in full flower in April and especially fragrant), with lesser quantities of winter savory and rosemary, closed with metal skewers, pierced at a good two inches to either side of the ventral slit, and laced up with wire. If two lambs are to be roasted, they are spitted facing in opposite directions to balance the weight. François prepares a bowl of basting liquid (salt, pepper, cayenne, the juice of six or seven pounds of lemons, and a cup of peanut oil) and a broom made of bundles of fresh thyme with a few branches of rosemary, wired tightly to the end of a long stick.

When there are no more flames, the spit is installed, at first about three feet above the coals, and put into motion; it is progressively lowered as the intensity of the coals' heat subsides. The coals are occasionally stirred, causing them to release more heat from beneath the ash-covered surface. The lambs are basted almost constantly with the broom, repeatedly dipped in the basting liquid, for from one and a half to two hours. Because they are surrounded with heat, they cook more rapidly and more evenly than when they are turned in front of flames; because the flesh is no longer that of a baby animal, it is best kept pink.

While the lambs are roasting, bagna cauda or grilled sardines are served with the apéritif. The lambs are kept on the spit, at a high notch above the dying embers, and carved, as needed, into small slices from different parts of the animal. François says, "Each person should receive a selection of cuts, but not too much at a time. It is better to return several times so that the meat is always hot." The most recent bottling of red Tempier is served, cool, with the *méchoui*.

The first of April, the cherry trees are in blossom; a month later,

François basting a méchoui.

the cherries are ripe. In May, and sporadically throughout the summer, shoals of anchovies rise to the sea's surface and are netted in quantity. Lulu puts her year's supply into salt and, often, serves the filleted fresh anchovies raw, like sardines. May is the month of petits pois. Lulu prepares little peas like those that accompany the pigeon squabs (page 249), substituting one ounce of butter, in pieces, for the olive oil. Often, she sweats pared and quartered young artichokes in a little butter, in a covered earthenware casserole, to add to the peas when they are done. In June, the green almonds are ready to be shelled and peeled, served with the apéritif or incorporated into desserts. Fresh garlic and the first sweet, orange-fleshed Charentais or Cavaillon melons appear.

SPRING MENUS

With the apéritif, Lulu often serves the stewed octopus cold. Sugar and cream are served at the same time as the strawberries; guests may add either cream or red wine to them, sugaring to taste.

Apéritif: Stewed Octopus with Aïoli, *Poulpe Confit à l'Aïoli*

Green Bean and Fresh Shell Bean Salad,
Salade de Haricot Verts et Egrenés

Roast Pork Loin with Sage and Onions,
Filet de Porc aux Oignons
Squash Gratin, *Gratin de Courge*

Curly Chicory Salad, Garlic Vinaigrette,
Salade de Frisé, Vinaigrette à l'Ail

Reblochon; Farmers' Goat Cheeses, *Chèvres Fermiers*

Strawberries, *Fraises*

Apéritif: Raw Vegetables with Hot Anchovy Dip, *Bagna Cauda*

Grilled Lamb Chops, *Côtelettes d'Agneau sur la Braise*
Potato and Sorrel Gratin, *Gratin de Pommes de Terre à l'Oseille*

Coulommiers; Farmers' Goat Cheeses, *Chèvres Fermiers*

Walnut Gâteau, *Gâteau aux Noix*

In late spring, and throughout the summer, Lulu often serves, among the appetizers, small melon cubes wrapped with strips of raw ham (prosciutto) and affixed with toothpicks; they are always accompanied by black olives.

Apéritif: Melon Cubes Wrapped with Raw Ham,
Bouchées de Melon au Jambon Cru
Black Olives, *Olives Noires*
Buttered Sardine Crusts, *Sardines Crues, Croûtons Beurrées*

Sautéed Squid with Parsley and Garlic, *Suppions à la Persillade*

Leg of Lamb on a Bed of Thyme, *Gigot sur Lit de Thym*
Sautéed Artichokes and Potatoes, *Artichauts Sautés aux Rattes*

Dandelion Salad with Garlic Croutons,
Salade de Pissenlit aux Chapons

Fresh Goat Cheeses, *Fromages de Chèvre Frais*

Cherries, *Cerises*

Lulu serves the endive, walnut, and apple salad at the same time as the Roquefort.

Apéritif: Mixed Fritters, *Beignets Panachés*

Hot Asparagus Vinaigrette, *Asperges Chaudes à la Vinaigrette*

Stuffed Baked Fish, *Poisson Farci au Four*

Endive, Walnut, and Apple Salad,
Salade d'Endives aux Noix at aux Pommes

Roquefort

Fruit Macédoine, *Salade de Fruits*

Caillette du Var is specific to the region around Bandol and Toulon. Each butcher makes his own. The caillette is composed of long, narrow strips of pork liver, pork fatback (about ¼ pound of fatback per pound of liver), and sometimes, pork sweetbreads, tossed well with salt, pepper, thyme, a hint of nutmeg, and a lot of garlicky persillade, sometimes a dash of *marc*. The strips are formed into a long bundle, 3½ to 4 inches in diameter, rolled in a sheet of caul, tied up like a rolled roast, and roasted for about 1½ hours at 350°F. The butcher sells caillette cold in slices. Lulu cuts the slices into bite-size squares and serves them with individual croutons.

Apéritif: Pork Liver Charcuterie, *Caillettes du Var*
Green Olive Tapenade, *Tapenade d'Olives Vertes*

Tuna Marseilles-Style, *Thon à la Marseillaise*

Grilled Chicken, *Poulet à la Crapaudine*
Squash Purée, *Purée de Courge*

Radicchio Salad with Garlic Croutons,
Salade de Trévisse aux Chapons

Beaufort; Farmers' Goat Cheeses, *Chèvres Fermiers*

Pears in Red Wine, *Poires au Vin Rouge*

SUMMER

From the time of the flowering, the hard, green grapes grow for two months, swelling in size from pinheads to marbles with no perceptible change in their chemical composition, while the branches continue to unfurl, new leaves constantly appearing. Abruptly, the vine's metabolic pattern shifts; from one day to another, just after the first week of August, growth is arrested, violet grapes suddenly appear, scattered throughout the green clusters of the red varietals, and the supple green branches begin to stiffen and to turn brown. Henceforth, all the vine's energy is devoted to ripening the grapes and to the lignification of the branches. The grapes' acidity diminishes as the sugar levels rise: six weeks later, the grapes are ready to be picked.

If left to its own devices, a vine will send its sap racing to the extremities of the branches to nourish newly forming leaves, to the detriment of the developing grapes. In July, a summer pruning consists in cutting back the branches to redirect the sap to the grapes. During this same period, François and his staff also pass through the vineyard several times for what they call "the green harvest" (*la vendange verte*), picking and discarding not only the *grapillons*— small bunches of grapes resulting from a retarded flowering—but a good number of large, healthy bunches as well, to make certain that the harvest will not be too abundant and that the vines will be able to nourish the remaining grapes to full maturity and maxi-

mum concentration of sugar and fruit. To produce the best the season can offer, François figures that no more than ten grape bunches
should be left on the vine.

Among the good things of summer are daily tomato salads. As
Lulu says, "It's not a recipe—it's just tomato salad." The tomatoes
are sliced, spread out, and seasoned with salt, pepper, and olive oil;
vinegar is optional. They can be garnished with rinsed and filleted
salt anchovies and black olives and scattered with fresh basil
leaves, chopped hyssop, or fines herbes. The thickly cigar-shaped,
sweet, violet Florence onions, which appear at midsummer, are a
precious addition, sliced in rings, to practically any salad. Male
zucchini flowers, which bear no fruit, abound in the morning markets. All the vegetables that, today, are on the market year-round
but that ripen in the Provençal garden only in the summer remind
one, then, of the taste of real food. Among the fruits are raspber-
ries, apricots, peaches, yellow and white, and figs: a large, reddish,
very sweet fig appears in July, the gray, black, and green figs ripen in
September. François cultivates a few vines that produce table
grapes.

Summer Menus

Because there are tomatoes in the ratatouille, eliminate them and
the 2 tablespoons of oil in which they are sautéed from the recipe
for Pilaf with Tomatoes. Stir a pinch of saffron into the rice before
moistening it.

A *faisselle* is a perforated cheese mold. Today it is fabricated
from discardable plastic. *Faisselles de chèvre* are molds filled with
fresh goat's milk that has been warmed and curdled by the addition
of rennet. They are sold while still draining and before being salted.
The delicate sweet cheeses tremble when unmolded at table. Children adore them with sugar and cream; wine drinkers prefer to season them with salt and pepper.

Apéritif: Grilled Sardines, *Sardines Grillées*

Ratatouille, *Ratatouille*

Grilled Lamb Skewers, *Brochettes à la Provençale*
Saffron Pilaf, *Riz au Safran*

Salad of Lambs' Lettuce and Curly Chicory with Garlic Croutons,
Salade de Mâche et de Chicorée Frisée aux Chapons

Faisselles de Chèvre

Apéritif: Grilled Mussels, *Moules à la Catalane*

Rabbit and Carrots in Aspic, *Lapin aux Carottes en Gelée*

Baked Bream with Fennel, *Daurade au Fenouil*

Green Salad, *Salade Verte*

Farmers' Goat Cheeses, *Chèvres Fermiers*
Reblochon, Saint-Nectaire, Fribourg

Apricot Compote with Vanilla, *Compote d'Abricots à la Vanille*

The peaches are simply peeled, sliced, sprinkled with sugar, covered with red wine, and chilled. If they are difficult to peel, dunk them first for a split second in boiling water and drain them immediately.

Apéritif: Raw Fish Salad, *Mérou à la Tahitienne*

Tart of Mixed Greens, *Tarte aux Herbes*

Roast Fillet of Beef, *Filet de Boeuf Rôti*
Tomatoes à la Provençale, *Tomates à la Provençale*

Saint-Nectaire, Comté

Peaches in Red Wine, *Pêches au Vin Rouge*

———✦———

When Lulu prepares a bouillabaisse, she likes to keep people busy first with a surprising variety of things to nibble with the apéritif. In addition to those mentioned here, and others, she often serves a platter of fried whitebait *(petite friture)* or of tiny fried red rock mullet *(rougets de roche)* (see introduction to Fried Zucchini and Eggplant, page 108). When she serves fresh figs, she serves fresh goat cheeses at the same time.

Apéritif: Plum Tomatoes with Basil, *Pendelottes au Pistou Figé*
Tapenade, *Tapenade; Dry-Cured Sausage, *Saucisson Sec*

Bouillabaisse, *Bouillabaisse*

Fresh Goat Cheeses, *Fromages de Chèvre Frais*

Fresh Figs, *Figues Fraîches*

Apéritif: Fried Zucchini and Eggplant,
Courgettes et Aubergines Frites
Flat Tomato Omelette, *Crespèu aux Tomates*
Black and Green Olives, *Olives Noires et Vertes*

Pasta with Basil and Anchovy, *Pâtes au Pistou à l'Anchois*

Stuffed Baked Squid, *Encornets Farcis*

Green Salad with Tarragon, *Salade Verte à l'Estragon*

Assorted Cheeses, *Fromages Assortis*

Apricot Pudding, *Clafoutis aux Abricots*

THE HARVEST

In early September, or in very precocious years like 1989 and 1990 in late August, François begins to visit the different parcels of the vineyard, collecting grape samples to test the juice for acid and sugar levels. Each year is different; the experience of previous years cannot always direct the decision for the opening date of picking. A potential alcohol content of 13.5 percent is considered ideal, on condition that there is sufficient acidity to create a balanced wine. If the level of acidity threatens to fall too low, the grapes must be picked with a lower sugar content. In unusual years, there may be good acidity when the mustimeter measures a potential of 14 percent or 14.5 percent alcohol. The fermentation of grapes with such a high sugar content may be long and difficult but the result can be extraordinary (one tun of 1971 was kept in the wood for five years before all the residual sugars were finally fermented out; today, it is one of the domaine's most glorious bottles). The opening date for picking is decided upon about a week in advance.

In vineyards with a single grape variety, soil structure, and exposition, the grapes ripen at the same time and must be picked as rapidly as possible; the grapes at Domaine Tempier, because of the different varietals and microclimates, ripen over a period of three weeks; in a three-week period there are fourteen days of picking. In the vineyard, François works with ten pickers, each with a *sécateur* and a *panier*, two carriers (*porteurs de seaux*—men who collect the grapes from the pickers' *paniers* and carry them in buckets to a dray for transport to the cellar), and the tractor driver, who transports the grapes. François instructs the pickers in the art of selection—only perfectly healthy and perfectly ripened grapes are picked—and keeps a sharp eye on all the grapes as they arrive at the dray, where they are emptied into cases, each containing about sixty pound of grapes, a precaution against any being crushed before arriving at the cellar. Grapes from one- and two-year-old vines are discarded. Grapes from three-year-old vines are picked and vinified separately to be sold in bulk as *vin de table*. Grapes from four- to eight-year-old vines are pressed for vin rosé. Only after the vines are eight years old are the grapes permitted to be used for red Appellation BANDOL Contrôlée.

A vineyard and its cellars are inhabited by yeasts that have established themselves there over the years. The grapes' bloom—an ashy veil that cloaks the skins—contains a dense population of yeasts. The Peyrauds believe that any tampering with natural yeasts, by the addition of commercial, laboratory-developed yeasts, robs a wine of its personality and disguises its origin. In the fermentation vats, as the yeasts feed on a fraction of the grape sugars and multiply, in contact with oxygen, they produce enzymes that break down the remaining sugars into approximately equal parts of carbon dioxide gas and alcohol. The density of the liquid diminishes from well over the weight of water for the unfermented grape juice to less than the weight of water for the finished dry wine.

Harvest 1963. Pickers relax at the casse-croûte matinal (breakfast break). Jean-Marie is second from right.

Harvesting the vines.

Less than a third of the production—about 36,000 bottles—goes into the vin rosé. As they arrive from the vineyard, the grape bunches are emptied immediately into a horizontal pneumatic press. The flesh, or pulp, of noble red grape varieties is colorless. Because all the pigment resides in the skins, which, when their cellular structure has not been broken down by fermentation, release very little color, the juice that flows from the pressed grapes is pale pink. It is pumped into a temperature-controlled vat and cooled to 53°F to prevent fermentation while solids in suspension settle to the bottom of the vat. Twenty-four hours later, the juice is pumped off its deposit into another vat. As it warms up, the yeasts begin to multiply at around 60°F, generating their own heat. The rosé is not permitted to rise above 77°F during the alcoholic fermentation, which demands about two weeks. The wine is pumped off its lees into another vat, where it is held at 72° to 73°F. Within the week or two to follow, a secondary, or malolactic, fermentation breaks down the malic acid into carbon dioxide and lactic acid, reducing and stabilizing the acidity. By mid-December, the malolactic fermentation is finished, the wine is filtered lightly, then stabilized by the addition of a solution of SO_2. Until a few years ago, the rosé was raised in wood until bottled. Changing fashions in taste have encouraged Jean-Marie to lodge it in 5,000- and 10,000-liter glass-lined vats that, because the wine is not altered by breathing as in the wood, allows him to bottle vats of wine progressively, whenever nature permits, from April until September. It is filtered at the time of bottling.

Today, great-grandmother Léonie's cellar contains, in addition to a number of tuns for aging red wine, eight 10,000-liter, temperature-controlled, clamp-lidded, stainless steel vats. The cellar is built into an incline. The entrance from behind opens onto a high platform, which stretches around three sides of the cellar, above the vats. It is there that the grapes for the red wines arrive. Because

Mourvèdre grape skins contain abundant tannin, less acerbic than that of the stems, the grapes are stemmed before going into the vats. A stemmer-crusher, which moves around the platform and can be positioned over any of the vats, rejects the stems and crushes the grapes lightly, and they fall into the vat. The vats are filled three-quarters full to allow for swelling volume during the fermentation.

Because of the Mourvèdre grape's natural antioxidant faculties, no antiseptic sulfur dioxide solution is added to the vats of fermenting red wine. Fermentation sets in after a few hours. On an average, it requires ten days. The vats' lids are left unclamped to permit the escape of carbon dioxide, whose pressure forces the pulp and skins to the surface, forming a "cap," or chapeau. The fermenting must is pumped up from the bottom of each vat over the chapeau every morning and evening *(remontage)*. One vat is equipped with a mechanical *pigeur*, metallic arms that periodically churn the must, immersing the chapeau and mixing it with the liquid; in the other vats, Jean-Marie uses a hand plunger. Wooden grills are also used, at times, to keep the chapeau immersed in liquid. Jean-Marie checks the temperature and the density two or three times a day. Until the last couple of days, by which time the density has fallen to just above that of water, the temperature is held beneath 86°F, after which it is permitted to rise to about 93°F to extract the maximum color and tannin from the skins. As the fermentation subsides, the chapeau settles to the bottom of the vat.

The free-run wine, or *vin de goutte,* is run off into oak tuns and the pomace, or *marc,* is carried by the *décuveur,* an endless screw, to the press to extract the press wine, or *vin de presse.* The *vin de presse* is thick and black. Its alcoholic content is lower than that of the free-run wine and its tannic content much higher. Most of it is added to the free-run wine to reinforce the tannic structure. Jean-Marie always puts aside a keg of *vin de presse* from a vat of pure, or nearly pure, Mourvèdre, which he puts into bottles before Christmas and which serves the family for cooking purposes throughout the year. It is with this wine that Lulu prepares her daubes and civets.

The red wine's malolactic fermentation takes place in the tuns and is usually finished by the first days of November. During the wine's sojourn in wood—from eighteen months to three years, depending on the *cuvée* and the vintage—there is an important loss of volume from evaporation through the pores of the wood. The tuns are topped up every fifteen days and the wine is racked—pumped from one tun to another to separate it from its lees, which settle into the belly of the tun, beneath the faucet level—six or seven times (the lees are sold to a distillery). For the first racking, in November, after the malolactic fermentation is finished, and for the second, in January, the wine is splashed from the tun's faucet into a large basin (to rid it of excess carbon dioxide, with which all new wine is impregnated), from which it is pumped into another tun. Succeeding rackings are conducted out of contact with air, the wine pumped directly from the orifice at the bottom of one tun into that at the bottom of the other. The tuns into which the wine is pumped are sterilized in advance by burning suspended sulfur wicks inside them, closing them, and later, scrubbing them out with a solution of water and sulfur dioxide. For the last racking, always with a new moon, the wine is pumped from the tun to one of several stainless steel vats, installed on a high platform. Two weeks later, as the moon begins to decline and on a day when the barometer is high, the wine is drawn by atmospheric pressure into bottles, as they move on the conveyor belt of a bottling and corking machine.

Marc is pomace, or the pressings left over from the *vin de presse*. By extension, the word also applies to the brandy that is distilled from the *marc*. Each year, François makes a 300-liter keg of *marc*. It is more avocation than profession, for profit is beside the point.

The antique still for making marc.

François, emptying the pomace from the cauldron of the still, after distillation.

He has an antique still, purchased years ago from a *bouilleur de cru. Bouilleurs de cru* were intinerant distillers who traveled with the still from property to property to distill each family's annual supply of *marc,* before the practice became illegal because of irregularities in the declarations to the state of alcohol production—today, licenses to distill are difficult to obtain and production is rigidly controlled. The oak keg, when new, is filled with sea water for three days before being used. Each vintage of *marc* remains in its keg three to four years before being bottled; the kegs are replaced after every third batch of *marc,* or every ten to twelve years.

Over a period of a week, when picking is done and the first vats of wine have finished fermenting, François does nothing, from dawn till nightfall, but distill his keg of *marc.* He uses the pomace of pure Mourvèdre, the domaine's principal grape variety, which, after the free-run wine has been drawn from the vat, is only lightly pressed, leaving the *marc* still saturated with wine. Before distillation, the pressed *marc* is spread into an open vat and covered with a tarpaulin for five or six days to rid it of its carbon dioxide.

The still is composed of three parts. A copper cauldron, reposing on a rocker, or *bascule,* permitting it to be tipped for emptying, is heated from beneath by a wood fire. A curved tube leads from the tightly closed lid of the cauldron into the bottom of a closed chamber, the rectifier (*rectificateur*), which is nearly immersed in a larger chamber of hot water. From the top of the rectifier, another tube leads into a coil, or condenser (*condensateur*), contained within a third vessel filled with cold water, from the bottom of which the condenser's spout releases the distilled *marc.*

In the cauldron, 30 liters of water are mixed with 120 kg (265 pounds) of pomace, from which is drawn 12 to 15 liters of finished *marc.* About an hour and a half is required to distill each batch. In all, 2,500 kg (5,500 pounds) of pomace, or 20 to 25 batches of distilled *marc,* are necessary to fill the keg. The fire is fed steadily, only enough to maintain a light boil within the cauldron. The vapors pass into the rectifier, leaving a deposit, or "phlegm" (*flegme*), then into the condenser. Because alcohol boils at a lower temperature than water, its vapors are the first to be distilled. The initial liquid delivered by the condenser is about 80 percent alcohol. If François were to distill the contents of the cauldron completely, the final liquid would measure only 30 percent alcohol. He arrests it at 50 percent (100 "proof"). When the *marc* leaves the still, it is colorless. It requires no care from the time it is put into the keg until it is bottled three to four years later, when its fragrance has refined and discovered new complexities and its color has turned amber.

The pomace emptied from the still after distilling is spread in the vineyard as compost.

Vin cuit is a traditional Provençal sweet wine whose origins are lost in the mists of time. It is always drunk with the thirteen desserts of Christmas at the Christmas Eve supper. Today, commercial *vin cuit* is nothing but reduced grape juice with brandy added to it and, if one can believe most Provençal cookbooks, contemporary family recipes are much the same, with or without the addition of brandy. The only published recipe, to my knowledge, in which there is question of a natural fermentation is that of René Jouveau, who reduces fresh, unfermented must by half, cools it, and pours it into glass jugs to remain uncorked until spring, an obvious invitation to unwanted bacteria.

This state of affairs was not to Lucien's liking, for he knew that *vin cuit* should be a genuine, naturally fermented and healthy wine. He spent many years questioning the oldest local vignerons to discover how their parents and grandparents made *vin cuit*. The result of his researches is more than convincing; Lucien's is the only *vin cuit* I have tasted that has the flavor of tradition. During the 1991 harvest, I found Lucien and his granddaughter, Valérie, outside the cellars. To the side was a huge pile of wood in reserve and a fire of

Lucien instructing Valérie in the occult secrets of making vin cuit.

oak logs burned beneath a 300-liter stainless steel cauldron filled nearly to the brim with purple must—unfermented grape juice that had been drawn off a newly filled vat—from which, with a large, flat, slotted spoon, its handle wired to a long stick, Valérie was skimming off the foam as it mounted to the surface. Lucien explained that the time had come for him to pass on the recipe for the family *vin cuit* to one of his grandchildren so that it would not be lost.

A couple of hours later, the surface was clear and the liquid simmering; Lucien threw in four fresh quinces, each stuck with several cloves, and a shovel-full of incandescent ambers from the fire to impart a smoky, caramelized flavor to the must. By the end of the day, the must had reduced by a third, the fire was left to die, the cauldron loosely covered, and left to cool overnight. In François's words, "This is strictly a folkloric process." The clearest of the cooled must, in which the yeasts have been destroyed by the previous day's heat, is transferred, with a pail and a funnel, to a keg, to fill it by about three quarters. It is brought into the cellar of fermenting vats, where the air is saturated with yeasts, and the keg is seeded with several liters of must, drawn from a vat in full fermentation, to hasten the yeasts' regeneration. The keg is left, with the bung hole unplugged, until the fermentation is completed, about one month, during which time wine may be drawn from the bottom of the keg and poured back in to aerate the mass and activate the fermentation. Because the grape sugars are concentrated by reduction, fermentation is arrested before they are all fermented out, leaving a sweet wine with a relatively low alcohol content—about 10.5 percent. When the wine falls clear, after two, three, or more months, it is bottled. A bottle of 1961, opened recently, was tile-hued with a flavor reminiscent of very old vintage port.

Picking is organized so that the last day's work winds up at noon, when everyone gathers for apéritif and the *repas des vendangeurs,* or pickers' meal; pickers, cellar workers, family, and friends add up to between twenty-five and thirty people. If the weather is beautiful, the table is set on the terrace in front of the house. If rain threatens, a long table is set in the old cellar amid the vats of fermenting wine. The emphasis is on abundance and the atmosphere is joyous.

THE HARVEST MENU

Apéritif: Black and Green Olives, *Olives Noires et Vertes*
Dry-Cured Sausage, *Saucisson Sec*
Celery with Anchovy Butter, *Céleri aux Anchois*

Aïoli, *Le Grand Aïoli*

Cheese Platter, *Plateau de Fromages*

Ice Creams and Sherbets, *Glaces et Sorbets*

Grapes, *Raisins*

LULU'S KITCHEN: RECIPES

Opposite: Lulu, with traditional Provençal cork fish paniers, 1968.

MEATS, POULTRY, GAME   189

VEGETABLES, SALADS, GRAINS, PASTA   255

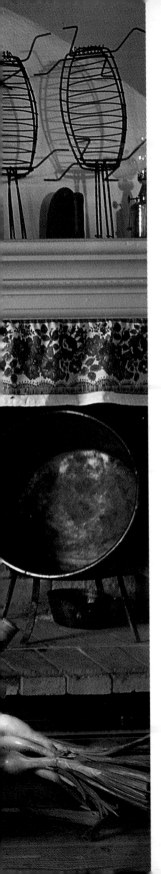

LULU'S KITCHEN

INTRODUCTION

LULU'S CUISINE IS at the same time traditional and intuitive. The names of the recipes will be familiar to anyone who has read a Provençal cookbook, but the flavors and textures of each preparation bear Lulu's signature. Her food is never complicated and the flavors are always direct and clean; she doesn't much believe in recipes, and many of her dishes are never twice prepared in the same way. She says, "You know, my food is nothing but plain old *cuisine de bonne femme.*" When I suggest that she is, after all, a rather special *bonne femme,* she counters, "Well, you understand, what makes it different from recipes in cookbooks and from restaurant cuisine is that I am always cooking for someone I love."

Fundamental to Lulu's cuisine are the marble mortars and wooden pestles, which serve daily, and the ancient Provençal table-height fireplace, whose hearth reaches the length of the kitchen wall and before which roasts are often slowly revolving. In fine weather, the kitchen fireplace is replaced by a barbecue, built against a wall of the house, outside the kitchen door.

I often feel guilty when writing recipes. To capture what one can of elusive, changing experience—a fabric of habit, intuition, and inspiration of the moment—and imprison it in a chilly formula, composed of cups, tablespoons, inches, and oven temperatures, is like robbing a bird of flight. Lulu doesn't measure. When describing liquid quantity, she speaks in terms of ladles, but, of course, she doesn't count out ladlefuls—she simply pours in liquid until it looks about right. When I ask what she means by "lots of garlic," the answer is, "Well, at least a head! But, naturally, when new garlic, which is crisp and fresh and sweet, comes into season, I use lots more than at the end of the season." The earliest fresh garlic, some white, some violet, appears in Provence in May. The skins are thick and tender. It peels easily. These varieties don't keep well but are exquisite when used very fresh. A few weeks later, the long-keeping varieties with dried husks, braided into tresses or tied in bundles, appear on the market. Lulu prefers purple-streaked husks. By late winter and early spring, even the most resistant garlic has lost its fresh flavor, the flesh is no longer crisp, and at the heart of each clove, a sprout begins to form. When using end-of-the-season garlic, Lulu splits or crushes the cloves and discards the sprouts. To peel garlic, first cut off a tip at the root end of each clove. Unless the cloves must be kept un-bruised, place the flat surface of a large knife blade on the clove and give it a light tap with the heel of your hand. This will rupture the skin, loosening it, and it will lift off easily, leaving the clove intact; to crush the clove, give the knife blade a more vigorous tap—or simply smack the clove with the heel of your hand and lift the skin free from the broken-up garlic clove. For liquids that are strained, peeling the crushed garlic cloves serves no purpose. Often garlic cloves are cooked, uncrushed, with roasts or stews and pressed or peeled at table.

I asked all the Peyrauds to prepare, separately, lists of their favorite dishes from Lulu's kitchen. The great classics—bouillabaisse, aïoli, bourride, anchoïade, tapenade, brandade—were on all lists.

Marion and Laurence noted "the floating islands of my childhood." Véronique wrote, following her list of favorite preparations, "When I was a child, Lulu taught me how to set a table for the pleasure of the eyes. From time to time Lulu would say to me, today we are going to learn how to make a sauce . . . a sauté . . . a gratin . . . this is how I acquired the taste for and the joy of cooking. What a pleasure to be joined around a beautifully laid table and to share a dish with those whom one loves. Thanks with all my heart to Lulu! *Ma maman.*" At the head of Lucien's list of favorite dishes was bougiettes. A *bougiette* is a spot or a stain, often of oil on clothing; Lucien's bougiettes are thin slices of semifresh bread, grilled over vine embers, transferred to a plate, and "stained" with fruity, still cloudy olive oil when it leaves the presses just after the new year. Next on his list was "Lulu's tomato sauces for pasta!" I asked Lulu how she made her tomato sauce. After a moment's silence, she said, "Well, there's no recipe—it's just tomato sauce, reduced and passed." Finally, she conceded that she uses "lots of garlic, more than most people." "Herbs?" "Oh yes, always *pebre d'aï* (winter savory), it grows just outside the kitchen door." "Thyme? Bay? Parsley?" "No, only *pebre d'aï* . . . of course the tomatoes have to be peeled!" "Why?" "Well, I don't want peels in my sauce!" "But, if the sauce is passed . . . ?" "When I say that I pass it, I don't mean that I pass it through a sieve or a food mill— that's too much work. I just mix it (with a hand-held electrical immersion blender), which is easier and, besides, that way the seeds stay in the sauce—I like to bite on a tomato seed. I make lots at a time and keep it in jars in the refrigerator because I use it every day for all kinds of things."

In the following recipes, pepper is always freshly ground and butter is unsalted. When using coarse salt, gray, unrefined sea salt is the best, but it can be used only in its coarse form as it contains too much humidity to pass through a salt grinder.

LULU'S TOMATO SAUCE
Coulis de Tomates

About 1 quart

TO PEEL TOMATOES, Lulu first strokes the skins with a small knife blade, in a scraping motion, before cutting out a cone at the stem end to remove the core, slitting a cross at the flower end and pulling off the skins from the flower end, holding a cross-tip of skin between thumb and knife blade. This method works easily only with garden-ripened summer tomatoes but, as she says, "Out of season, canned tomatoes are better anyway. If a wood fire is burning, you can pierce the tomatoes at the stem end with a long-handled kitchen fork and turn them around for a few seconds over the embers—this loosens the skins and gives the tomatoes a nice smoky taste. I would never hold tomatoes over a gas flame."

To seed tomatoes, first cut each in two horizontally, exposing a cross section of the seed pockets. So as not to deform the shape of the tomato halves, loosen the seeds in the pockets with your little finger and give each half an upside-down shake. If the tomatoes are destined to be cut up or chopped, as here, the halves can be simply squeezed and shaken. To coarsely chop a tomato, place each half, cut side down, slice through it a couple of times, give it a quarter turn, and slice through again.

The *poêlon* in which the tomatoes are cooked is a traditional Provençal earthenware casserole, low, wide, and round-sided. The wide surface is important for evaporation—the less time required for the tomatoes to reduce, the fresher the flavor. Like all earthenware, the *poêlon* should be protected from direct contact with heat by an asbestos pad or other heat disperser. If substituting another utensil, it should be wide, heavy, and of a nonreactive material.

3 tablespoons olive oil
1 pound sweet summer onions, coarsely chopped
1 large head garlic, cloves separated, crushed, and peeled
Several sprigs of fresh winter (perennial) savory, tied together
4 pounds garden-ripe tomatoes, peeled and quartered
  (or substitute Italian canned chopped tomatoes—polpa
  di pomodoro)
Large pinch of coarse sea salt (gray, unrefined, if available)

Warm the olive oil in a large earthenware *poêlon* over low heat, add the onions, and as they begin to soften, add the crushed garlic cloves. Stir regularly with a wooden spoon until the onions and garlic are melting, yellowed, but not browned. Add the savory, tomatoes, and salt; turn up the heat and stir regularly until the tomatoes have begun to fall apart and to bubble; cook, uncovered, adjusting the heat when necessary to keep the sauce bubbling lightly. Stir often to prevent its sticking to the bottom or browning around the edges. When all the tomato liquid has evaporated—after about 1 hour—discard the savory bouquet and blend or process the sauce for a couple of seconds—not too much, a bit of texture is a good thing.

APÉRITIF AND AMUSE-GUEULES

In the flowering garden, the apéritif awaits us, a glass of rosé in hand—what will we nibble before going to table?

Dans le jardin en fleurs l'apéritif nous attend, un verre de rosé en main, qu'allons-nous grignoter avant de passer à table?

Lulu

LULU IS ALWAYS in search of new additions to her repertory of *amuse-gueules,* which might, not very elegantly, be translated as "mouth-amusers"—the little appetizers whose role is to excite the appetite and the imagination in anticipation of the meal to follow. Although they are only a prelude to a menu, the first taste surprise encountered by a virgin palate is often the most firmly engraved in a guest's memory.

Opposite: Mussels on the grill.

Tapenade ingredients.

CRUSTS AND SPREADS

TAPENADE
Tapenade

Serves 6 to 8

LULU'S TAPENADE is the simplest (no tuna, no lemon, no brandy, no mustard) I know—and the best. It contains only one herb, *pebre d'aï,* or winter savory, which is a Lulu signature. For aïoli, rouille, or pistou, the mortar and pestle are sacred, but Lulu figures that a food processor produces a perfect tapenade in no time—and she usually prepares one several times a week. Spread on croutons, it is one of the trademark Tempier appetizers served with the apéritif, but it is also incorporated into a vinaigrette for composed salads, it accompanies warm or room temperature roasts, and serves as a stuffing for a boned leg of lamb (page 221). Lulu prepares a green tapenade in precisely the same way, substituting green picholine olives for black.

> *½ pound large Greek-style black olives, pitted*
> *2 salt anchovies, rinsed and filleted, or 4 fillets*
> *3 tablespoons capers*
> *1 garlic clove, peeled and pounded to a paste with a pinch of*
>   *coarse salt*
> *Small pinch of cayenne*
> *1 teaspoon tender young savory leaves, finely chopped, or a*
>   *pinch of crumbled dried savory leaves*
> *4 tablespoons olive oil*

In a food processor, reduce the olives, anchovies, capers, garlic, cayenne, and savory to a coarse purée. Add the olive oil and process only until the mixture is homogenous—a couple of rapid whirs.

ANCHOVY CRUSTS
Anchoïade

Serves 8

GROWING UP in an Iowa farm community, I imagined that I did not like preserved anchovies, for I was familiar only with the little cans of harsh, salty, oil-packed anchovies, from which no amount of soaking can draw the excess salt. I discovered anchovies packed in coarse salt while living in New York, south of Greenwich Village, in the neighborhood then known as Little Italy. They opened up a new dimension in the kitchen. Look for them in Italian, Spanish, or Greek markets. For anchoïade and other recipes calling for anchovies, substitute canned, oil-packed anchovies only if you cannot find anchovies packed in salt.

Salted anchovies are a recurrent seasoning agent in the Peyraud kitchen. Canned anchovies have never crossed the threshold. Throughout the summer, when fresh anchovies appear on the market, Lulu buys them in quantity to salt down for the year to come. She pinches off the head of each at the back, drawing it forward to pull out whatever gut remains attached. The bodies are spread out on trays sprinkled with coarse sea salt, more salt is scattered over them, and they are left for 3 or 4 hours to release a certain amount of liquid, which is discarded, before being tightly packed, spiral fashion, into large, wide-mouthed glass preserving jars, between alternating layers of coarse sea salt with sprigs of fresh winter savory tucked in here and there. A portion of the salt dissolves, creating just enough brine to completely immerse the layers of anchovies and salt crystals. When used within the year, they are never so salty as to require soaking. Each is rubbed gently beneath running water to remove clinging salt crystals, the fillets are pried loose from the backbone with thumbnail and fingertips, rinsed again to remove any clinging fin bones, and laid out, briefly, on paper towels, another paper towel pressed on top to sponge them dry.

To permit the anchoïade to thoroughly penetrate the croutons, Lulu prepares them ahead, using split baguettes, the crust of which prevents the anchoïade from soaking through the bottoms of the croutons. Chilled Tempier rosé from the most recent vintage sings with the anchoïade.

> *Pinch of coarse salt*
> *Freshly ground pepper*
> *1 garlic clove, peeled*
> *1 teaspoon fresh winter savory leaves, or a pinch of dried*
>   *savory*
> *About 20 salt anchovies, rinsed and filleted (40 fillets)*
> *About ⅔ cup olive oil*
> *2 baguettes, each cut across into 3 sections, each section*
>   *split lengthwise*

In a marble mortar, pound the coarse salt, pepper, garlic, and savory leaves to a smooth paste with a wooden pestle. Add the anchovy fillets, pound to a paste, and add olive oil slowly, stirring briskly with the pestle until the paste is quite fluid. Spread it on the split surfaces of the baguettes and put aside for 3 to 4 hours before grilling.

If possible, grill the crusts over a dying bed of wood embers veiled in white ash (or beneath an electric or gas grill), first on the crust sides, then on the anchoïade surfaces. Cut the baguette sections into 2-inch lengths and serve hot, accompanied by a dish of black olives.

GARLIC CRUSTS
Croûtons à l'Ail

GARLIC CRUSTS, anointed with fruity olive oil, are adored wherever olive trees grow. They are never so good as when accompanied by black olives. If you buy Greek-style black olives, put them in a terrine, add 3 or 4 bay leaves, grind over pepper, and pour over a little olive oil—about 2 tablespoons per pound of olives. Stir them around, turning them over, at least once a day to keep them coated in oil.

Lulu usually uses baguettes for garlic crusts. Large, round, country loaves of semifresh, firm-crumbed sourdough bread, thinly sliced and lightly grilled, can be rubbed with garlic, then cut into bite-size squares before being transferred to a platter and dribbled with olive oil. Lulu sometimes places a slice of plum tomato, topped with a basil leaf, on each crust.

Garlic crusts profit by being dried at a good distance (6 to 8 inches) from a bed of wood embers. It is important to understand that crusts and toast are not the same thing. Crusts, in some instances, may be lightly colored but they are never browned. They are subjected to lower—and more distant—heat than toast and for a longer time. For her bouillabaisse, for instance, Lulu prefers to dry her crusts in the sun.

¹⁄₂-inch-thick slices of fresh baguette or 2- to 3-day-old
    country loaf
Peeled garlic cloves
Olive oil

Partially dry the slices of bread in a slow oven or grill them lightly at a good distance from a heat source. Stroke a garlic clove over one surface of each slice, never twice in the same place. If the garlic-rubbed bread slices are large, cut them into squares. Spread the crusts out on a platter and dribble a fine thread of olive oil over the garlic-rubbed surfaces. Serve while still warm.

SALT COD PURÉE
Brandade

Serves 8

GOOD SALT COD is filleted but not skinned before salting. If buying a section of fillet, avoid the tip of the tail and the abdominal flaps. The best part lies directly behind the abdomen. It may require from 24 to 36 hours soaking in repeated changes of cold water, preferably placed skin side up in a colander immersed in a large basin. Check with your merchant for soaking times. When it is ready, it will have doubled in volume and noticeably whitened.

Brandade is often served as a first course, scattered with tiny croutons fried in olive oil. Except for the Christmas Eve *gros souper,* Lulu nearly always serves it spread on individual croutons to accompany the apéritif. She emphasizes the importance of including the skin, whose gelatinous content binds the purée while lending it, at the same time, a soft, voluptuous texture.

(continued)

Brandade ingredients.

COURT-BOUILLON
Sections of wild fennel stalk, or a pinch of fennel seeds
1 bay leaf
4 garlic cloves, crushed
3 cups water

1 pound salt cod, soaked (see above)
4 tablespoons olive oil
3 tablespoons milk
Thin slices of baguette, partially dried in a slow oven or in
    the sun and rubbed lightly with garlic

Combine the fennel, bay leaf, garlic, and water in a saucepan, bring to a boil, and simmer, covered, for 30 minutes. Strain the court-bouillon and leave it to cool. Place the salt cod, skin side down, in a saucepan just large enough to contain it, pour over the cold court-bouillon, and if necessary to completely immerse the cod, some cold water. Bring slowly to a boil, cover the pan tightly, turn off the heat, and leave to poach in the cooling liquid for 15 minutes. Remove the fish, drain it, and pick it over, removing any bones, flaking the flesh and tearing the skin to pieces.

In a food processor, process the flesh and skin for a few seconds. In a small pan, heat about 1 tablespoon of olive oil until very hot. At the same time, put the milk to warm. Add the hot olive oil to the fish, process, warm the remaining oil to hot but not smoking, and whir in about 2 tablespoons. Add about 2 tablespoons hot milk and, if necessary, a little more olive oil and milk until the purée is creamy and consistent, neither too firm nor too loose. Spread it on the garlic croutons and serve warm.

EGGPLANT-TOMATO SPREAD
Bohémienne

Serves 8

A BOHÉMIENNE can be eaten hot, tepid, or cold. Some cooks spread it into a shallow oven dish, sprinkle it with dried bread crumbs and olive oil, and transform it into a gratin. Lulu serves it tepid or cold, spread on garlic croutons, with the apéritif. The eggplant should be ripe but firm, with seeds undeveloped, the skin tight-stretched and glossy. The wide-surfaced cooking vessel is important for evaporation and reduction.

> *6 tablespoons olive oil*
> *1 large onion, halved and finely sliced*
> *3 garlic cloves, crushed and peeled*
> *2 pounds eggplant, peeled, sliced into rounds, salted on both sides for 30 minutes, and pressed dry between paper towels*
> *2 pounds tomatoes, peeled, seeded, and coarsely chopped*
> *3 salt anchovies, rinsed and filleted, or 6 fillets*
> *Salt and pepper*

In a large earthenware *poêlon* or heavy sauté pan, warm 4 tablespoons olive oil. Add the onion and cook over low heat, stirring regularly with a wooden spoon, until softened but not colored. Add the garlic and eggplant; cook until softened, stirring regularly. Add the tomatoes, turn up the heat, and stir until they begin to disintegrate and the mixture begins to boil. Lower the heat to maintain a simmer, uncovered, for an hour or more. Stir regularly, crushing the contents with the wooden spoon and, after about 45 minutes, crush regularly with a fork to create a coarse purée from which all liquid has evaporated. Toward the end, it should be stirred almost constantly to prevent sticking and the heat should be progressively lowered.

Pour 2 tablespoons olive oil into a small pan, lay out the anchovy fillets in the bottom, and hold over very low heat until they begin to disintegrate when touched or when the pan is shaken. Remove the eggplant-tomato purée from the heat and stir in the anchovies and their oil. Taste for salt and grind over pepper. If prepared in advance, transfer the bohémienne to a bowl and leave, uncovered, to cool completely before covering and refrigerating.

ONION TART
Pissaladière

Serves 8

PISSALADIÈRE derives from the word *pissala*, a purée of tiny, salted anchovy and sardine fry that was, in Nice, traditionally mixed with the cooked onions before spreading them onto rolled-out bread dough. Today, nearly everyone uses anchovies instead of *pissala* for the confection of a pissaladière; Lulu prefers short crust to bread dough. She uses large white summer onions, very sweet with a high water content. Niçois olives are small ripe and semiripe (mixed black, brown, and violet) olives preserved in an aromatic brine; they are now commonly available on the American market.

PASTRY
1 cup flour
Salt
10 tablespoons cold butter, diced
About 4 tablespoons cold water

4 tablespoons olive oil
2 pounds sweet onions, finely sliced
Salt and pepper
8 salt anchovies, rinsed and filleted, or 16 fillets
1/2 cup (2 ounces) niçois olives

(continued)

Sift the flour and salt into a mixing bowl, add the diced butter, and crumble the flour and butter together, lightly and rapidly, picking up portions and rubbing loosely between thumb and fingertips. Above all, don't overwork the pastry. Gather it together with a fork and a little cold water, wrap it in plastic, and refrigerate for at least 1 hour before rolling it out.

Warm 2 tablespoons olive oil in a large earthenware *poêlon* or heavy sauté pan, add the onions and salt, and cook, covered, over very low heat, stirring occasionally with a wooden spoon, for an hour or more, or until they are so soft as to form a semi-purée. Remove the lid and continue to cook until much of the liquid has evaporated; the onions should remain absolutely uncolored. Season with pepper.

Preheat the oven to 375°F. With the palm of your hand, flatten the ball of pastry on a generously floured marble slab or other work surface, sprinkle over plenty of flour, and roll it out to a thickness of approximately $\frac{1}{8}$ inch. Roll it up on the rolling pin and unroll it onto a large baking sheet. Roll up the edges and crimp them, either with your thumb, dipped repeatedly in flour, or with the tines of a fork. Spread the onion purée evenly over the pastry, press the anchovy fillets into place in a simple design—latticework or wheel spokes—and push the olives into the purée to complete the design. Dribble olive oil over the surface and bake for about 30 minutes, or until the edges of the pastry are golden and crisp. Serve hot or tepid, cut into small wedges or squares with the apéritif, or in large wedges as a first course.

PLUM TOMATOES WITH BASIL
Pendelottes au Pistou Figé

Serves 6

THESE BITE-SIZE tomato halves, stuffed with a pistou solidified by the cold, whose flavor explodes only as the olive oil begins to melt in the mouth, never fail to enchant. Lulu insists that there must be "lots of basil—the leaves from at least three plants." When I suggested that "3 packed cups" or "3 large handfuls" might be a more specific measure, she figured that might not be enough.

> *Large pinch of coarse salt*
> *Freshly ground pepper*
> *3 garlic cloves, lightly crushed and peeled*
> *4 cups fresh basil leaves*
> *½ cup olive oil*
> *12 firm, summer-ripe plum tomatoes, plunged into boiling*
>   *water, drained immediately, and peeled*

Assemble the coarse salt, pepper, garlic, and basil in a marble mortar and, with a wooden pestle, pound them to a fine paste (a roughly textured purée). Slowly incorporate the olive oil, turning the mixture rapidly with the pestle—it will not form an emulsion but should be intimately combined.

If the stem and flower ends of the tomatoes are not flat enough to form a base, remove a tiny slice from each. Cut each tomato in two horizontally to expose a cross section of the seed pockets. With the handle of a teaspoon, remove the seeds and liquid. With a small spoon, fill the empty seed pockets with the pistou mixture, first stirring it to keep it homogenous. Arrange the tomato halves closely, touching, on a platter and chill in the coldest part of the refrigerator (not the freezer) for about 3 hours, or until the olive oil of the pistou has solidified from the cold. Remove from the refrigerator only at the moment of serving.

RAW VEGETABLES WITH HOT ANCHOVY DIP
Bagna Cauda

Serves 8

"IT'S VERY MESSY," says Lulu. "It is best eaten out-of-doors and it has to be eaten standing up, with the apéritif. Each time one dips a vegetable into the sauce, a piece of bread must be held beneath the dripping vegetable between the pot and the mouth. You need lots of anchovies and lots of olive oil, not so much garlic, and very little vinegar. These proportions are all right for 8 well-bred people, but there are always some *gens mal éléves* who dip their bread in the sauce—for them, you need to make a lot more."

Prepare a table away from that at which lunch will be served. Place a hot plate or other warming device at the center, a basket of thinly sliced baguettes, and platters containing bouquets of raw vegetables all around. Except for the artichokes, from which leaves should be torn, one by one, as they are eaten, all the vegetables should be cut, ready for dipping. Forks should be handy for any vegetables or vegetable ends that are difficult to dip by hand. Choose from among the following (washed, crisped in ice water, if necessary, but served dry):

Inner leaves of romaine lettuce, plus the hearts, split into quarters (or, better, whole 3- to 4-inch untransplanted garden romaine, freshly pulled, yellowed baby leaves removed and roots trimmed)

Belgian endive, blemished outer leaves removed, bottoms trimmed and split into quarters

Hearts of celery, split into quarters

Small, very white heads of cauliflower, broken into florets

Spring onions (green onions; scallions)

*Fennel bulbs, outer stalks removed, split, and sliced into
    vertical sections*
Radishes, freshly pulled, leaves attached
*Small carrots, peeled (not scraped), stems attached (or carrot
    sticks)*
*Small zucchini, split in two, each half sliced lengthwise into
    strips*
*Elongated sweet green salad (Italian) peppers, split in two,
    core and seeds removed, and cut into strips*
Baby artichokes, outer leaves removed
*Cherry tomatoes (or plum tomatoes, peeled and seeded),
    forks needed*

Large pinch of coarse sea salt
Pepper
Large pinch of fresh savory leaves or crumbled dried savory
4 garlic cloves, lightly crushed and peeled
10 salt anchovies, rinsed and filleted, or 20 fillets
1 teaspoon red wine vinegar
1½ cups olive oil

In a marble mortar with a wooden pestle, pound the salt, pepper, savory, and garlic to a smooth liquid paste. Add the anchovy fillets and pound to a paste. With the pestle, stir in the vinegar, then the olive oil, and transfer to a *poêlon* or other earthenware casserole. Heat gently, stirring the while, until hot but far from boiling (test with your finger). Remove to the hot plate at the service table. Throughout the service, the sauce should remain hot, but it should never boil; each time that a vegetable is dipped in the sauce, it should be stirred around to keep the anchovy and the oil from separating.

FLAT OMELETTES
Crespèus

A FLAT OMELETTE is a thick pancake in which the principal element is usually a vegetable. Eggs are present in relatively small quantity to act as a binder. It should be firm enough to hold its shape when cut into sections. If the pan in which the vegetable garnish has been first sautéed is absolutely clean when emptied, it can be used for the omelette; if any trace of vegetable sticks to the pan, this will cause the omelette to stick—the pan should be rapidly cleaned and dried or replaced by another pan. I asked Lulu if she sometimes tossed an omelette to turn it. She said, "Oh, no—I'd be afraid of its landing on the floor. Besides, you have to be strong to do things like that—your American women are big and strong but I'm only a little bit of a woman (*un petit bout de bonne femme*)." She usually serves these omelettes, cut into squares or small wedges, with the apéritif. A flat omelette that can serve 8, in combination with other appetizers, will serve 4 as a first course.

CHARD OMELETTE
Omelette de Blettes

Serves 8

"SIX CLOVES OF GARLIC" is my translation of *beaucoup d'ail*. Adjust the quantity to taste. I asked Lulu if we should suggest spinach as a possible alternative to chard. She said, "Oh, I don't think so—chard is so much better."

3 eggs
Salt and pepper
7 tablespoons olive oil
6 garlic cloves, crushed, peeled, and finely chopped
1 pound chard greens (without ribs), parboiled for a few
  seconds, drained and refreshed beneath cold running
  water, squeezed thoroughly, and chopped

Break the eggs into a mixing bowl, add salt and pepper, and hold them beside the stove in readiness. Heat 3 tablespoons olive oil in a large heavy frying pan over high heat. Add the chopped garlic and let it sizzle for 2 or 3 seconds. Add the chard and salt and sauté for several minutes, shaking the pan and tossing the chard repeatedly. Before removing it from the heat, whisk the eggs briefly with a fork. Add the hot chard, stirring rapidly at the same time; continue to stir until there is no visible separation of egg and chard.

Heat 3 tablespoons olive oil in a clean, large heavy frying pan over high heat and rotate the pan to oil the sides. Add the omelette mixture, stir rapidly without permitting the fork to touch the bottom or sides of the pan, spread the mixture in the pan, and even the surface with the tines of the fork. Cover the pan and lower the heat for several minutes, or until the body of the omelette has noticeably thickened. Gently jerk the pan back and forth to make certain that the omelette slides freely, hold a flat lid firmly against the top of the pan, turn pan and lid upside down together, and return the pan to high heat. Add a tablespoon of olive oil and slip the omelette back into the pan, cooked side up. A minute later, make certain that the omelette moves freely in the pan and slide it onto a platter. If the pan is in good shape, the omelette will not stick; if it should stick, slip a supple spatula beneath to loosen it.

ZUCCHINI OMELETTE
Omelette aux Courgettes

Serves 8

¹/₂ cup olive oil
1 pound sweet onions, finely sliced
Salt
3 eggs
Pepper
1 pound zucchini, cut into ¹/₃-inch dice
Persillade (small bouquet of flat-leaf parsley, 2 garlic cloves,
*   lightly crushed and peeled, each chopped separately,*
*   then finely chopped together)*

In a *poêlon* or heavy saucepan, warm 2 tablespoons of olive oil, add the onions and salt, and sweat, covered, over very low heat, stirring occasionally with a wooden spoon, for about 30 minutes, or until melting but uncolored.

Break the eggs into a mixing bowl; season with salt and pepper.

In a large heavy frying pan, heat 3 tablespoons olive oil and sauté the zucchini, salted, over high heat, tossing often, for 5 minutes, or until lightly colored. Add the persillade and sauté for less than a minute, or until the characteristic garlic-parsley scent fills the kitchen. Add the softened onions and toss a couple of times again. Whisk the eggs briefly with a fork and add the zucchini mixture, stirring briskly with the fork at the same time.

In a clean, large heavy frying pan, heat 2 tablespoons olive oil over high heat, rotate the pan to coat the sides with oil, pour in the egg mixture, and stir rapidly with the fork, tines pointed up, in a circular, swirling motion, taking care not to touch the bottom or sides of the pan with the fork (this can cause an omelette to stick). Lower the heat and cover the pan for a minute, or until the omelette has noticeably thickened but remains moist on the surface. Shake the pan to make certain the omelette slides freely. Hold a flat lid firmly over the pan, invert pan and lid together, return the pan to high heat, add 1 tablespoon of olive oil, and slip the omelette back into the pan, cooked surface up. A few seconds later, shake the pan, making certain that the omelette slides freely, and slip it from the pan to a platter.

FLAT TOMATO OMELETTE
Crespèu aux Tomates

Serves 8

THIS OMELETTE can be prepared only at high summer with garden-ripe tomatoes. The goodness of the omelette depends on the tomatoes being hardly cooked and, at the same time, nearly dry and caramelized. To achieve this, they are first salted to draw out as much liquid as possible, then thrown into very hot oil in the widest possible pan for rapid evaporation.

6 tablespoons olive oil
2 garlic cloves, lightly crushed, peeled, and finely chopped
1 pound garden-ripe tomatoes, peeled, seeded, cut-up, salted,
    and layered in a colander for at least 1 hour
Large pinch of fresh savory leaves, finely chopped, or
    crumbled dried savory
4 eggs
Salt and pepper

Heat 3 tablespoons olive oil in a large heavy frying pan. Add the garlic and, when it is sizzling, add the tomatoes. Sauté over very high heat, jerking the pan back and forth and tossing the tomatoes repeatedly, until there is no liquid left in the pan and the tomatoes have begun to stick and brown. Add the savory, toss once again, empty the tomatoes onto a plate, and leave until tepid.

In a mixing bowl, briefly whisk the eggs, salt, and pepper with a fork and stir in the tomatoes. In a clean, large heavy frying pan, heat 2 tablespoons olive oil over high heat, rotating the pan to coat the sides, pour in the egg mixture, and swirl with the fork, tines turned up, taking care not to scrape against the bottom or the sides of the pan. Tilt the pan repeatedly in all directions, each time lifting the edge of the omelette with the tines of the fork to let liquid egg run beneath. When no more will run, lower the heat and cover the pan for perhaps 30 seconds to let the omelette partially set. Shake the pan to make certain the omelette slides loosely back and forth, then hold a flat lid firmly on top of the pan, turn lid and pan over together, holding the overturned omelette on the lid while returning the pan to high heat. Add 1 tablespoon olive oil to the pan and slip the omelette back in for a few seconds to seal the uncooked surface. Shake the pan to make certain the omelette is not sticking and slide it onto a round platter.

ARTICHOKE OMELETTE
Omelette "Clair de Lune"

Serves 8

To the Peyraud family, "clair de lune" means artichoke omelette. It was baptized years ago by François's youngest son, Jérome, for whom the pattern of artichoke slices on the omelette's surface represented moon crescents.

Lulu emphasises the importance of using tender young artichokes in which the chokes have not yet begun to develop. If these

are not available, buy the freshest looking, thick-stemmed artichokes the market has to offer. After turning them (page 257), cut
each in two vertically and, with a small, sharply pointed stainless
steel knife, cut out the chokes before slicing the halves vertically.

1/2 cup olive oil
1 pound sweet onions, finely sliced
Salt
3 eggs
Pepper
1 pound tender artichokes, pared (page 257), finely sliced,
   and tossed in a bowl with a little olive oil to coat them

In an earthenware *poêlon,* warm 2 tablespoons olive oil, add the
onions and salt, and cook, covered, over very low heat, stirring occasionally with a wooden spoon, for 30 minutes, or until melting
but uncolored. Break the eggs into a mixing bowl, season with salt
and pepper, and hold in readiness. In a large heavy frying pan, heat
3 tablespoons olive oil and sauté the artichokes, salted, over high
heat, tossing repeatedly, until lightly golden and beginning to crisp
at the edges. Add the onions to the artichokes and toss together until intimately intermingled.

With a fork, whisk the eggs briefly, only enough to break them
up. Add the sautéed onions and artichokes, stirring rapidly with
the fork at the same time to prevent the eggs coagulating in contact
with the heat.

In a clean, large heavy frying pan, heat 2 tablespoons olive oil
over high heat, rotating the pan to make certain that the sides are
coated with oil. Add the omelette mixture and stir it rapidly, taking
care that the back of the fork does not touch or scrape against the
bottom of the pan. With the tines of the fork, lift the edges of the
omelette all around, tilting the pan to let loose egg run beneath.

(continued)

Lower the heat and cover the pan for 2 to 3 minutes, or until the body of the omelette has begun to thicken noticeably but the surface remains liquid. Shake the pan gently to make certain that the omelette slides freely back and forth without sticking. Hold a plate or a flat lid firmly over the top of the pan and turn plate and pan upside down together. Return the pan to high heat, add 1 tablespoon olive oil, and slip the omelette back into the pan, cooked side facing up. Cook for less than 1 minute, making certain that the omelette slides freely in the pan, and slip it onto a serving platter. Best tepid, but also good cold or at room temperature.

GRILLED MUSSELS
Moules à la Catalane

Serves 8

"THE WHOLE FAMILY joins in, opening the live mussels and, as soon as they are removed from the embers, eating them straight from the grill. It's a marvelous ambience," says Lulu.

To clean the mussels, put them to soak in cold water to which a handful of coarse sea salt has been added. Scrape them, if necessary, or simply rub them beneath the water. Pull out the beards. To open a mussel, force the two shells in opposite directions between thumb and forefinger and slip a knife blade between the shells—when it touches the muscle, the shells open out. With knife tip, loosen the flesh from one half shell and fold it into the other. Twist the empty half shell free and discard it. As they are ready, arrange the mussel-filled half shells in rows, touching, on a large grill.

François makes a bonfire from several large bundles of dry branches—at the Domaine, bundles of grapevine branches, rescued from winter pruning, are reserved for fast grilling. There is a moment of fierce blaze before the flames die, leaving a mound of glowing embers that are spread out enough to create a flattened surface on which to place the grill.

> 4 *quarts mussels, cleaned and opened, half shells arranged on grill (see above)*
> *Pepper*
> *Olive oil*

Grind pepper over the mussels, pour a few drops of olive oil over each mussel, and place the grill directly on the bed of hot coals. When the mussels contract, releasing liquid that begins to boil almost immediately, combining with the olive oil to form an exquisite little sauce, they are done. Remove the grill from the coals before the mussels' liquid has evaporated. Pour well-chilled Tempier rosé and place a bucket on the ground to receive the empty mussel shells.

GRILLED SARDINES
Sardines Grillées

Serves 6 to 8

"THEY MUST BE grilled just as they come from the sea, neither scaled nor gutted," says Lulu. "These sardines could not possibly be as good served at table and eaten with knives and forks. They have to be eaten out-of-doors, standing up, straight from the grill. Each person rubs off the scales with fingers, lifts off and eats the fillets, and discards the carcass and guts. No seasoning is necessary—they are seasoned by the sea. Of course, you have to have a large pile of paper napkins handy, a communal finger bowl, and a bucket on the ground in which to throw the carcasses and the napkins." Lulu's communal finger bowl is a huge glass compotier filled with tepid water, thin slices of lemon, and floating rose petals. A 16-inch-square, flat, double-faced grill will very neatly hold 24 sardines, placed side by side, in two rows.

2 pounds (about 24) freshly fished sardines

Prepare a solid bed of incandescent wood coals. Arrange the sardines on one face of a flat, double-faced grill, close it, clamp it, and place it over the coals. Turn the grill after 2 minutes, grill on the other side for less than 2 minutes, remove from the coals, open up the grill on a rustic surface, and invite your guests to serve themselves.

BUTTERED SARDINE CRUSTS
Sardines Crues, Croûtons Beurrées

Serves 6

FRESHLY NETTED SARDINES are always abundant and always in-expensive in the Bandol market; they recur often in Lulu's menus. To fillet sardines, first cut off the heads with a small sharp knife, slit the abdomens and gut them, then hold each under cold running water, rubbing the surfaces gently from tail to head end to remove the scales. Hold the sardine on a flat surface and slide the knife blade flat between the fillet and the central bone, from tail to head end. Turn the fish over and remove the other fillet in the same way. Rinse each fillet under running water, pulling off any clinging frag-ments of fin bones. Lay the fillets out on paper towels and press pa-per towels on top to sponge them dry. Lulu often peels off the skin from each fillet, but she admits that this is time-consuming and, perhaps, unnecessary. The flesh beneath the skin of very fresh sar-dines is iridescent; the beauty alone justifies skinning the fillets.

> *Thin slices of baguette (as many as there are sardine fillets)*
> *Butter, softened at room temperature*
> *1 pound (about 12) very fresh sardines, filleted (see above)*
> *Salt*

Grill the baguette slices, over hot coals, in a hot oven, or beneath a broiler, until crisp and lightly colored on both sides. Smear a bit of butter on one side of each, fold or twirl a raw sardine fillet on top, sprinkle lightly with salt, and serve immediately, while the toasts are still warm.

RAW FISH SALAD
Mérou à la Tahitienne

Serves 10 to 12

DURING THE 1950S, the Peyrauds' diver friends, former wartime frogmen appointed to the recently created CIPS (Centre International de Plonger Sousmarine) in Bandol, whose business is the study of the sea floor the world round, established a tradition of each year celebrating François's birthday with a grouper (*mérou*), chosen from a colony that they called their *troupeau*, or herd, and that they visited regularly. The grouper's weight in kilograms was supposed to approximate François's age in years. The last great celebration was for his twenty-first birthday and his age imposed two groupers. Lulu recalls with sentimental delight the arrival of the divers carrying the two huge fish and the hours that she, they, and a number of family members spent separating the fish's firm flesh from the skin and bones, slicing it and cutting it first into strips, then into tiny cubes. The recipe was also furnished by the divers, who had returned from an expedition to Tahiti with its memory; it has, inevitably, been somewhat Mediterraneanized.

> *3 pounds grouper fillet or other firm, white-fleshed fish
>   (anglerfish, halibut, cod, hake), skinned, boned, and cut
>   into approximately ⅓-inch cubes*
> *Juice of 4 lemons (or more)*
> *1 pound tomatoes, peeled, seeded, diced, salted for 30
>   minutes, and drained*
> *Handful of fresh mint leaves, finely chopped*
> *Large handful of flat-leaf parsley, finely chopped*
> *4 garlic cloves, lightly crushed, peeled, and finely chopped*
> *1 large white sweet onion, finely chopped, or 1 cup finely
>   sliced or chopped scallions*

2 large sweet peppers (1 yellow, 1 red), split, stemmed, seeded, white ribs removed, cut into slivers lengthwise, and diced

Salt and freshly ground pepper

4 dried cayenne peppers, pounded to a powder in a mortar with a pinch of coarse salt, or 1/8 teaspoon (or a large pinch of) cayenne

1 teaspoon fennel seeds added to the mortar with the cayenne and coarsely crushed

3/4 cup olive oil

Crisp, cupped leaves from the hearts of head lettuce, white cabbage, radicchio, etc.

Put the cubes of raw fish into a large bowl, pour over enough lemon juice to immerse them, and leave for about 45 minutes, tossing them lightly a couple of times with your fingertips. Drain them, discarding the lemon juice, rinse them in cold water, drain again, and sponge them dry between towels or paper towels (soaking in lemon juice has a similar effect to poaching—the semitranslucent flesh turns opaque, firms up, and discards a certain amount of albuminous material, the equivalent of the gray scum thrown off during poaching). Return them to the cleaned and dried bowl. Scatter over the vegetables and herbs, sprinkle with the seasoning, and dribble over the olive oil. Toss repeatedly, lifting with splayed fingers, taste for salt and lemon juice, adding more of each if necessary, toss again, cover, and refrigerate for at least 3 hours before serving. Toss again as before, taste again for salt and lemon—you may want to add more olive oil also. Prepare a number of salad and cabbage leaves, each filled with about 1 tablespoonful of the mixture, lay them out on a large platter, and present the remainder of the salad and the leaves apart so that guests may serve themselves.

DEEP-FRIED APPETIZERS
Amuse-gueules Frites

DEEP-FRIED MOUTHFULS—of vegetables and seafood, in particular—are among the classics of Lulu's apéritif "finger-food" repertoire. She says, "I always serve them with the apéritif because you can fry only a few at a time and they have to be served immediately, still crisp, to be wonderful, so I, or whoever is helping me in the kitchen, have to be running back and forth all the time with each new batch. If they are held in an oven until all are fried, they turn limp."

In the course of writing this book, "Trying to Pin Lulu Down" has evolved into an ongoing game. I asked her to describe her system of deep-frying. She said, "Well, I always use a beer batter—I dip things in it and fry them . . . I don't much like eggplant slices in batter so I just flour them and fry them." The next time around, I decided to ask about more specific materials . . . "Squid, for instance?" "I cut it up, flour the pieces, and fry them." "But, you said that you used beer batter." "Well, I do, but not always . . . anyway, anything that is moist, like squid or zucchini slices, I flour first because the batter clings better that way—if you like, you can dip floured things in beaten eggs instead of batter and fry them. They are very crisp that way—large, fresh sage leaves are delicious dipped, dry, in batter and fried." "Do you dip zucchini flowers in batter and fry them?" "No. I know that everyone else does that, but I like to stuff and braise zucchini flowers—fried, they have no taste . . . but, clusters of acacia (locust) flowers are delicious dipped in batter and deep-fried."

FRITTER BATTER
Pâte à Frire

Enough for 8 servings

THE PROPORTIONS of flour to liquid are, to a certain extent, a question of personal taste. A relatively thin batter will produce a crisper coating, with greater loss of batter in the oil; a thicker batter will hold better but the coating will be spongier. Whisking the batter makes it elastic; it should be whisked no more than necessary to combine the ingredients. The resting period relaxes the batter, permitting it to cling better to the foods that are dipped in it.

1 cup flour
Salt
3/4 cup tepid beer
2 tablespoons olive oil
1 egg white

Sift the flour and salt into a mixing bowl, and whisk in the beer and the olive oil, working from the center out, until smooth. Cover with a plate and leave the batter to rest for 1 hour. Just before using, whisk the egg white until it holds soft peaks and fold it gently into the batter.

MIXED FRITTERS
Beignets Panachés

Serves 8

FRITTERS ARE PERFECT only when fried in fresh oil. Lulu uses olive oil, which flavors them exquisitely. A tasteless vegetable oil—corn, for example—will produce very good results at a price that permits one to discard the oil after using it once. Lulu often dips langoustine tails in batter and fries them—in America, one would substitute large shrimp, shelled to the tail and deveined. Tiny, whole cuttlefish, with cuttlebones and beaks removed, are another favorite.

Deep-fryers are equipped with thermostats. The correct temperature for these fritters and for the floured vegetables in the following recipes is 375°F. Any large wide pot, filled to no more than half with oil (a 5-quart pot with 2 quarts of oil, for instance) will work as well. When a drop of batter sizzles on contact with the oil, it is ready. Don't try to use a basket—battered foods will stick to it and it takes up unnecessary space. The ideal instrument for removing deep-fried foods from the oil is a large, round, flat wire skimmer, called a spider. Next best is a slotted spoon.

After each batch of fritters is removed from the oil, fragments of fried batter will remain behind. They should be skimmed out and discarded before adding the next batch.

Oil for frying (see above)
Flour
1 1/2 pounds small squid, cleaned (see Stuffed Baked Squid,
    page 182), body pouches cut across into 1/2-inch rings,
    head and tentacle sections split in two, and well drained
1 pound young artichokes, turned (page 257), split to
    remove chokes (if necessary), sliced thin (1/8 to 1/4 inch),
    and tossed in a little olive oil to coat them

Salt and pepper
1 recipe Fritter Batter (page 105)
Handful of large, fresh sage leaves

Put the oil to heat.

Sprinkle a tray with flour. Sponge the squid sections with paper towels to remove excess moisture and pat the artichoke slices with paper towels to remove excess oil. Season both with salt and pepper and spread them out on the floured surface. Sprinkle flour lightly on top. Drop a few of each into the bowl of batter and, holding the bowl next to the hot oil, lift the pieces out, one by one, with a fork or with tongs, and slip them into the oil. Dip a few leaves of sage in the batter, one by one, holding the leaf by the stem end, and slip them into the oil. As the edges turn golden, after 2 or 3 minutes, flip each element over in the oil with the tines of a fork. A couple of minutes later, when golden and crisp on both sides, remove with a spider or a slotted spoon to paper towels to drain for a couple of seconds, transfer to a napkin-lined basket or platter, and send it to your guests while preparing the next batch.

Fried Zucchini and Eggplant
Courgettes et Aubergines Frites

Serves 8

Fried zucchini is equally good battered or floured. Eggplant is better simply floured. Floured whitebait (*petite friture*) or fillets of small flat fish (sole, lemon sole, gray sole, flounder), sliced on the bias into ½-inch widths, are delicious prepared in this way. Because of their size, the easiest way to flour them is to shake them in a paper bag with seasoned (salt, pepper, cayenne) flour, then toss them in a sieve to rid them of excess flour before adding them to the hot oil. Lulu often prepares tiny, 2-inch-long red mullets (*rougets*) like this, to everyone's ravishment. If frying these small articles, there is no question of turning each over individually in the oil—simply stir them around to turn all sides crisp.

> *Oil for frying*
> *Flour*
> *1½ pounds zucchini, stem and flower tips cut off, sliced*
> *   lengthwise into ¼-inch-thick strips*
> *1½ pounds elongated, firm, seedless eggplant, stem and*
> *   flower ends cut off, sliced into ¼-inch-thick rounds*
> *Salt*

Put the oil to heat.

Sprinkle a tray with flour. Distribute the slices of zucchini and eggplant on the bed of flour, sprinkle flour over, and give each slice a shake in hand before slipping it into the hot oil. Add no more slices than can float freely in the oil. Flip each over with the tines of a fork after a couple of minutes and, when the slices are unevenly golden and brown, remove them with a spider to paper towels, transfer immediately to a napkin-lined basket or platter, sprinkle with salt, and serve, while preparing the next batch.

ANCHOVY PUFFS
Choux aux Anchois

Serves 8

THESE PUFFS are particularly good served warm; they and a chilled Tempier rosé do wonders for each other. Lulu prepares gougères in the same way, substituting 3 ounces of diced Gruyère for the anchovies.

1 cup water
Salt
5 tablespoons butter, cut into small pieces
1 cup flour
4 eggs
5 salt anchovies, rinsed, filleted, and chopped, or 10 fillets

Preheat the oven to 375°F.

Combine the water, salt, and butter in a saucepan, place over medium heat, bring to a boil, and as soon as the butter is melted, remove from the heat. Add the flour all at once, stirring with a wooden spoon. Return to the heat, stir vigorously, then beat until the mixture pulls away from the sides of the pan in a smooth mass. Remove from the heat and leave to cool for 2 or 3 minutes.

Beat in the eggs, whole, one at a time, continuing to beat each time until the egg is completely incorporated and the paste smooth before adding the next egg. Add the chopped anchovies at the same time as the last egg and beat well. At 3-inch intervals, drop teaspoonfuls of the paste onto an ungreased baking sheet and bake for 25 minutes without disturbing. Turn off the oven, prick each puff with a sharply pointed knife, and leave them in the oven for 10 minutes to dry out.

Provençal Celebrations

To be meaningful, certain dishes in Provence must gather together all the family or very dear friends around a single dish—but what a dish!

Il y a des plats en Provence qui n'ont un sens que dans le fait de réunir toute la famille ou des amis très chers autour d'un plat unique—mais quel plat!

Lulu

Bouillabaisse and aïoli are mythical dishes. The words, themselves, are magic—musical and salivating as the liquid syllables roll round one's tongue—and, to all the world, they symbolize the exuberance of Provence, its bright colors and white light, its sky as blue as the Mediterranean.

When Lulu gathers family and friends around a single dish, that means that there are no preceding courses at table; amuse-gueules with the apéritif and the cheese platter are sacred, and dessert is never sacrificed.

Opposite: Bouillabaisse.

BOUILLABAISSE
Bouillabaisse

Serves 8

A BOUILLABAISSE DAY at Domaine Tempier is a finely orchestrated celebration. Behind the scenes, the day begins with Lulu's visit to Bandol to meet the fishing boats as they return with the night's catch. When the catch has been unusually rich, the special fish that appear in that day's bouillabaisse are noted in Lulu's menu diary—in particular, the pastel-splashed, sinister-looking *murène* (moray eel), firm-fleshed with a wild sea taste unlike any other, is always noted, as are *Saint-Pierre* (John Dory) and *mérou* (grouper). Always present are *baudroie* (anglerfish), *rascasses* (scorpion fish), *vives* (weevers), *rouquiers* (wrasses), and *serrans* (combers).

At least as important as the choice of fish to be presented are the elements that enter into the preparation of the *soupe,* the moistening agent in Lulu's bouillabaisse. Fish merchants in the region carry crates, labeled "soupe," of freshly netted tiny rockfish, varying from less than 1 inch to 3 or 4 inches in length. It's a pity that guests are never able to admire the extraordinary beauty of these fish before they are transformed into broth. Many of them duplicate, in miniature, the fish that are served whole with a bouillabaisse: thorny black rascasses and red rascasses, grotesque weevers with eyes popping from the tops of their heads, the lovely *girelle,* or rainbow wrasse, with a wavy, luminous ribbon of orange reaching from mouth to tail, other wrasses, bright green or multicolored, dappled or striped, and dozens of combers, among which the *serran écriture,* with blue and lilac scribbles against a red background, is especially striking; tiny soles are often present as well as the blunt-nosed slipper lobsters, called *cigales de mer* (sea cicadas), whose flesh is the sweetest of all the crustaceans. Also for the soup, kept in closed crates to prevent their escape, are *favouilles*—scuttling green shore crabs—whose distinctive spicy, peppery flavor

Soup fish.

will be recognized immediately by lovers of *soupe de poissons* or bouillabaisse. Slices of conger eel are usually served with a bouillabaisse but, because its flesh is thickly threaded with fine bones, Lulu prefers to cut up the conger and lose it in the soup. When serving the soup on its own, as a first course, she adds parboiled fresh egg noodles to the strained, reheated soup, dosed with saffron, and sometimes serves giant shrimp tails, grilled in their shells over wood embers, at the same time.

Part of the magic of Lulu's bouillabaisse depends on beautiful weather and guest participation in the final steps of its preparation. The table is set on the long terrace in front of the house. Vin rosé and tapenade crusts are served on the terrace while François prepares a fruitwood fire in the nearby garden path. Mortars of rouille are placed at table and the fish, some whole, others sliced or filleted, aglint in their saffron–olive oil marinade, are presented on a huge platter to be admired. The soup is poured into an antique copper cauldron, gleaming inside, blackened on the outside from the smoke of a hundred bouillabaisse fires. It is placed on a tripod over the fire and everyone gathers around, glass in hand, to watch the ritual addition of potatoes, mussels, anglerfish, rascasses, and the other fish, in that order. "Maybe the mussels are overcooked," says Lulu, "but it is the flavor that counts—I put them into the pot before adding the fish so they won't get in my way when I serve the fish onto a platter. I don't count different cooking times for the different fish because I use only firm-fleshed varieties—anglerfish and rascasses take a little longer than the others so they go in first and come out last." Shortly after taking these notes, I assisted at the preparation of a beautiful bouillabaisse in which the mussels were added after the fish. More recently, a couple of octopus, cleaned and deep-frozen in advance to tenderize the flesh, unfrozen overnight, cut into small pieces, and simmered for an hour in a court-bouillon (which was then added to the fish soup base), were added to the boiling broth at the same time as the fish, with the mussels thrown on top. Never has a bouillabaisse been more sumptuous.

In the summer of 1973, as part of the supplementary program to my cooking classes in Avignon, I organized a bouillabaisse lunch for my students in Carry-le-Rouet, near Marseilles, at L'Escale, a restaurant whose chef-proprietor, Charles Bérot, was famous for his bouillabaisse. Domaine Tempier offered the wine and Lulu joined us for lunch. The 1972 rosé was poured to accompany a variety of little seafood hors d'oeuvre, but at my request, the 1972 red, which would not be bottled for sale until a year hence, was put into bottles to wash down the bouillabaisse. The day was hot and the tables were set on a high open terrace juttied above the Mediterranean. At each table, an ice bucket was filled with cold water and a few ice cubes, to keep the wine cool but not over chilled. Madame Bérot kept a sharp eye on the buckets and, as ice cubes began to disappear, she would order another handful to be added. Throughout the bouillabaisse service, the untamed red Tempier, still slightly prickly from its young residue of carbon dioxide, flowed at a constant 50°F. A 1966 Tempier, somewhat less cool, accompanied the cheese platter. It was the kind of day that assumes greater importance in retrospect, memory distilling the limpid blue sky, the intermingled scents of the sea air, the bouillabaisse, and the cool fruit of the wine into a sort of abstract symbol of well-being. Lulu was ravished. With her next bouillabaisse, she insisted that Jean-Marie serve cooled red Tempier from the most recent vintage. The entire family was seduced by the alliance of the cool wine's wild fruit, the saffrony bouillabaisse, and the garlicky rouille. For twenty years, Lulu's bouillabaisse has been escorted by cool, young, red Tempier — with rosé always present for those who prefer it. The final line of her bouillabaisse recipe reads, "With this rich dish, which was once a poor fisherman's dish (*un*

Lulu making rouille for the bouillabaisse.

plat de pauvre), drink either a very cool rosé or a young red, just as cool!" The tradition is maintained in Berkeley, California; in *Chez Panisse Cooking*, Paul Bertolli writes, "Fish and shellfish soup, as served at Chez Panisse, would not be the same if not accompanied by the wines (both red and rosé) of Domaine Tempier. . . ."

Part of the bouillabaisse mystique resides in the persistent claim that no bouillabaisse is possible away from the Mediterranean coast or without the presence of rascasses (on a recent trip to Australia I found quantities of red rascasses in the Sydney fish market, called red rock cod; I was told that black rascasses also exist in the Australian waters). Lulu and Paule returned recently from a week's celebration of Domaine Tempier wines and Chez Panisse food in Berkeley. The week's menus, the first of which featured Bouillabaisse for Lulu, were printed beneath the title "Domaine Tempier at Chez Panisse. Celebrating the Visit of Lulu Peyraud and Paule Peyraud. April 27— May 2, 1992." Lulu's verdict: "The bouillabaisse was marvelous! Of course it was not like mine because the fish were not the same—they were all large fish that were filleted and cut into serving portions. The heads and carcasses were used to make the broth. It came as a surprise because I'm used to seeing whole fish in a bouillabaisse. Most of the fish were flown in from the East Coast, but they were absolutely fresh, the seasoning was perfect, the flavors wonderful! Paul not only pounded anglerfish livers in the rouille as I do, but he poached slices of anglerfish liver in the bouillabaisse; that was new to me—they were *dé-li-cieux!*"

Anglerfish, also called monkfish, which was practically unknown in America twenty years ago, is quite common on the market today. The texture of its flesh is often compared to that of lobster. When filleted, the cartilaginous central bone, chopped small, and the trimmings and the head, chopped to pieces, are precious additions to the fish broth (the heads are in such demand in the south of France that fishmongers no longer give them away). The large pinkish-beige liver, whose mysterious flavor and sumptuous texture characterize Lulu's rouille and all her fish stuffings, is as velvety and voluptuous as foie gras—no other liver can replace it. Because fish merchants often receive anglerfish already beheaded, gutted, and skinned, heads and livers may have to be ordered in advance.

Oily fish do not mix well in a bouillabaisse, but most fish in American waters are suitable. Some of the best, among them John Dory and conger eel, are rarely marketed, probably because any fish of unusual appearance is considered suspect by the fishing industry. Any fish called rockfish, rock cod, redfish, ocean perch, sea perch, red snapper, sea trout, ocean catfish, scrod, tom cod, croaker, or drum is good bouillabaisse fish; grouper, porgy, tautog, cunner, spot, black bass, striped bass, sheepshead, halibut, hake, haddock, sea robin, sculpin, skate wings, and stargazers are but a few of the other possibilities.

Lulu does not like to mix up too many scents and flavors. Because the principal herb is fennel, thyme and bay leaf are, typically, absent from her bouillabaisse (when describing a fish preparation, she often indicates "lots of herbs"; if asked "Which herbs," the answer is invariably, "Well, fennel, of course!"). Wild fennel (Foeniculum officinale) grows everywhere in the south of France. In spring, the tender new shoots are used, in summer, the fresh green stalks, and in autumn, the tall, flowered stalks are collected, cut or broken into short lengths, tied in bundles, and used throughout the winter (cultivated Florence bulb fennel does not have a sufficiently pronounced flavor to replace wild fennel). As for dried orange peel, a common element in most bouillabaisse bouquets, Lulu is categorical: "Dried orange peel is necessary in a Provençal daube and it gives a wonderful tang to a red wine game stew, but I would never use it with fish." Carrots, on the other hand, absent from other Provençal fish soups, always count among the aromatic elements in Lulu's fish soup, whether it be served as such or as a base for bouillabaisse. Other distinguishing characteristics are lots of garlic, not too much tomato, and the caress of wood smoke, a memory of the original fisherman's bouillabaisse cooked over a driftwood fire at the seaside; when weather prevents the bouillabaisse from being finished out-of-doors, François prepares the wood fire in the kitchen fireplace.

With the exception of the anglerfish, all the fish in Lulu's bouillabaisse are whole. She counts 20 minutes from the time the potatoes and mussels are added. Because most of the filleted fish will require shorter cooking, I have adjusted the timing.

> *2 pounds anglerfish, filleted, trimmed of flabby membranes*
> *and belly flaps (reserve for soup), and cut into 8 sections*
> *4 pounds fillets of white-fleshed saltwater fish (see above),*
> *cut into serving portions (Lulu: "8 rascasses, 5 weevers,*
> *3 each of 2 or 3 other varieties—wrasses, combers, John*
> *Dory, etc.")*

MARINADE
1 bouquet of fresh wild fennel or several sections fennel
stalk, or a large pinch of powdered fennel seed
About ⅛ teaspoon powdered saffron
4 to 5 garlic cloves, crushed and peeled
About 4 tablespoons olive oil

FISH SOUP
4 tablespoons olive oil
1 large onion, sliced or coarsely chopped
1 head garlic, cloves separated and each crushed with heel of
hand or beneath a large knife blade
2 tomatoes, quartered

(continued)

2 to 3 pounds reserved fish heads and carcasses, gills
    removed, rinsed, and chopped or broken into small
    pieces (Lulu: "2 pounds soupe"—small, whole,
    ungutted soup fish)
1 thick slice (about ½ pound) conger eel (if available), cut
    into small pieces
8 small, lively blue crabs (Lulu: "8 favouilles")
3 quarts water
Salt and pepper
1 bouquet of fennel, or 1 teaspoon fennel seeds
1 leek, trimmed of tough green parts, partially slit, rinsed,
    and finely sliced
1 celery branch, sliced
2 carrots, peeled and finely sliced

ROUILLE
1 cup fresh bread crumbs (without crusts)
¼ teaspoon powdered saffron dissolved in 2 or 3
    tablespoons hot fish soup
2 dried cayenne peppers, or a large pinch of powdered
    cayenne
Large pinch of coarse salt
3 garlic cloves, peeled
1 anglerfish liver, poached for a minute in a ladle of fish
    soup, until firmed up but still pink
1 egg yolk
About 2 cups olive oil, at room temperature

¼ teaspoon saffron
8 medium potatoes (about 2 pounds), peeled and quartered
1 large sweet white onion, sliced paper-thin
2 tomatoes, peeled, seeded, and coarsely chopped

4 to 5 garlic cloves, crushed and peeled
1 bouquet of fennel (use the fennel from the marinade), or a
large pinch of fennel seeds tied in a piece of cheesecloth
1 ½ pounds mussels, soaked in water with a handful of
coarse sea salt, scraped, bearded, and rinsed
24 thin slices of crusty elongated French bread (baguette),
preferably sour dough (pain au levain), partially dried
out in a slow oven or, on a hot clear day, in the sun,
stroked on each side with peeled garlic cloves

Spread the pieces of fish out on a platter, distribute the fennel branches among them or sprinkle with the powdered fennel seed, sprinkle with saffron, add the fragmented crushed garlic, and dribble olive oil all over. Turn the fish around and over several times in its marinade, rubbing the surfaces gently until evenly yellowed with saffron and coated with oil. Marinate for a couple of hours, turning the fish over two or three times, while preparing the fish soup and the rouille.

For the fish soup: In a large heavy pot, warm the olive oil over medium-low heat, add the onion and the crushed, unpeeled garlic cloves, and stir regularly with a wooden spoon until the onion is softened but not colored. Add the tomatoes, the broken-up heads and carcasses, and the cut-up conger eel, raise the heat to medium, and stir regularly, mashing with the spoon or a wooden pestle, until the contents of the pot are reduced to a coarse debris. Add the live crabs and stir until they turn red. Pour over water to cover generously, stir to make certain nothing is sticking to the pot, bring the water to a boil over medium-high heat, and skim the foam from the surface. Add salt, pepper, fennel, leek, celery, and carrots. Adjust the heat to maintain a light boil, lid ajar, for 45 minutes. After 5 or 10 minutes, remove the crabs, one or two at a time, to a marble mortar. Pound them with a wooden pestle, breaking up the shells thoroughly, and spoon them back into the soup. Rinse out the mortar with a ladle of soup and pour it back into the pot.

Remove the bouquet of fennel and pass the contents of the pot, a couple of ladles at a time, through a fine sieve into a large bowl, pressing with the wooden pestle to extract the liquid without passing any of the debris into the purée. Spoon the pressed debris from the sieve, discard it, and pour the sieved soup into another bowl before beginning again. When all the soup has been passed, rinse the sieve, making certain that no tiny fish bones remain, and pass the soup again, loosely, shaking the sieve gently, to separate the broth from any puréed solids or fish bones that may have passed through the first time.

For the rouille: Put the bread crumbs in a bowl and, with a fork, mash them with the dissolved saffron, adding a bit more fish soup, if necessary, to form a loose paste. In a mortar, pound the cayenne peppers to a powder with a wooden pestle. Add the coarse salt and the garlic, pound to a paste, add the anglerfish liver, and pound to a consistent thick smooth paste. Add the egg yolk and the saffron-bread paste and turn briskly with the pestle until the mixture is smooth and homogenous. Mount it like a mayonnaise, adding the oil in a thin trickle to the side of the mortar, while turning constantly with the pestle.

Reheat the fish soup, dissolve the saffron in a ladle of boiling soup, and stir it in. Add the potatoes, onion, tomatoes, garlic, and fennel and return to a boil. Five minutes later, add the mussels, then the marinated pieces of anglerfish. Five minutes later, add the remaining fish and boil for 10 minutes longer (boiling produces a liaison between the broth and the olive oil).

With a large, flat, slotted skimming spoon or a spider, lift the pieces of fish onto a large heated platter, the mussels and potatoes onto another platter (never mind if they get a bit mixed up), and ladle part of the broth into a heated soup tureen, leaving the remainder over heat for the second servings. At table, smear garlic crusts thickly with rouille, place a couple of crusts in each soup plate, and pour over a ladle of soup. In separate plates (or the same), serve potatoes, mussels, and fish; pass the rouille and the broth.

GRAND AÏOLI

AÏOLI—garlic-oil—is two things. First of all, it is the more or less mild or powerful garlic mayonnaise that Lulu serves with any number of individual preparations—cold roasts, poached fish, boiled vegetables, fritters, etc. Secondly, it is an abundant meal, a traditional cornucopia of products of the earth and the sea, accompanied by an aïoli sauce. The traditional meal, or Grand Aïoli, at the Peyraud table, is a mad, joyous circus. Lulu rarely prepares a Grand Aïoli for fewer than 15 or 20 people, and there are always three mortars of aïoli sauce at table: one, relatively mild, for *les estrangers* (Parisians, Americans, etc.); one, generously dosed with garlic, for the Provençaux; and one, overpowering, for Lucien, who likes a "bite" in his aïoli (the Parisians and the Americans invariably end up wiping Lucien's mortar clean). As with the bouillabaisse, vin rosé is always present, but it is cool, young red that flows most freely.

While taking notes for the following recipe, I was puzzled when Lulu called for "3 or 4 cloves of garlic." I asked if that was enough. She said, "Well, you know, Richard, that I always use at least a head—and a lot more for Lucien—but I was thinking of your American readers."

AÏOLI SAUCE
Sauce Aïoli

About 2 cups

Large pinch of coarse sea salt
1 head (more or less to taste) garlic, cloves separated,
  crushed, and peeled
2 egg yolks, at room temperature
2 cups olive oil, at room temperature
1 to 2 teaspoons water, at room temperature

In a marble mortar with a wooden pestle, pound the salt and garlic
to a smooth, liquid paste. Add the egg yolks and stir briskly with
the pestle until they lighten in color. Begin to add the oil in a tiny
trickle, to the side of the mortar so that the oil flows gradually into
the yolk and garlic mixture, while turning constantly with the pestle.
As the mixture begins to thicken, the flow of oil can be increased to
a thick thread, always to the side of the mortar. Never stop turning
the pestle, with a rapid, beating motion. When the aïoli is quite
thick, add a teaspoon or two of water to loosen it, while turning,
and continue adding oil until you have obtained the desired quantity and consistency. Cover and refrigerate until serving.

GRAND AÏOLI

Serves 8

1 recipe Aïoli Sauce (page 124)
2 pounds salt cod, soaked and poached (see Brandade,
    page 83)
1 pound green beans, parboiled (5 to 8 minutes) in salt water
16 small carrots, peeled and parboiled (12 to 15 minutes) in
    salt water
8 small new potatoes, parboiled (about 20 minutes) in salt
    water
1 cauliflower, broken into florets and parboiled (3 to 4
    minutes) in salt water
8 young artichokes, parboiled (about 30 minutes) in salt
    water, split in two, and chokes removed
4 medium beets, baked at 375°F for about 45 minutes,
    peeled and quartered
8 sweet potatoes, baked at 375°F for about 45 minutes
8 hard-boiled eggs (cover raw eggs with cold water, bring to
    a boil, hold at a simmer for 10 minutes), refreshed in
    cold water and shelled
8 firm ripe tomatoes, peeled
1 recipe Stewed Octopus (page 177)

The star preparation of Lulu's Grand Aïoli is the stewed octopus, a dish that arouses passions, not only in the Peyraud family but in all who have tasted it—when octopus sauce and aïoli meet, flavors explode. Lulu serves the stewed octopus very hot, directly from its earthenware *poêlon*. The cod, vegetables, and eggs are arranged on large platters, the cod and the vegetables as warm as possible, and placed at table. Often Lulu, Paule or Catherine serve up the plates from a separate table and pass mortars of aïoli at table.

SOUPS

From time immemorial, soups have nourished our ancestors and continue to cast a spell over young generations.

Du fond des ages il est un mets qui a nourri tous nos ancêtres et qui continue à encorceler les jeunes générations, ce sont les soupes.

Lulu

FOR THE PEYRAUD FAMILY, as for most of France, soup is meant to be eaten in the evening, an undemanding, comforting, easily digestible prelude to a good night's sleep, which is no less delicious for possessing these homely qualities. The only soup that I have encountered (quite often) at Lulu's lunch table is fish soup (*soupe de poissons*), the recipe for which is not included in this chapter because it is one of the elements in her bouillabaisse and has been incorporated into that recipe.

Lulu prefers to receive at midday, but circumstances may impose guests for the evening meal as well. On these occasions, she often opens a meal, in the summer, with a soupe au pistou or a chilled summer soup; in other seasons, a fish preparation or a vegetable ragout or gratin.

The simple vegetable soups are reserved for the family. A pity perhaps, for their purity of flavor is wondrous. Lulu says, "I never use stock in my vegetable soups because I hardly ever prepare pot-

---

Opposite: Soupe au Pistou.

au-feu these days." But then, she hastens to add, "Of course, I prefer soups prepared with water—with stock, you can't taste the vegetables."

CROUTONS FOR SOUPS
Croûtons pour les Potages

OFTEN WITH PURÉED vegetable soups, sometimes with others, Lulu serves little croutons to the side, either crisped in butter or fried in olive oil, depending on whether one or the other has entered into the soup's preparation. "Whether or not I serve croutons depends on how thick the soup is," she says. "Sometimes I don't know until I have finished it." The croutons are cut from $\frac{1}{3}$-inch-thick slices of semifresh (1 or 2 days old), firm-crumbed country bread (crusts removed) and diced. If crisped in butter, they are sautéed over very low heat in about 2 tablespoons butter to start, with more butter added when necessary (they absorb a lot), until golden and crisp on the surfaces but not dried out—they should remain tender at the heart. If fried in olive oil, they are added to a pan containing about $\frac{1}{3}$ inch hot olive oil and stirred around until colored on all sides, then drained on paper towels. Count about 1 slice of bread, or a small handful of croutons, per person.

GARLIC BROTH
Aïgo Boulido

Serves 4

IN PROVENCE, *aïgo boulido* (garlic broth) most often serves to soothe systems worn thin from an enthusiastic celebration of the table. Lulu says, "I often rub the slices of bread with a clove of raw garlic—its flavor is very different from that of cooked garlic."

> *1 quart water*
> *Salt*
> *2 bay leaves*
> *1 head garlic, cloves separated and crushed*
> *2 tablespoons olive oil*
> *4 egg yolks*
> *Thin slices of baguette, partially dried in a slow oven or in*
> *   the sun or lightly grilled*

In a saucepan, bring the water, salt, bay leaves, garlic, and olive oil to a boil and hold, lid ajar, at a light boil for 15 minutes. With a wire whisk, whisk the egg yolks briefly in a soup tureen. Strain the broth, discard the bay leaves and garlic, and slowly pour the broth over the egg yolks, whisking at the same time. To serve, place a couple of crusts in each soup plate and ladle over the broth.

VEGETABLE SOUP WITH GARLIC AND BASIL
Soupe au Pistou

Serves 8 to 10

IN HER SOUPE AU PISTOU, Lulu's signature is evident in the absence of all herbs except the basil in the pistou and, above all, in the presence of a lamb shank, whose soft flavor and gelatin reinforce the velvety quality drawn from the squash and the shell beans. She says, "The lamb shank is there only for flavor and texture. With family, I leave it in the soup and anyone who wants to eat the meat can have it; when I have guests, I remove the meat from the bone, cut it into small pieces, and return it to the soup. I always prepare the soup in the morning for the evening meal—it is better reheated."

The shops in Provence carry a number of large, tough-skinned yellow, orange, or red-fleshed squashes, all sold in slices or wedges for use in soupe au pistou. Lulu uses a large, flat, elongated green bean (about 1 inch wide and 8 to 10 inches long), called *haricot pape,* which appears in the markets of Provence in June. Dried beans never have the finesse of fresh shell beans but, if the latter are unavailable, substitute a couple of handfuls of dried beans, soaked overnight in cold water, drained, covered with cold water, brought slowly to a boil, boiled for 15 minutes, drained, and added to the soup when it comes to a boil.

3 quarts water
1 lamb shank
Handful of coarse sea salt
1 dried cayenne pepper pod, or a pinch of cayenne
1 pound Hubbard or pumpkin squash, seeded, peeled, and
  diced
1 pound (unshelled) fresh cranberry beans, shelled

1 pound (unshelled) fresh white shell beans, shelled
½ pound onions, finely sliced
2 carrots, peeled and diced
6 garlic cloves, crushed and peeled
1 pound potatoes, peeled, quartered lengthwise, and sliced
½ pound tomatoes, peeled, seeded, and coarsely chopped
½ pound runner beans (or other green beans), topped,
  tailed, strings removed if necessary, and cut into ¾ inch
  lengths
½ pound zucchini, quartered lengthwise and thickly sliced
1 cup small elbow macaroni

PISTOU
Large pinch of coarse salt
Freshly ground pepper
3 garlic cloves, lightly crushed and peeled
2 packed cups fresh basil leaves
1 tomato, peeled, seeded, and quartered
5 tablespoons olive oil

Freshly grated Parmesan or Gruyère or half of each

In the morning, put the water and the lamb shank into an earthenware pot-au-feu or a large enameled ironware pot, bring slowly to a boil, skim off the gray scum from the surface, and add the salt, the cayenne, and all of the soup vegetables (not the macaroni). Return to a boil and adjust the heat to maintain a simmer or light boil, lid ajar, for about 2 hours. Leave to cool, uncovered. Remove the lamb shank, separate the flesh from the bone, cut the flesh into small pieces, and add them to the soup.

In the evening, reheat the soup. When it reaches a boil, add the macaroni and cook at a light boil for from 12 to 15 minutes (check the cooking instructions on the package and count a couple of minutes extra). If the soup seems too thick (it should be thick), add a bit of boiling water and taste for salt.

Meanwhile, prepare the pistou: in a marble mortar, pound the coarse salt, pepper, garlic, and basil to a liquid paste with a wooden pestle. Add the tomato and crush, pound, and stir until well mixed, then stir in the olive oil, adding it slowly. Remove the soup pot from the heat and stir the pistou into the soup (wash out the mortar with a ladle of soup and pour it back into the pot). Serve directly from the soup pot (Lulu pours the soup into a preheated, giant antique soup tureen), accompanied by a dish of grated cheese to be passed at table.

FRESH FAVA BEAN SOUP
Soupe aux Fèves Fraîches

Serves 4

"I ALWAYS purée this soup," says Lulu, "because Lucien likes his soups puréed, but, if the favas are young and tender, they need cook only a couple of minutes and I like the soup better when they are left whole." If the soup is not puréed, the beans should be fully developed (about the size of a thumbnail), the peels should still be green, not yellowing, and when each bean is peeled, the flesh should be a bright, clear green, tender enough to be easily cut into with one's thumbnail. At a more advanced stage, while the peeled beans are still a fine green color but hardening and beginning to turn starchy, they can still make a delicious soup, but it is then better puréed.

4 cups water
Salt
1 large sweet onion, finely sliced
1 large potato, peeled, quartered lengthwise, and finely sliced
*   crosswise*
2 pounds fava beans, shelled, each bean peeled
Pepper
1 tablespoon finely chopped fresh mint leaves
2 tablespoons cold butter, diced

Bring the water to a boil in a saucepan, add the salt, onion, and potato, and cook at a light boil, lid ajar. If the favas are tender (enough to be eaten raw), cook the onion and potato for 30 minutes before adding the beans, boil for a minute or two, grind over pepper, stir in the mint and butter, and serve. If the beans are hardening and beginning to turn starchy, add them to the pot after 15 minutes and cook for another 15 to 20 minutes, until all the vegetables are purée-tender. Pass through a vegetable mill, reheat, and finish with pepper, mint, and butter.

CABBAGE SOUP
Soupe aux Choux

Serves 6

1 small white cabbage
6 cups water
Salt
½ pound carrots, peeled and thickly sliced
1 large sweet onion, sliced or coarsely chopped
1 pound potatoes, peeled, quartered lengthwise, and thickly
*   sliced*
2 garlic cloves, crushed, peeled, and coarsely chopped
1 bay leaf
½ teaspoon olive oil
1 thick slice (½ pound) lean, streaky salt bacon or pancetta,
*   cut crosswise into 12 sections, covered with cold water,*
*   brought to a boil, drained, and rinsed in cold water*
Pepper

Remove blemished outside leaves from the cabbage, split it from top to bottom, cut a wedge from the bottom of each half to remove the core, pull the leaves apart, and cut away and discard the thick ribs from each leaf. Stack the leaves, a few at a time, cut them into ½-inch strips, and cut the strips across into squares.

Put the water to boil, add the salt, cabbage, carrots, onion, potatoes, garlic, and bay leaf, and adjust the heat to maintain a light boil, lid ajar.

Warm the olive oil in a frying pan, add the bacon wedges, and cook over low heat, turning them regularly, until lightly browned but not crisp. Add them, without their rendered fat, to the soup, simmer for 1 hour, grind over pepper, and serve.

LENTIL SOUP
Soupe aux Lentilles

Serves 6

"LENTIL SOUP needs *lots* of garlic" (Lulu). If available, use the small French lentils labeled *lentille vertes* or *lentilles du Puy.*

1 ¼ *cups (¹/₂ pound) lentils, soaked in cold water for 2 or 3
        hours*
2 *quarts boiling water*
1 *head garlic, cloves separated, crushed, and skins discarded*
4 *tablespoons olive oil*
Salt
2 *cups small croutons, cut from ¹/₃-inch-thick crustless slices
        of semifresh bread, fried in olive oil until golden and
        crisp*

Drain the lentils, put them into an earthenware, enameled iron-ware, or stainless steel pot, cover generously with cold water, bring to a full boil, and drain. Return the lentils to the pot, pour over the boiling water, return to a boil, add the garlic and olive oil, and adjust heat to a simmer, with lid slightly ajar. Salt to taste after 45 minutes. When the lentils are purée-tender, but still intact—after about 1 hour, 15 minutes—pass them through the fine grill of a vegetable mill. Reheat the purée, pour it into a heated soup tureen, and serve, at table, accompanied by the bowl of croutons.

LUCIEN'S SOUP
Soupe pour Lucien

Serves 6

AFTER A PASSING reference to Lucien's soup, I asked Lulu, "What is Lucien's soup?" "Oh," she said, "it doesn't have a name—there's no recipe for it. It's just the soup I fix for Lucien every evening when we're alone. I think it's just as good with the vegetables left in pieces, but Lucien likes his soups puréed."

6 cups water
Salt
3 tablespoons olive oil
2 leeks (10 ounces), trimmed, green ends slit, soaked, washed, and sliced
2 medium potatoes (12 ounces), peeled, quartered lengthwise, and sliced
½ pound carrots, peeled and sliced
½ pound crisp young turnips, peeled and quartered or chopped
2 large celery stalks, diced
1 large onion (½ pound), halved and sliced
2 garlic cloves, crushed
Pepper

In a large saucepan, put the water, salt, and 1 tablespoon olive oil to boil. Add the vegetables, as they are prepared, in any order. Adjust the heat to a light boil, lid ajar, and cook for at least 45 minutes, or until all the vegetables are purée-tender. Pass through a vegetable mill, taste for salt, return to a boil, grind in pepper, add 2 tablespoons olive oil, and serve.

Lucien, in his role of Grand Cellerier of L'Ordre Illustre des Chevaliers de Méduse, 1992.

SPLIT PEA SOUP
Soupe aux Pois Cassés

Serves 6

ALTHOUGH SPLIT PEAS are less sensitive to hard water than chick-peas, Lulu prefers to use bottled Volvic water, both for soaking and for cooking all dried legumes.

1¾ cups (12 ounces) split peas, soaked in cold water for
several hours or overnight
6 cups water
Salt
1 large onion, coarsely chopped or cut up
1 large potato, peeled and quartered or cut up
1 fresh mint sprig
1 tablespoon olive oil
1 tablespoon chopped fresh mint leaves
4 tablespoons butter, cut into small pieces

Drain the split peas, put them in a large saucepan with 4 cups cold water, place over medium heat, and bring to a boil. Add the salt, onion, potato, sprig of mint, and olive oil, cover, and cook over very low heat, at a simmer, for 2 hours. Add boiling water if the soup becomes too thick. Discard the sprig of mint, stir in the chopped mint leaves, pass the soup through a vegetable mill, and adjust its consistency by the addition of boiling water. Taste for salt, reheat, and, off the heat, stir in the butter.

SORREL SOUP
Soupe à l'Oscille

Serves 6

LULU'S ADVICE: "If the sorrel leaves are young and tender, use them raw. If they are large and dark green, remove the stems and, after the leaves are cut into a chiffonade, plunge them into boiling water for a second, then drain them well before adding them to the sweated onions." If you raise your own sorrel, you need only to pick it regularly to have a constant supply of young and tender leaves—it is better to pick the older leaves and to discard them, if necessary, to encourage the production of young leaves. To remove the stems, fold the two sides of the face of each leaf together, grasping them in one hand, while pulling the stem backward with the other hand—the stem and the central vein of the leaf will pull away together from the leaf wings. To cut the leaves into chiffonade, stack them, roll up the stacks, and shred the rolls, slicing thin.

> *4 tablespoons butter*
> *1 large sweet onion, finely sliced*
> *1 pound sorrel, stemmed, cut into chiffonade (parboiled for a*
> *   split second and drained, if necessary)*
> *1 large Idaho potato, peeled, quartered lengthwise, and*
> *   thinly sliced crosswise*
> *Salt*
> *2 quarts boiling water*
> *Pepper*
> *Butter croutons*

In a heavy saucepan over low heat, melt 2 tablespoons butter, add the onions, and cook, covered, stirring from time to time with a wooden spoon, until melting but uncolored. Add the sorrel chiffonade, potato, and salt and cook, stirring regularly, until the sorrel has melted into a gray-green semipurée. Pour over boiling water and simmer, lid ajar, for 30 to 40 minutes, or until the potato slices collapse when pushed against the side of the pan with the spoon. Remove from the heat, grind over pepper, stir, and add the remaining butter, diced or shaved (or, if serving from a soup tureen, place the chopped butter in the bottom and pour over the soup). Scatter over croutons at the last minute or pass a dish of croutons at table.

SQUASH SOUP
Soupe de Courge

Serves 8

LULU: "Just enough potato to give a little body to the soup, lots of celery to season the squash—no other herbs except for the parsley at the last minute."

8 tablespoons butter
2 large sweet onions, finely sliced
3 large celery stalks, diced
1 large potato, diced or finely sliced
2 pounds pumpkin, Hubbard, or other firm, red or yellow-
    fleshed squash, peeled, seeded, and diced
Salt
2 quarts boiling water
¼ cup finely chopped flat-leaf parsley
Pepper

In a heavy saucepan, melt 4 tablespoons butter over low heat, add the onions and diced celery, and cook, covered, stirring occasionally with a wooden spoon, until the onions are melting but uncolored. Add the potato, squash, and salt and continue to cook over

low heat, stirring regularly, until the squash begins to disintegrate.
Pour over boiling water and cook, lid ajar, for about 30 minutes.
Pass through a vegetable mill, reheat, add the parsley, grind over
pepper, and, off the heat, add the remaining butter, cut into small
pieces. (Lulu: "But I forgot to say that, instead of parsley, this soup
is wonderful finished with chopped fresh mint.")

SUMMER SOUP
Soupe d'Eté

Serves 6

"THE PEARL BARLEY gives this soup a smoothness that, when
chilled, makes it wonderfully refreshing on a hot summer day"
(Lulu).

1 quart water
1 tablespoon coarse sea salt
¼ cup pearl barley
1 head garlic, cloves separated and crushed
4 tablespoons olive oil
3 bay leaves
Small pinch of cayenne
2 pounds tomatoes, rinsed and quartered

Put the water to boil, add all the other ingredients, adjust the heat
to maintain a light boil, lid slightly ajar, for about 1 hour and 15
minutes, or until the pearl barley crushes easily between the back of
a wooden spoon and the side of the saucepan. Discard the bay
leaves and pass the soup through the fine blade of a vegetable mill
into a large bowl. Cool, uncovered, at room temperature and refrigerate, covered, for 2 or 3 hours before serving.

SQUASH AND MUSSEL SOUP
Soupe de Courge aux Moules

Serves 6

2 quarts mussels, cleaned and bearded (see Grilled Mussels,
    page 98)
1 teaspoon fennel seeds, or several sections of wild fennel
    stalk
$^1/_2$ cup white wine
2 tablespoons butter
1 large sweet onion, finely sliced
4 garlic cloves, crushed and peeled
2 pounds pumpkin or similar squash, peeled, seeded, and
    diced
4 cups boiling water
Salt
Pepper
$^1/_2$ cup heavy cream

Put the mussels, fennel, and white wine in a large pot with a tight-fitting lid and place over high heat. Shake the pot several times over a period of 3 or 4 minutes and remove from the heat as soon as nearly all the mussels have opened. Pour the contents of the pot into a colander placed over a bowl to collect the liquid. Slip a knife blade between the shells of any mussels that remain unopened, remove the mussels from their shells, and collect them in a small bowl. Decant the mussel liquid through a cheesecloth-lined sieve, discarding any sediment that has settled to the bottom of the bowl. Pour a little liquid over the mussels to keep them moist.

In a heavy saucepan, over low heat, melt the butter, add the onion, and sweat, covered, stirring occasionally with a wooden spoon, until melting but uncolored. Add the garlic and the squash and continue to cook over low heat, stirring regularly, until the squash begins to disintegrate. In another saucepan, bring the mussel cooking liquid to a boil, add it to the squash, and pour in the boiling water. Cook at a light boil, lid ajar, for about 30 minutes. Pass the soup through a vegetable mill, taste for salt, return it to its saucepan, bring back to a boil, grind over pepper, add the mussels, stir in the cream, and serve.

TURNIP SOUP
Soupe aux Navets

Serves 6

4 tablespoons butter
1 large sweet onion, finely sliced
2 pounds crisp young turnips, peeled, split, and finely sliced
Salt
5 cups boiling water
Pepper
1/2 cup heavy cream
Croutons crisped in butter

In a heavy saucepan, over low heat, melt the butter, add the onion, and sweat, covered, stirring occasionally with a wooden spoon, until softened but uncolored. Add the turnips and salt and continue to sweat over low heat, stirring regularly, for about 15 minutes. Pour over boiling water and cook, lid ajar, at a light boil for 30 to 45 minutes, or until the turnips collapse when pressed to the side of the pan with the spoon. Pass through a food mill, reheat, grind over pepper, stir in the cream, and serve with a dish of croutons.

FISH

So close to the Mediterranean, how can we not rejoice in the fruits of this nourishing sea! Fish!

Si près de la Méditerranée, que pouvions nous nous offrir d'autre que les fruits de cette mer nourrissière! Le poisson!

Lulu

Because *mer* (sea) and *mère* (mother) are pronounced alike, Lulu has indulged in a typically frivolous pun, nonetheless serious for she shares the Provençal almost mystical attachment to the Mediterranean sea, provider of life and joy, Provence's nursing mother. She adores, above all, anything that comes from the sea and willingly serves, as a main course, a large fish, packed with one of her stuffings that she claims are all alike and that are always different, often preceded by another fish preparation as well as the live sea urchins, vioulets, mussels, and other bivalves that she serves as *amuse-gueules* with the apéritif.

When fish is served as a main course, Jean-Marie chooses a relatively young red wine (five or six years old) to accompany it, reserving an older red for the cheeses.

Opposite: Lulu at the Bandol fish market, 1992.

BOURRIDE
Bourride

Serves 6

MOST RECIPES for bourride call for a liaison of aïoli to which extra egg yolks have been added and more aïoli served apart. Lulu is categoric: "The liaison for a bourride must contain much less garlic than an aïoli—it has to be specially prepared." Lulu prepares her broth with an anglerfish head.

BROTH
The broken-up heads and carcasses of the fish to be poached
1 leek, finely sliced
1 large onion, finely sliced
2 carrots, finely sliced
3 garlic cloves, crushed
1 small celery branch
Bouquet of wild fennel stalks, or 1 teaspoon fennel seed
6 cups water
Salt

LIAISON
Pinch of coarse salt
2 garlic cloves, peeled
6 egg yolks, at room temperature
1 cup olive oil, at room temperature

4 pounds filleted, white-fleshed fish (anglerfish, halibut, cod, porgy, etc.), cut into serving portions
12 slices of baguette, partially dried out in a slow oven or in the sun

Place the broken-up fish heads and carcasses in the bottom of a large saucepan, the aromatic elements on top. Pour over water, add salt, bring to a boil, skim off any gray foam that rises, and cook at a simmer or light boil, lid slightly ajar, for 40 minutes. Strain, discard the solids, and leave the broth to cool.

In a mortar, pound the coarse salt and garlic to a paste with a wooden pestle. Add the egg yolks and stir briskly with the pestle until they lighten in color. Mount exactly like an aïoli, adding the oil in a slight trickle to the side of the mortar, turning the while with the pestle. Hold in readiness.

Arrange the fish in the bottom of a very large sauté pan, pour over the cooled broth, bring slowly to the boiling point, and hold, covered, beneath the boil, at the lowest possible heat, for 10 minutes (if the liquid reaches a boil, despite all precautions, cover the pan tightly and turn off the heat). Remove the fish to a warmed platter and hold it, covered, in a warm place. Transfer about 1 cup of the broth to a small saucepan and put it aside.

Slowly add a ladleful of the broth to the liaison in the mortar, stirring at the same time. Transfer this mixture to a saucepan and add the remaining broth, stirring with a wooden spoon. Place the saucepan over low heat and stir constantly until the liquid thickens enough to coat the spoon—it must not boil. Pour it into a soup tureen. Spread the bread slices in the bottom of a heated platter. Bring the small saucepan of broth to a boil, pour it evenly over the bread slices, place the fish on top, and serve, accompanied by the tureen of soup. A portion of fish is served into a soup plate with its soaked crust beneath and some soup is ladled over.

FISH IN COURT-BOUILLON
Murène au Court-bouillon

Serves 4

WITH THIS SPICY court-bouillon, Lulu likes to prepare *murène*, or moray eel, since ancient times one of the most admired Mediterranean fish. Grouper, dolphinfish (not to be confused with dolphin), or tilefish is an ideal substitute or, as Lulu says, "almost any white-fleshed fish—a section of fresh cod tail, for instance." Sea bass should not be considered—because of the delicacy of its flesh, it is best simply poached in salt water. For the same company, count twice the weight for a whole fish with its head than for fillets or sections of solid flesh. Whole fish or sections of larger fish are best poached unscaled—the skin and scales slip off easily once the fish is cooked. Whether the fish be whole, filleted, or cut crosswise in a single section, cooking time relates to thickness rather than to weight. It is said that one may count 10 minutes per inch of thickness, but intuition and tactile sense must play a role, for the fish is cooking as the court-bouillon warms to the near boiling point and it continues to cook when the heat is turned off. Most importantly, the court-bouillon must never boil—the ideal poaching temperature is about 185°F (when poaching a large fish, some 5 inches thick at the back, behind the gills, a thermometer that clips to the side of the fish kettle is practical).

The leftover court-bouillon provides a wonderful, if unorthodox, base for a fish soup, in which small fish or chopped fish heads and carcasses, shrimp shells, small crushed crabs, etc., may be cooked for about 40 minutes before the broth is sieved and flavored with dissolved saffron.

COURT-BOUILLON
1 quart water
2 cups white wine
1 large onion, finely sliced
2 tomatoes, coarsely chopped
2 bay leaves
Bouquet of wild fennel, or 1 teaspoon fennel seeds
2 dried cayenne peppers
Salt and pinch of peppercorns
2 tablespoons olive oil

2 pounds sectioned or filleted fish, or 4 pounds whole fish,
about 3 inches at thickest part

Combine all of the ingredients for the court-bouillon in a saucepan, bring to a boil, and cook, lid slightly ajar, at a light boil for 45 minutes. Strain and leave the broth to cool.

Place the fish in a fish kettle or other vessel of a size and shape to just contain it without wasted space. Pour over the cold court-bouillon—if the fish is not completely immersed, add water. Bring the liquid to a near boiling point, turn the heat very low, and hold beneath the boil, lid ajar, for about 15 minutes. Turn off the heat, cover the kettle tightly, and leave to poach for 10 minutes or longer. Serve, accompanied by steamed or boiled potatoes and a cruet of olive oil.

GRILLED FISH
Poissons Grillés

AMONG THE LARGE FISH for grilling, Lulu chooses a sea bass or one of the Mediterranean breams. Usually, but not always, a bundle of wild fennel is tucked into the body cavity. This is the only artifice. The fish is unscaled and unseasoned. As it grills, the scales and skin are transformed into a brittle scabbard that protects the flesh from the desiccating effect of direct heat, permitting it to steam in its own moisture, trapped beneath the seal of scales and skin, which is then lifted off intact after being slit the length of the back and the abdomen, at the tail, and around the gill. For a 4- to 6-pound fish, a solid bed of embers should be prepared and the fish should be grilled at a good 6-inch distance from the heat source. If you do not have a double-faced fish grill in the shape of the fish, a regular, preheated grill can be used—the scales will prevent the fish from sticking to it. The cooking time is a function of the thickness of the fish's back behind the gills—the thickest point. Count about 10 minutes per inch of thickness and test for doneness by piercing the fish at this point with a skewer, remembering that underdone is better than overdone.

Lulu grills large Mediterranean shrimp, called *gambas,* and small, lively spiny lobsters (*langoustes*) in the same way about 4 inches from the bed of coals. Unshelled jumbo shrimp can replace the *gambas;* they are done after about 4 minutes, when the shells have turned pink on all sides. Spiny lobsters, each an individual portion weighing no more than 1 pound, are grilled for no longer than 15 minutes. At first, they flip around a bit and curl up their tails, which must be flattened out several times until they relax. The legs begin to come loose from the body after 2 or 3 minutes and should be removed from the grill then, before drying out.

Lulu figures that sea bass is of such delicacy that it should be eaten without the support of seasoning or sauces. She often serves a sauce or, as in the following recipe, two sauces with grilled bream.

GRILLED FISH WITH TWO SAUCES
Sar à la Braise, Tapenade et Tomates Confites

Serves 4

A 4-POUND FISH should be grilled for about 15 minutes on each side (see above), turning two or three times. Don't worry if the scales are charred. If you prefer, the tomato sauce can be prepared in advance, but the anchovy fillets should be added only at the last minute.

1 4-pound porgy, red snapper, etc., gutted, gills removed but unscaled

TOMATO SAUCE
3 tablespoons olive oil
1 medium onion, finely chopped
4 garlic cloves, crushed and peeled
1 1/2 pounds tomatoes, peeled, seeded, cut into pieces, and salted in a colander for 1 hour
3 salt anchovies, rinsed and filleted, or 6 fillets
Salt
Pepper
1/2 teaspoon fennel seeds, pounded to a powder in a mortar

1 recipe Tapenade (page 79)

Prepare the bed of coals and put the fish to grill.
In a wide heavy frying pan, warm 2 tablespoons olive oil, add the

onions and garlic, and cook, covered, stirring occasionally with a wooden spoon, until softened but uncolored. Uncover, raise the heat, add the tomatoes, and sauté, shaking the pan regularly and tossing the tomatoes, until their liquid has disappeared and they form a roughly textured sauce.

Put the remaining tablespoon of olive oil into a small pan, lay in the anchovy fillets, and place over very low heat until they melt, falling apart when the pan is shaken. Taste the tomato sauce for salt, grind over pepper, add the powdered fennel, and stir in the melted anchovies.

Serve the grilled fish accompanied by the two sauces. After lifting off and discarding the top surface of scales and skin, cut with a knife tip the length of the lateral line and lift the fillets from the bone with a spatula. Lift the bone and head free from the fillets on the underside, separate them along the lateral line, push the fin bones aside, and lift away the other fillets. Don't forget to serve the cheeks to two lucky guests.

Baked Halibut with Mushrooms and Cream
Turbot ou Flétan au Four, Champignons à la Crème

Serves 6

LULU USES TURBOT for this preparation. Turbot is flown to America, at vast expense, to appear on the menus of luxury French restaurants, but common sense suggests the choice of another fish. Halibut doesn't exist on the Mediterranean market but, judging from that eaten in America, Lulu figures that its fine, firm texture makes it the best substitute. She scatters dried bread crumbs over all fish to be baked and over most vegetable gratins and insists that they must be slightly coarse and irregular in texture. To achieve this texture, she rubs together two broken ends of dried-out baguette over the dish. Blenders or food processors are unsatisfactory because they produce a mixture either too fine or too coarse, or if whirred for longer, a powder of dried bread. If the shape of your bread doesn't lend itself to the rubbing method, use a rough, old-fashioned cheese grater.

3 pounds halibut fillet, about 2 inches thick
1 tablespoon olive oil
Salt and pepper
½ cup white wine
Dried bread
1 lemon, cut across into thin slices, ends discarded
4 tablespoons butter
¾ pound mushrooms, stem ends trimmed, rinsed rapidly,
*   dried in a towel, and finely sliced*
1 cup heavy cream

Preheat the oven to 450°F. Choose a shallow oven dish, round or oval, depending on the shape of the fish fillet.

(continued)

Rub the fish with olive oil, season with salt and pepper, place it in the dish, and pour the white wine in the bottom. Grate dried bread over the fish, arrange the lemon slices, slightly overlapping, and distribute about 1 tablespoon cold butter, cut into thin blades, on the surface. Bake for 20 minutes, basting several times during the last 10 minutes. If the liquid threatens to dry up, add some boiling white wine to the dish.

A few minutes before removing the fish from the oven, add 2 tablespoons butter to a large heavy frying pan, over high heat. When the butter begins to foam, add the mushrooms, season with salt and pepper, and toss repeatedly. The mushrooms will release an abundant liquid and begin to boil; continue tossing until all the liquid has evaporated. Remove from the heat.

Remove the fish from the oven and distribute the remaining butter, cut into blades, on top. Tilt the dish and spoon all the liquid in the bottom over the mushrooms. Return the mushrooms to high heat and reduce the liquid, shaking and tossing, until they are coated in a syrup. Add the cream, bring to a boil, and reduce, shaking the pan and stirring with a wooden spoon, to the consistency of a light-bodied sauce. (American heavy cream, which has milk homogenized into it, requires more reduction than crème fraîche, which hardly needs any reduction at all.) Pour into a heated serving dish.

Serve the fish directly from its baking dish, first removing the lemon slices, onto heated plates. Spoon creamed mushrooms to the side of each serving.

Lulu at table with baked fish.

BAKED BREAM WITH FENNEL
Daurade au Fenouil

Serves 4

LULU SPECIFIED *daurade royale* (gilt-headed bream) for this recipe, but she prepares many fish in the same way. Wild fennel is abundant in California and perhaps elsewhere. In the spring, Lulu uses the tender shoots, throughout the summer the green stalks and feathery leaves from the summits, and in late summer she cuts and dries the winter's provision, mainly the stalk summits in flower and partially gone to seed, the seeds still green. If you cannot find wild fennel, fresh or dried, substitute fennel seeds, sprinkled into the abdominal cavity, over the bottom of the oven dish, and on the surface of the fish.

Lulu always uses the same general style of white wine in the kitchen, but only occasionally does she insist on the importance of its being young, very dry, and acidic. This is one of those instances.

4 tablespoons olive oil
1 medium sweet onion, finely sliced
4 garlic cloves, peeled and finely sliced
Large handful of wild fennel stalks and summits, fresh or
*   dried, depending on the season, or 1 teaspoon fennel*
*   seeds*
3 bay leaves
Salt and pepper
2 lemons, ends cut off and thinly sliced
Coarsely grated dried bread crumbs
1/2 cup young, dry, acidic white wine (Sauvignon Blanc,
*   Entre-Deux-Mers, Muscadet, Gros Plant, etc.)*
2 tablespoons butter

Preheat the oven to 400°F.

Choose a gratin dish of a size to just hold the fish (don't worry about the tip of the tail). Smear olive oil in the bottom of the dish, mix together the onion and the garlic, and spread them evenly over the bottom. Scatter the fragments of fennel and a couple of bay leaves. Season the fish inside and out with salt and pepper, dribble a little olive oil into the body cavity, and stuff it with a bay leaf and a bundle of fennel (with the gills removed, the abdominal area and the head form a single cavity). Rub the fish all over with olive oil and place it on the bed of aromatics. If the tail overlaps the edge of the gratin dish, wrap it loosely with a piece of aluminum foil to prevent it from charring. Arrange the lemon slices, overlapping, in a row from the head to the tail, sprinkle the surface of the fish with bread crumbs, dribble olive oil over the surface, and pour the white wine into the bottom of the dish.

Bake for 30 to 35 minutes, basting several times with the wine— if it threatens to dry up, add a little bit of boiling wine to the dish. Test for doneness by piercing the flesh at the thickest part with a skewer. When removing the dish from the oven, disperse small pieces of butter over the surface of the fish. Remove the foil from the tail and serve directly from the oven dish: lift off the lemon slices, slit the skin with a knife tip the length of the back and the abdomen, against the fin bones, cut to the bone along the lateral line, and lift the fillets free from the central bone with a spatula. Push the fin bones aside with the knife blade (for those who are willing to suck on the fin bones, the flesh is succulent), lift off the central bone and the attached head, and serve the underlying fillets. The head is also rich in sucking matter and the cheeks are a great delicacy. Spoon juices from the gratin dish over each portion.

STUFFED BAKED FISH
Poisson Farci au Four

Serves 8

LULU'S FAVORITE FISH for stuffing is a *chapon de mer* (sea capon), a large red rascasse with a huge head, short, stocky, and thick-bodied with very firm flesh, which, because of its shape when stuffed, lies naturally on its belly with the arch of the back uppermost. Its large blond liver, along with that of the anglerfish, she says, are the only Mediterranean fish livers that are wonderful to cook with (rouget livers are also a great delicacy, but they are always eaten with the ungutted fish). For her stuffings, she always supplements the chapon's liver with an anglerfish liver. She says, "My fish stuffings are always the same—of course, sometimes I add sorrel, quite often some parboiled chopped chard, and I might add a little tomato, some chopped mussels opened in white wine, chopped black olives, or a couple of chopped anchovy fillets . . . they don't always contain hard-boiled eggs." In fact, the "sameness" resides mainly in the presence of anglerfish liver. If you are unable to obtain anglerfish liver, don't worry about it—the stuffing will be delicious, if less velvety; doctor it to taste with the above suggestions—a chopped fish fillet can be added to lend more body. Lulu's fish stuffing is always quite loose—semiliquid—which means that the abdomen must be laced up to contain it. It firms up in the cooking but, when the fish is served out, a bit of stuffing always escapes into the cooking juices to form a sumptuous, roughly textured sauce.

STUFFING
2 tablespoons butter
1 medium onion, finely chopped
1 garlic clove, finely chopped

Handful (about 2 ounces) of young sorrel leaves, finely
   shredded
Large pinch of fennel seeds, pounded to a powder in a
   mortar
1 teaspoon finely chopped fresh savory, or a pinch of
   crumbled, dry
1 anglerfish liver (about 7 ounces), poached in salt water for
   about 1 minute, or until firmed up but still pink, cut into
   pieces
4 ounces semifresh bread, crusts removed, soaked in milk,
   and lightly squeezed
2 hard-boiled eggs, shelled and quartered
1 raw egg
Salt and pepper

1 4-pound red snapper, porgy, etc., scaled, gutted, and gills
   removed
Salt and pepper
2 tablespoons olive oil
Fresh or dried wild fennel stalks (if available)
½ cup dry, acidic white wine (Muscadet or Sauvignon Blanc,
   for instance)
2 lemons
Dried bread crumbs
2 tablespoons butter

Melt the butter in a frying pan, add the chopped onion and garlic,
and stew gently over low heat, stirring regularly with a wooden
spoon, until softened and lightly colored. Add the sorrel and stir regularly for a few minutes more, or until the sorrel has collapsed into
a near purée. Assemble all the ingredients of the stuffing in a food
processor and process very briefly to a coarsely textured purée.

(continued)

Preheat the oven to 400°F.

Season the abdominal cavity of the fish generously with salt and pepper and spoon in the stuffing, forcing it up into the head cavity so as to create a single unit of stuffing in head and abdomen. Pierce the belly flaps with 4 or 5 small skewers (bamboo skewers, cut into 3 ½-inch lengths and sharpened are ideal) and, with kitchen string, lace the belly up, bootlike, and tie the string. Rub the fish all over with olive oil and place it, belly down or on its side, depending on its shape, in a long gratin dish. Scatter the fennel stalks around. Season the fish with salt and pepper. Pour the white wine into the bottom of the dish. Cut off the ends of the lemons. If the fish is lying on its side, slice the lemons thin and place the slices, slightly overlapping, the length of the fish. If its back is in the air, cut to the center of each lemon lengthwise before slicing it crosswise; fit the lemon slices upright, horseback-like, along the crest of the back. Sprinkle the fish with bread crumbs, dribble with a bit more olive oil, and bake for about 40 minutes, basting several times. If the liquid threatens to dry up, heat some more white wine and add to the dish. The fish is done when, at its thickest part, the flesh shows little resistance to a skewer or trussing needle.

Remove the fennel stalks from the dish, place fragments of butter the length of the fish, and present it in its baking dish. Remove the lemon slices before serving one half fillet, a spoonful of stuffing, and a spoonful of the cooking juices per person. At the Peyraud table, Lucien receives the head and offers the delicate cheeks to guests.

ROAST ANGLERFISH
Rôti de Lotte

Serves 8

I ASKED LULU why she called this dish *rôti de lotte* (French) instead of *rôti de baudroie* (Provençal). She said, "Because that's the way you always see it on restaurant menus—but, of course, we always call it *baudroie*." She always roasts the fish surrounded with ("lots of") wild fennel stalks, fresh or dried, depending on the season, but, she says, "If using pounded fennel seeds, mix some of the powder with salt to coat the garlic slivers before inserting them into the flesh." Lulu most often accompanies roast anglerfish with a chard and sorrel gratin (page 266); it is also delicious served on a bed of hot ratatouille (page 287). Anglerfish is sold already skinned, but a superficial flabby tissue is often left clinging to the flesh. It should be removed.

> *1 teaspoon fennel seeds, pounded to a powder in a mortar*
> *Salt*
> *4 garlic cloves, peeled and cut into thick slivers*
> *4 pounds cross section of anglerfish, unboned, trimmed if*
> *   necessary*
> *2 tablespoons olive oil*
> *Dry bread crumbs*
> *1 tablespoon butter*

Preheat the oven to 400°F.

In a small bowl, mix together a pinch of the powdered fennel seed and a large pinch of salt, add the garlic slivers, and toss until they are well coated with the mixture. With a small, sharply pointed knife, pierce the fish's flesh repeatedly on all surfaces, tucking a seasoned garlic sliver into each vent. Sprinkle the surfaces of the fish with salt and powdered fennel. In a small oven dish, smear the fish (or *rôti,* as Lulu calls it) on all sides with olive oil, sprinkle the surface with dry bread crumbs, and roast for 25 minutes, turning it three or four times and sprinkling the unbreaded surfaces with crumbs. Turn off the oven and leave it for another 5 minutes or so. Transfer the fish to a heated serving platter and place a couple of strips of butter on top to melt before serving.

ANGLERFISH GRILLED IN FIG LEAVES
Baudroie en Feuilles de Figuier

Serves 4

ONE OF THE FAVORITE dishes at all of the Peyraud tables is small, 3- to 4-ounce, freshly fished red rock mullets (*rougets de roche*), ungutted, unscaled, and unseasoned, each wrapped in a grapevine leaf and grilled in a double-faced grill for a couple of minutes on each side over grapevine embers. Each guest unwraps the fish (3 or 4 per person) at table. Most of the scales and skin cling to the leaf (which is discarded), exposing the moist fillets that slip easily from the bone. The only seasoning is the liver and the innards, which are spread onto the fillets as they are eaten. A pure and exquisite thing.

On a recent trip to California, Lulu was seduced by the delicate sweet scent and flavor imparted to filleted striped bass by the fig leaf in which it was wrapped and grilled. Back at Domaine Tempier, her version of the dish, anglerfish in fig leaves, appeared on her first menu.

(continued)

Fish wrapped in vine leaves on the grill.

*4³/₄-inch-thick slices (1¹/₂ to 2 pounds) of filleted fish
    (anglerfish, grouper, halibut, sea bass, for instance)
Salt and pepper
1 lemon
2 tablespoons olive oil
4 large fig leaves, stems removed, rinsed but undried*

Season the slices of fish with salt and pepper, a few drops of lemon juice on each side, and coat them with olive oil. Place each slice on a moist fig leaf, underside facing up, and fold the lobes of the leaf up and over the top side of the fish. Place the packages, folded sides down, on a double-faced flat fish grill and grill about 4 inches above hot coals for 4 minutes on each side. Serve the packages directly from the grill, to be unwrapped by each guest at table. The moisture clinging to the leaves creates steam within the packages and prevents the exteriors from charring.

ANGLERFISH AND MUSSELS WITH CHARD
Baudroie et Moules aux Blettes

Serves 6

HALFWAY THROUGH our notes, Lulu exclaimed, "But you can do exactly the same thing with endives!" And after a moment's reflection, "I forgot to say that sorrel is a wonderful seasoning for chard—I often add sorrel to chard and, of course, chard needs a lot of garlic, but I would never add sorrel or garlic to endives . . . and I never include mussels or saffron with endives." Briefly, the endives are sliced lengthwise into slivers, added raw to melted butter, salted, and braised gently, covered, for about 45 minutes, a little white wine added as they begin to color, finished with a few spoon-fuls of heavy cream, and the sautéed anglerfish slices are placed on top.

If you choose to incorporate sorrel into the following recipe, count a large handful of leaves, stems and central ribs torn out, washed and coarsely chopped. If the leaves are young and tender, add them raw to a pan containing a bit of melted butter and stew over low heat for a couple of minutes, or until gray and falling apart. If the leaves are no longer in their first youth, plunge them into boiling water for a couple of seconds and drain. In either case, add the sorrel to the sauté pan at the same time as the parboiled chopped chard.

To prepare the chard in advance, cut the ribs from the green parts, wash and drain both, trim the ribs, and cut them into $1/2$ x 2-inch sticks. Add the ribs to a large pot of salted boiling water and cook at a light boil for 10 minutes. Bring the water to a rolling boil, add the chard greens, push them with a wooden spoon repeatedly beneath the water's surface, stirring at the same time, until the water has returned to a full boil and the leaves are completely limp. Drain in a colander, refresh beneath cold running water, and squeeze repeatedly in your hands to form a firm ball. To chop, slice the ball thin, give it a quarter of a turn, and slice through it again. (If using small-leaf ribless chard, pull off the stems and discard them, parboil the leaves for a few seconds, as above, refresh, squeeze, and chop.)

To prepare the mussels, soak them in a basin of cold water to which has been added a handful of coarse sea salt. Depending on whether the shells are encrusted with sea growth, scrape them or simply rub them beneath the water to clean them. Discard any whose shells are broken or gaping. Pull out the beard—the tough, grassy attachment near the hinge—from each, rinse, assemble them in a large pot with a tight-fitting lid, and pour over the white wine.

(continued)

Place, covered, over high heat and, after a couple of minutes, shake the pot repeatedly until the liquid inside reaches a full boil and the shells are gaping. Empty into a colander placed over a bowl. Remove the mussels from their shells, collecting them in a small bowl. Discard the shells. Decant the liquid, pouring all but the sediment that has settled to the bottom of the bowl through a sieve lined with several thicknesses of moistened cheesecloth. Pour a bit of the liquid over the mussels to keep them moist. Reserve the remaining liquid (some will be used to finish the dish, the remainder can serve elsewhere).

6 tablespoons butter
4 garlic cloves, peeled and finely chopped
2 pounds chard, parboiled, squeezed, and chopped (see above)
Flour
1 cup heavy cream
2 pounds anglerfish, boned, trimmed, fillets cut crosswise into ¹/₂-inch slices
Salt and pepper
2 pounds mussels, opened over heat with ¹/₄ cup white wine, removed from shells, cooking liquid decanted (see above)
¹/₄ teaspoon powdered saffron

In a large heavy sauté pan, melt 2 tablespoons butter, add the garlic over medium-low heat, stir it around with a wooden spoon, and when it begins to sizzle and turn lightly golden, add the chard and cook for about 15 minutes, stirring and scraping the bottom of the pan regularly. Add a little more butter if the chard becomes very dry. Sprinkle with a scant tablespoon of flour and stir for a couple of minutes longer. Add the cream, a few spoonfuls at a time, stirring and waiting until the chard has absorbed it before adding more. The mixture should not be liquid. Hold it over low heat.

Season the anglerfish slices with salt and pepper, dredge them in flour, and toss them lightly in your hands to rid them of excess flour. In a large frying pan, heat 4 tablespoons butter and sauté the fish slices over medium heat for about 2 minutes on each side, or until lightly colored and resilient to the touch.

Meanwhile, drain the mussels and stir them into the chard to reheat them. In a small saucepan, bring about ⅔ cup of the mussel cooking liquid to a boil, add the saffron to a tablespoon, and with a teaspoon, stir in enough of the boiling liquid to dissolve it, then stir the dissolved saffron into the mussel liquid.

Empty the chard and mussels onto a heated deep platter, distribute the sautéed fish slices on top, and spoon the saffron-flavored mussel juice evenly over the fish and the chard.

ANGLERFISH WITH GINGER
Baudroie au Gingembre

Serves 8

LULU PREPARES fresh salmon in the same way. Raw, filleted sardines or fresh anchovies are dressed with the same sauce and topped with peeled, seeded, chopped, salted, and drained tomatoes.

2 pounds filleted anglerfish
Salt and pepper
Juice of 2 limes
6 tablespoons olive oil
4 tablespoons peeled and grated fresh ginger
2 firm ripe tomatoes, thinly sliced

Put the anglerfish into the deep freeze for about 20 minutes—long enough to firm it up. Slice it as thin as possible and lay out the slices on a large platter. Mix together the salt, pepper, lime juice, olive oil, and grated ginger, spread the sauce over the slices of fish, and decorate with tomato slices.

GRATIN OF SALT COD AND CHARD RIBS
Brandade sur Lit de Blettes

Serves 4

FOR THIS PREPARATION, only the ribs of the chard are used. The green parts can be parboiled, refreshed, squeezed, wrapped in plastic film, and refrigerated for other uses.

COURT-BOUILLON
1 onion, finely sliced
4 garlic cloves, crushed
Bouquet of parsley or parsley root
Salt
3 cups water

1¼ pounds chard ribs, strings removed as for celery stalks,
    cut into ¾ x 3-inch sections
2 tablespoons butter
1 recipe Brandade (page 83)
Dried bread

Assemble the ingredients for the court-bouillon in a saucepan, bring to a boil, simmer covered for 30 minutes, strain, and return the court-bouillon to the saucepan. Add the chard ribs (pour over some boiling water, if necessary, to completely immerse them) and cook at a light boil, lid ajar, for about 12 minutes, or until tender. Drain.

Preheat the oven to 400°F. Butter a gratin dish and spread half the chard ribs in the bottom, half the brandade on top, add the remaining ribs, and finish with the remaining brandade. Grate a good layer of dried bread over the surface, cover with fine shavings of butter, and bake for 20 minutes, or until the surface is golden.

Sautéed Small Eels
Anguilles de Martigues

Serves 6

EELS ARE ABUNDANT in American waters, but it is the fishing industry's decision that they should be exported rather than sold on the American market. Eels are always sold alive. Large eels have to be stunned and skinned. Small eels (not to be confused with elvers, which are miniature, transparent eel fry), no more than a foot long, if sautéed or grilled, need not be skinned—they are simply beheaded, gutted, and cut up. These are called *Martigues* eels because it is a traditional Christmas Eve preparation in the town of Martigues, near Marseilles. When small eels turn up on the Bandol market, Lulu never fails to bring them home and sauté them. Martigue eels were on nearly all the family lists of preferred dishes. If flesh can be firm and melting, moist and succulent, all at the same time, this is the answer.

> 4 tablespoons olive oil
> 6 live eels, about 12 inches long, beheaded, gutted, and cut
>   into 2-inch sections
> Salt and pepper
> Persillade (a handful of flat-leaf parsley, chopped, then
>   chopped again with 3 finely chopped garlic cloves)
> 1/2 lemon

In a large heavy sauté pan, heat the olive oil, add the eel sections, season with salt and pepper, and sauté over medium heat, jerking the pan back and forth regularly and flipping the eel sections over occasionally with the tines of a fork, for about 15 minutes, or until a toothpick or skewer meets with little resistance when piercing a section. Turn up the heat, add the persillade, shake the pan back and forth for a few seconds, until the scent of frying parsley and

garlic fills the kitchen, squeeze over a bit of lemon, and serve immediately, directly from the sauté pan onto hot plates.

MUSSEL AND SPINACH GRATIN
Gratin de Moules aux Epinards

Serves 4

*2 pounds mussels, soaked in water with a handful of coarse
    sea salt, cleaned, and bearded*
1/2 cup dry white wine
4 tablespoons butter
2 garlic cloves, crushed, peeled, and chopped
*2 pounds spinach, stemmed, washed, parboiled for a few
    seconds, refreshed under cold running water, squeezed
    well, and chopped*
1 tablespoon flour
1 cup heavy cream
Salt and pepper
Dried bread crumbs

Put the mussels and the white wine in a large pot with a tight-fitting
lid, place over high heat, and as soon as the wine comes to a boil,
shake the pan repeatedly for 2 or 3 minutes, or until most of the
mussels are open. Empty the pot into a colander placed over a large
bowl. Remove the mussels from their shells, first slipping the knife
blade between the shells of those that have not opened. Pour the
liquid through a cheesecloth-lined sieve, discarding any sediment
that has settled at the bottom of the bowl.

Preheat the oven to 400°F.

In a *poêlon* or heavy sauté pan, melt half the butter over

medium-low heat, add the garlic, and when it begins to sizzle, add the spinach. Cook, stirring with a wooden spoon, for about 5 minutes, or until the spinach has lost its superficial moisture. Sprinkle with the flour, stir, and cook, stirring, for another couple of minutes. Add the mussels' cooking liquid slowly, stirring the while, and cook, stirring, until the spinach has absorbed all the liquid and is quite thick. Add the cream, in small quantities at a time, stirring, and cook until the mixture is consistent. Taste for salt and grind over pepper.

Butter a gratin dish, spread the mixture into it, poke little holes repeatedly into the surface, and place a mussel in each. Sprinkle the surface generously with dried bread crumbs, scatter over shavings of cold butter, and bake for 20 minutes, or until the surface is golden.

MUSSEL AND CRAB RISOTTO
Rizotto de Moules et Favouilles

Serves 8

THE BODY WIDTH of the Mediterranean shore crabs that Lulu uses averages $2\frac{1}{2}$ inches. They are packed with spicy flavor but short on flesh. She notes that, to extract the flavor, the crabs must be crushed, but for the beauty of the thing, she always holds back a few whole cooked crabs for garnish. Mussels' natural saltiness is variable; often no additional salt is needed. The mussel and crab cooking liquid will have to be supplemented by boiling water. The rice will absorb something over two and a half times its bulk in liquid—its final consistency should be that of a very thick, barely pourable soup. Lulu does not hold with the Italian theory that a seafood risotto should contain no cheese.

2 pounds mussels, cleaned (page 98)
1 teaspoon fennel seeds
¹/₂ cup white wine
16 small blue crabs or sand crabs
2 tablespoons olive oil
1 large sweet onion, finely chopped
4 garlic cloves, peeled and finely chopped
1 tomato, peeled, seeded, and coarsely chopped
3 cups round-grain Italian rice
Pinch of cayenne
¹/₄ teaspoon powdered saffron, or a large pinch of saffron
*   threads*
Salt
Boiling water
6 tablespoons cold unsalted butter, diced
¹/₂ cup freshly grated Parmesan cheese

Assemble the mussels, fennel seeds, and white wine in a large pot with a tight-fitting lid, place over high heat, and after a couple of minutes, shake the pot at brief intervals, holding the lid firmly in place and tossing the mussels. After another 2 or 3 minutes, when nearly all have opened, remove from the heat and pour the contents of the pot into a colander, reserving the liquid. Remove the mussels from their shells. Any that remain unopened can be opened with a knife blade (do not heed the superstition that unopened mussels should not be eaten—they are often the best). Discard the shells and put the mussels aside in a small bowl, moistened with a bit of their cooking liquid.

Decant the cooking liquid, passing it through a cheesecloth-lined sieve. In a saucepan, bring the liquid to a boil and add the crabs. Add boiling water, if necessary, to completely immerse them. When they turn red, remove 8 crabs and put them aside. With a wooden pestle, pound the others, two or three at a time, in a mortar, spoon them back into the boiling liquid, and simmer, covered, for about 15 minutes. Pass the contents of the saucepan through a sieve, pressing the crushed crab pulp firmly to extract as much liquid as possible. Discard the debris.

Warm the olive oil in a large heavy saucepan, add the onion and, a few minutes later, the garlic. Stir regularly with a wooden spoon until they are soft and yellowed, but not browning. Add the tomato and, when its liquid has evaporated, the rice, cayenne, saffron, and if necessary, a bit of salt. Stir regularly until the rice is well coated with oil. Bring the mussel and crab cooking liquid to a boil apart and add enough to just immerse the rice. Cook for 20 minutes, uncovered, over medium-low heat, the liquid maintained at a light bubble, stirring often and adding more liquid as the previous batch is absorbed. When there is no more mussel and crab liquid, begin adding boiling water, in smaller quantities toward the end to control the consistency. If the rice is nearly dry when it is cooked, stir in a bit more boiling water, then stir in the reserved crabs and mussels. Hold over heat long enough for the crabs and mussels to reheat, remove the saucepan from the heat, and stir in the butter and cheese, mixing thoroughly. Serve directly from the saucepan onto heated plates.

MACKEREL AND VEGETABLES BAKED WITH WHITE WINE
Maqueraux à la Chartreuse

Serves 4

1 pound tomatoes, peeled, seeded, and sliced
1 large onion (¹/₂ pound), sliced into thin rings
4 garlic cloves, crushed, peeled, and coarsely chopped
Fragments of wild fennel, or a large pinch of fennel seeds
4 small fresh savory sprigs, or a pinch of dried savory
2 bay leaves
Salt and pepper
6 tablespoons olive oil
1¹/₂ pounds small mackerel, heads and tails removed, gutted,
  washed, and dried
¹/₂ cup young acidic white wine
Dried bread crumbs

Preheat the oven to 400°F.

Choose an oven dish just large enough to hold the mackerel, laid side by side, about 4 inches deep. Layer half the tomato slices on the bottom, press half the onion rings on top, scatter with half the garlic, half the fennel, 2 sprigs of savory and a bay leaf, season with salt and pepper, dribble olive oil back and forth over the surface, and press the mackerel into place on this bed. Dribble more olive oil over the mackerel, season with salt and pepper, scatter over the remaining garlic and the onion slices, then the remaining herbs. Press the remaining tomato slices over the surface, pour over the white wine, dribble over a bit more olive oil, season the surface with salt and pepper, sprinkle generously with bread crumbs, dribble olive oil crisscross across the surface, and put the dish in the oven. Lower the oven setting to 325°F and bake for 45 minutes. Serve hot or tepid.

SARDINE FILLETS IN ESCABECHE
Filets de Sardines en Escabeche

Serves 8

THE CLASSIC ESCABECHE recipe calls for sardines, beheaded and gutted but unboned, fried for a few seconds in olive oil, removed to a dish, more olive oil added to the pan, herbs, crushed garlic, and seasoning added to the boiling oil. Vinegar is added, boiled, and the mixture thrown over the sardines. Lulu figures that raw sardine fillets, coated with uncooked olive oil and heated through by their immersion in aromatic boiling vinegar, produce a superior result; it is very good, indeed.

*2 pounds fresh sardines (about 24), filleted (see Buttered
     Sardine Crusts, page 101)*
4 tablespoons olive oil

MARINADE
1 cup red wine vinegar
*Several fresh savory sprigs or a large pinch of crumbled,
     dried savory*
1 medium onion, thinly sliced
4 garlic cloves, crushed
3 dried cayenne peppers
Large pinch of coarse sea salt
1/2 teaspoon coarsely crushed peppercorns

Choose a deep serving dish or a gratin dish large enough to contain the sardine fillets in a single or at most in two layers. Put in the sardine fillets, add the olive oil, turn them around, and spread them out.

In a small saucepan, combine all the elements of the marinade, bring to a boil, and cook at a simmer until the vinegar is reduced by about half—15 minutes or so. Pour the boiling marinade over the sardine fillets, leave to cool, cover, and hold, refrigerated, for a day or two before serving.

Stewed Octopus
Poulpe Confit

Serves 8

LULU OFTEN SERVES stewed octopus out of context of Grand Aïoli, but always accompanied by a mortar of aïoli sauce, either with apéritif, escorted by individual croutons on which to place a piece of octopus coated with its sauce, a dab of aïoli on top, or as a first course, accompanied by baked sweet potatoes. For Lulu, the combination of stewed octopus, aïoli, and baked sweet potato is a summit of perfection.

Lulu emphasizes the importance of using small octopus, weighing less than 2 pounds each, preferably about 1 pound. She cleans them, removing eyes, beaks, and innards, but insists that they must not be skinned, the skins adding both flavor and smooth consistency to the sauce. To tenderize the flesh, she deep-freezes the cleaned octopus, tightly wrapped in plastic, overnight or for a couple of days and unfreezes them slowly in the refrigerator before cooking them, uncovered. When I asked if the degree of simmer could not be better controlled if they were partially covered, the lid kept ajar, she answered, "Oh no—the sauce would not reduce enough. Octopus throws off a tremendous amount of liquid and, when it is finished cooking, there must be only enough sauce to coat the pieces. You see, when I prepare my octopus confit, I never leave it—I nurse it all the time, turning the heat up and down regularly to keep the simmer right and stirring it often. I always prepare it ahead and, when left to cool, uncovered, the sauce continues to reduce. Before serving, I reheat it very slowly, stirring regularly, and the sauce reduces some more, until it coats the pieces of octopus, with no loose liquid remaining." Lulu always cooks the octopus in an earthenware *poêlon;* it is cooled, reheated, and served in the same *poêlon.* If a heavy sauté pan is used, the stew should be transferred to a nonmetallic container to cool and reheated in a clean pan.

If octopus is not available, large squid can be prepared in the same way. They need not be prefrozen and require only about 40 minutes cooking time.

5 tablespoons olive oil
1 large sweet onion, finely chopped
4 garlic cloves, crushed and peeled
2 tomatoes, peeled, seeded, and coarsely chopped
Salt
2 or 3 small octopus (about 3 pounds), cleaned but
  unskinned, deep-frozen, defrosted in refrigerator, bodies,
  heads, and tentacles cut into small bite-size pieces
1 bay leaf
4 tablespoons marc de Provence or Cognac
½ cup acidic white wine

In a large frying pan, warm 3 tablespoons olive oil, add the onion and garlic, and cook over low heat, stirring with a wooden spoon, until soft and golden but not browned. Turn up the heat, add the tomatoes and salt, and sauté, tossing regularly, until the tomato liquid has evaporated.

At the same time, in a large earthenware *poêlon* or heavy sauté pan, heat 2 tablespoons olive oil, add the octopus, salt, and bay leaf, stir with a wooden spoon, and shake the pan regularly until the liquid thrown off by the octopus has come to a full boil. Add the brandy, ignite it, and stir until the flames die. Bring the white wine to a boil in a small saucepan and add it. Boil for a few minutes, stirring, to partially reduce it and to rid the wine of its alcohol and stir in the sautéed onion, garlic, and tomatoes. Bring back to a boil and adjust the heat to maintain a gentle simmer, uncovered, stirring regularly, for about 50 minutes, or until the octopus pieces are quite tender but still resilient. If preparing the stew ahead, leave to cool uncovered and reheat over very low heat, stirring the while. If prepared the previous day, cool uncovered and refrigerate covered before reheating, uncovered.

SAUTÉED SQUID WITH PARSLEY AND GARLIC
Suppions à la Persillade

Serves 6

FOR THIS, Lulu uses tiny cuttlefish (*suppions*), because the size and shape permit the bodies and tentacles to be left whole. For the more elongated bodies of squid, it is practical to cut them into sections or rings, depending on the size. Very large squid, whose body pouches may be well over a foot long, are best braised, like stewed octopus (page 177), but most squid on the market can be treated in the following manner. Like many fleshes, which are tender when raw, small squid or cuttlefish are exquisite when only seized by heat; on contact with heat, they throw out an abundant and succulent liquid, but if permitted to cook in their juices, the flesh toughens and then requires a subsequent braising period to become tender again. For years, I dumbly respected the instructions of cookbooks, which insist on removing the membranelike skin from cephalopods. The only justification is cosmetic. Lulu is right—skinned, they lose in subtlety of flavor.

(continued)

*2 pounds small squid, cleaned (page 182), pouches cut into
    wide rings or sections, heads and tentacles left whole or
    split in two, depending on size*
3 tablespoons olive oil
Salt and pepper
*3 tablespoons persillade (chopped flat-leaf parsley, chopped
    again, with 3 chopped garlic cloves)*

Put the squid in a large heavy frying pan or sauté pan over high
heat, cover, shake two or three times, and as soon as the liquid they
release arrives at a boil, remove them with a skimmer or slotted
spoon to drain in a colander placed over a bowl. Reduce the juices
over high heat, adding those that drain from the squid, to a syrup—
about 2 tablespoons—and put them aside. In another large heavy
frying pan, heat the olive oil over high heat, add the squid, season
with salt and pepper, and sauté, tossing them repeatedly, for 20 to
30 seconds. Add the persillade, toss a few times, until the scent of
fried parsley and garlic permeates the kitchen, add the reduced
cooking juices, toss once again, and serve.

LITTLE SQUID IN THEIR INK
Suppions ou Calmars à l'Encre

Serves 4

THIS WAS HIGH on the family's list of favorites. As in the preceding recipe, Lulu uses tiny cuttlefish (*suppions*), which do not exist in American waters. Squid have narrower, more elongated body pouches and longer tentacles than cuttlefish, and clinging to the inside body wall, a transparent, celluloid-like "pen" instead of a cuttlebone. The flavor and texture of the flesh is practically identical. For this preparation, the pens are pulled out and discarded, the eyes are cut out with scissors, and the beaks, at the base of the tentacles, are squeezed out, but the head and tentacles remain attached to the body pouches, which are not cleaned.

2 tablespoons olive oil
1 head garlic, cloves separated, crushed, and peeled
*1 pound very small squid (body pouches about 3 inches
    long), pens, eyes, and beaks removed (page 182), rinsed
    and well drained*
1 bay leaf
Salt and pepper

In a heavy sauté pan, heat the olive oil, add the garlic, squid, and bay leaf, season with salt and pepper, and sauté over high heat, shaking the pan and stirring with a wooden spoon, for about 10 minutes, or until the ink sacs break and the squid are bathed in black juice. Serve directly from the pan.

Stuffed Baked Squid
Encornets Farcis

Serves 8

LULU: "It's true that all my fish stuffings are the same . . . but for squid I often add a handful of parboiled (refreshed and squeezed) chard leaves, chopped and sautéed in olive oil with finely chopped garlic . . . and very often, a peeled, seeded, and chopped tomato and a couple of salt anchovies (rinsed and filleted), chopped, are added to the white wine . . . also a handful of chopped parsley."

8 medium squid

STUFFING
2 tablespoons olive oil
The squid wings, heads, and tentacles, wings diced, head and
*   tentacles cut into small fragments*
Salt
1 recipe fish stuffing (page 158)
3 tablespoons olive oil
Salt and pepper
1/2 cup dry, acidic white wine
Pinch of fennel seeds or powdered fennel seeds
1 lemon, thinly sliced crosswise
Dried bread crumbs

Clean the squid in a basin of water: Pull the heads and tentacles and the attached innards out of the body pouches. Pull out the transparent pen that is loosely attached to the inside wall of each pouch. Pull off the triangular wings from the outsides of the pouches. Separate the heads and tentacles from the loosely attached intestinal material, cut out the eyes with scissors, and pinch out the beaks from each orifice at the base of the tentacles. Rinse the pouches, wings, heads, and tentacles and drain them in a colander. Do not remove the brownish violet membrane from the bodies and tentacles.

Heat 2 tablespoons olive oil in a frying pan, add the chopped wings, heads, and tentacles, season with salt, and sauté over medium heat until the liquid from the squid has been reabsorbed and the pan is nearly dry. Empty the pan into the fish stuffing and mix thoroughly.

Preheat the oven to 400°F.

With a teaspoon, stuff the pouches, forcing small quantities at a time into the pouch tips to leave no air pockets. Stuff to within 1 inch of the top of each pouch without packing—the stuffing will swell and the pouches will shrink during cooking. Tack the tops of the pouches with a trussing needle and kitchen string, once through opposite sides and again, after a quarter turn, through the other opposite sides. Pull the ends of the string together, tie, and clip.

On a plate, roll the stuffed pouches around in a bit of olive oil to coat them on all sides, season with salt and pepper, and arrange them in a gratin dish of a size to just contain them without forcing. Pour in the white wine, put fennel seeds between the pouches, place a lemon slice on each squid, sprinkle with bread crumbs and a dribble of olive oil, and bake for 40 to 45 minutes, basting regularly. Serve directly from the gratin dish.

TUNA MARSEILLES STYLE
Thon à la Marseillaise

Serves 4

A TUNA STEAK, or cross section of the body, cut from behind the abdomen, presents a structure that falls naturally into 4 serving sections (if the tuna is small). Lulu often prepares this for 8 or more people, but she then needs a separate pan for each steak of 4 servings. She notes, "You'll need slices of tuna about two fingers thick. Above all, cook each side for no more than 5 minutes—the tuna must be 'rosé' or it will be dry and boring."

1 tuna steak (about 3 pounds and 1 1/2 inches thick)
1 tablespoon olive oil
Several fresh savory sprigs
4 bay leaves

SAUCE
3 tablespoons olive oil
1 medium onion, finely chopped
4 garlic cloves, crushed and peeled
1 1/2 pounds tomatoes, peeled, seeded, coarsely chopped, and layered, salted, in a colander for 1 hour
Salt and pinch of cayenne
Large pinch of fresh savory leaves, finely chopped, or dried, powdered savory
2 tablespoons capers, chopped
3 ounces Greek-style large black olives, pitted and coarsely chopped
3 salt anchovies, rinsed and filleted, or 6 fillets

1 tablespoon olive oil
Salt and pepper

In a shallow dish, rub the tuna steak with 1 tablespoon of olive oil and press savory sprigs and bay leaves to the surfaces. Cover and leave in a cool place for 3 or 4 hours—if refrigerated, remove from the refrigerator 1 hour before cooking.

For the sauce, warm 2 tablespoons of olive oil in a large heavy sauté pan, add the onion and the garlic, and cook over low heat, stirring with a wooden spoon, until soft but uncolored. Turn up the heat, add the tomatoes, salt, cayenne, and savory, and cook, shaking the pan and stirring often, until the sauce is thick with no loose liquid remaining. Lower the heat and stir in the chopped capers and olives. Over very low heat, warm the remaining tablespoon of olive oil and the anchovy fillets in a small frying pan for a few seconds, or until the fillets fall apart when the pan is shaken. Stir the anchovies and their oil into the sauce.

In a heavy frying pan only slightly larger than the tuna steak, heat the 1 tablespoon of olive oil over high heat. Discard the sprigs of savory and the bay leaves, season the steak on both sides with salt and pepper, and fry for about 5 minutes on each side, adjusting the heat, as necessary, to avoid burning. Use a large wide spatula to turn the steak and to transfer it to a heated platter. Remove and discard the skin and spoon the sauce over the steak's surface.

GRILLED STURGEON WITH SPICY TOMATO SAUCE
Esturgeon Grillé, Sauce Pablo

Serves 8

THE SAUCE PABLO is an invention of a friend of the Peyraud family. Lulu was delighted with the simplicity of the preparation and with the sauce's versatility. She also recommends it with grilled swordfish or with pasta.

SAUCE
3 tablespoons olive oil
1/2 pound onions, chopped
1 head garlic, cloves separated, crushed, and peeled
3 pounds tomatoes, peeled, seeded, and coarsely chopped
Salt
*Several winter savory sprigs, tied together, or a large pinch of
    dried, crumbled savory*
Handful of chopped parsley
4 salt anchovies, rinsed, filleted, and chopped, or 8 fillets
2 tablespoons capers, chopped
Juice of 1/2 lemon
1 tablespoon red wine vinegar
1 tablespoon Dijon mustard

*8 sturgeon steaks, approximately 3/4 inch thick (about 3
    pounds)*
Olive oil
Salt and freshly ground pepper

In a large earthenware *poêlon* or a heavy sauté pan, combine all the sauce ingredients, bring slowly to a boil, stirring occasionally with a wooden spoon, and cook at a light bubble, stirring regularly, for about 1 hour, or until reduced and consistent.

Coat the sturgeon steaks thinly with olive oil, season with salt
and pepper, enclose them in a double-faced flat fish grill, and grill
over hot coals for about 4 minutes on each side. Serve accompanied
by the sauce or, if you prefer, pour the sauce into a large heated
platter and place the grilled steaks on top.

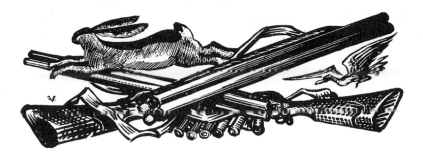

Meats, Poultry, Game

The seasons beckon us to choose not only very different kinds of meats, but also different methods of preparation; autumn is the moment for game, winter for daubes and stews, spring and summer for grilled meats and spicy ragouts.

Les saisons nous invitent à choisir des viandes bien différentes et les façons de les apprêter, aussi à l'automne c'est le gibier, en hiver les daubes et les ragoûts, au printemps et en été les grillades ou les assortiments épicés.

Lulu

Grilled meats are, of course, not reserved only for spring and summer, and simple roasts, above all, are served year-round, transformed each season by the vegetable preparations that accompany them. A red Tempier, older than that served with the fish, is a welcome accompaniment to any meat, and one still older will be poured with the cheeses.

Opposite: Gigot à la Ficelle.

LULU'S POT-AU-FEU
Pot-au-feu à la Provençale

Serves 8

LULU'S POT-AU-FEU is unusual in that it contains white wine. Lamb is traditional in a Provençal pot-au-feu. The tang of the wine (Lulu insists that it should be young and quite acidic, a Muscadet, for instance) and the soft, slightly sweet flavor of the lamb mingle with the beef and aromatic elements to produce a very special and subtle broth.

3 pounds beef shank from hind leg, boned, in a single piece, and tied

3 pounds beef short ribs, in three pieces, tied

1 lamb shank, unboned

1 beef marrow bone, wrapped and tied in a piece of cheesecloth

1 cup young, acidic white wine

Water

Handful of coarse sea salt

Large bouquet garni (leek greens, celery stalk, savory, bay leaf)

6 garlic cloves, crushed and peeled

1 large onion, stuck with 3 cloves

2 pounds young freshly dug carrots, peeled

2 pounds leeks, white and light green parts only, cleaned (upper parts slit, soaked in water), tied in a bundle

2 pounds small yellow-fleshed potatoes, peeled

1 pound small, tender, crisp turnips, peeled

16 thin slices of baguette, partially dried out in a low oven

3 cups tomato sauce (page 74)

Arrange the meats and the marrow bone in a large (8- to 10-quart) earthenware "pot-au-feu" or a heavy, deep soup pot closely but without packing. Add the white wine, pour over cold water to cover by about 2 inches, place over medium-low heat, and bring to a boil (this may require about 1 hour). As the liquid approaches the boil, skim off and discard the gray foam that rises to the surface. Add the salt, the bouquet garni, garlic, and onion stuck with cloves and, when the water again approaches the boil, adjust the heat to maintain a bare simmer, lid kept slightly ajar, for about 3 hours.

After 2½ hours, add the carrots, leeks, potatoes, and turnips, raise the heat until the liquid approaches a boil again, and adjust again to a simmer. With a trussing needle, test the beef shank for doneness—it should not resist the needle but should remain slightly firm. Discard the bouquet garni and the onion stuck with cloves.

Serve the broth first. Pour part of it into a soup tureen, keeping the meats and vegetables hot in the remaining broth. Remove the marrow bone from its wrapping, slip the marrow out of the bone onto a plate, and spread small pieces of marrow onto the slices of bread. At table, place 2 slices of marrow crust in each soup plate and ladle over broth.

Carve the meats in the kitchen. Slice the beef shank quite thin, slice the short ribs between each rib, and arrange the pieces on a very large heated platter. The meat from the lamb shank will be falling off the bone—tuck it at the end of the platter. Lift the bundle of leeks to the platter, cut the strings, and arrange them around the meats. Remove the other vegetables to the platter with a slotted spoon and scatter them around the meats. Serve, accompanied by the hot tomato sauce.

MEAT AND POTATO GRATIN
Hachis à la Purée de Pommes de Terre

Serves 4

2 pounds potatoes, peeled and quartered
Salt
1 tablespoon olive oil
8 tablespoons (1 stick) butter
1 onion, finely chopped
1 pound leftover beef from pot-au-feu, thinly sliced, cut into
* thin strips, then cut across into tiny dice*
Pinch of fresh savory leaves, finely chopped, or dried savory
Pepper
Persillade (handful of flat-leaf parsely leaves, finely chopped,
* chopped again with 2 finely chopped garlic cloves)*
1 cup milk, heated to the boiling point
1/2 cup freshly grated Parmesan cheese

Boil the potatoes in salted water for about 30 minutes, or until just done.

At the same time, warm the olive oil and 2 tablespoons butter in a *poêlon* or heavy sauté pan, add the onion, and cook over low heat, stirring regularly with a wooden spoon, until soft but not colored. Add the meat, savory, and salt and cook over medium-low heat, stirring regularly for about 10 minutes, or until lightly colored but not browned. Grind over pepper, stir in the persillade and remove from the heat.

Preheat the oven to 400°F.

Drain the potatoes and, with a wooden pestle, push them through a sieve. Add 4 tablespoons butter, cut into small pieces, and stir in enough hot milk to render the purée very supple, not quite pourable. Taste for salt, grind over pepper, and stir in the cheese without beating.

Spread the meat mixture in the bottom of a gratin dish. Spread the potato purée on top, smooth with the tines of a fork to create a ripply surface, scatter over shavings of remaining 2 tablespoons butter, and bake for 20 minutes, or until golden.

GRILLED HANGER STEAK WITH ANCHOVY BUTTER
Onglet Grillé au Beurre d'Anchois

Serves 4

WHEN LULU WAS a little girl, in Marseilles, she sought adult company. She cherishes memories of an old seamstress who enjoyed a child's company and was happy to recount her souvenirs of Marseilles, of its life, its scandals and its cuisine, and to share her lunch with the child. The lunch was often a salad and *onglet grillé au beurre d'anchois*.

The butcher's piece, or the butcher's cut, sometimes called bloody skirt or hanging tender, is considered by many to be the most succulent cut of beef for grilling. It is a single, internal muscle that, depending on the animal, weighs 3 to 4 pounds. When trimmed, it falls apart into two elongated, thick, completely lean strips of meat, devoid of nerve tissue, which butchers usually split partially and open out to form 1-inch-thick steaks. Like skirt and flank, it is cut with the grain and not across. It is firm but not tough, it contains its juices better than most cuts, and is wonderful only when grilled rare.

The anchovy butter should be rustic—imperfectly puréed. The individual serving plates should be very hot. The steak should be seared, grill-marked, very hot on the surface, but only warm inside.

(continued)

ANCHOVY BUTTER
4 salt anchovies, rinsed and filleted, or 8 fillets
8 tablespoons butter (1 stick), softened at room temperature

2 pounds hanger steak (butcher's piece), cut into 4 steaks (see
*   above), at room temperature*
1 tablespoon olive oil
Salt and pepper

In a plate, mash the anchovies with a fork—or pound them in a mortar with a wooden pestle. Add the butter and mash or pound until well mixed.

Heat the grill over a solid bed of glowing embers. Rub the steaks with olive oil, season with salt and pepper, and grill them at a 4-inch distance from the coals for 2 to 3 minutes on each side.

While the steaks are grilling, spread a spoonful of anchovy butter onto each preheated plate, remove the steaks from the grill to the plates, dab a spoonful of anchovy butter on top of each steak, and serve immediately.

ROAST FILLET OF BEEF
Filet de Boeuf Rôti

Serves 8

LULU'S ROAST BEEF is no different from anyone's roast beef. It is what she serves with it that makes it her own—and makes the roast beef taste different. Favorite garnishes are: Chard Gratin, Gratin of Eggplant and Tomatoes, Grilled Eggplant with Garlic Cream, Potato Soufflé, Gratin of Celeriac and Potatoes, Scalloped Potatoes with Olives, Potato and Sorrel Gratin, Squash Gratin, Purée of Sweet Potatoes, Tomatoes à la Provençale, and Zucchini Gratin. Lulu roasts in one oven and prepares her gratins in another.

> *1 beef tenderloin (fillet), about 5 pounds, trimmed of all
>   superficial fat and nerve tissue, at room temperature*
> *2 tablespoons olive oil*

Preheat the oven to 500°F.

So that the roast will be of the same thickness from one end to the other, fold over the narrow tip of the tenderloin, or filet mignon, and tie it with a loop of kitchen string. With your hands, coat the roast with olive oil, place it in a shallow, heavy, elongated roasted pan, and put it in the oven. A couple of minutes later, turn the oven down to 325°F. After 15 minutes, turn the oven off, open the door for a minute to slightly cool it, and leave the roast in the oven to rest for 15 minutes (if your oven is very well sealed, you can put the roast into a 500-degree oven, turn it off, and remove the roast after 30 minutes). Carve the tenderloin in the kitchen, lay the slices out, overlapping, on a warm platter and serve.

PROVENÇAL BRAISED BEEF
Daube à la Provençale

Serves 8

IN PROVENCE, it is considered essential while a daube is cooking to keep the *daubière* covered with a soup plate containing red wine, which is regularly replenished as it evaporates. Lulu remains faithful to this tradition, although she admits that water would probably serve the same purpose, causing the steam inside the *daubière* to condense on the underside of the soup plate and fall back into the daube. She often prepares daube in advance, leaves it to cool, uncovered, and reheats it very slowly on the day following its preparation. With leftover daube, she stuffs ravioli (page 313).

When Lulu prepares a daube to be served cold, unmolded, in its jelly, she adds a calf's foot to reinforce the gelatinous content of the juices. In the United States, pig's trotters are often easier to find— two pig's trotters will replace one calf's foot. They should be split in two, covered abundantly with cold water, brought to a full boil, drained, and rinsed in cold water before being assembled with the marinated meats in the *daubière*. A rounded or slant-sided metal mixing bowl (*cul de poule*) is an ideal mold for *daube en gelée*. Drain the daube into a colander. Pour a tablespoon of cooking liquid into a saucer and refrigerate until set to test for gelatinous content. If it does not set firmly, reduce the liquid until it does, at the same time skimming off any fat that rises to the surface. Bone the trotters, cut the flesh into small pieces, and distribute it evenly with the other meats in the mold, or molds. Pour over the hot juices, cool to room temperature, and refrigerate, uncovered, overnight before unmolding.

*4 pounds boned beef shank and chuck, in approximately
equal proportions, cut into 3-ounce pieces*

4 ounces lean, streaky salt bacon, in a single slice, cut across
    into ⅓-inch-thick lardons, or slab bacon, unsmoked
1½ cups peeled and thinly sliced carrots
½ pound onions, sliced into thin rings
3 branches thyme, 2 bay leaves, parsley stems
1 strip dried orange peel
1 tablespoon olive oil
3 cups (1 bottle) young, deeply colored, tannic red wine
Coarse sea salt
Bouquet garni (thyme, bay leaf, strip of dried orange peel,
    celery stalk, parsley)
1 pound large elbow macaroni, penne rigate, tortiglioni, etc.
Freshly grated Parmesan (served separately)

In a large bowl, intermingle the meats, vegetables, herbs, and dried orange peel, sprinkle over the olive oil, and pour over red wine to cover. Marinate, covered, for several hours or overnight, turning the contents of the bowl around in the marinade two or three times.

Strain the marinade into another bowl. Discard the carrots, onions, herbs, and orange peel. In a *daubière* or other heavy pot, preferably earthenware, layer the meats, sprinkling with salt, and place the bouquet garni between layers. Pour over the marinade and, with a heat disperser placed over the heat source, bring slowly to a boil over medium heat—this will require about 1 hour. Adjust the heat to maintain a slight simmer—the barest ripple of movement at the liquid's surface—for 6 hours, the pot covered with a soup plate containing about ½ cup red wine (or water), which should be replenished as it evaporates (if the shape of your pot doesn't lend itself to being covered by a plate, cover it with a sheet of foil with a lid pressed atop). Lift off as much floating fat from the surface as possible. Discard the bouquet garni.

(continued)

Boil the macaroni in abundant salted water, according to the instructions on the package (about 12 minutes), drain well, empty it into a deep, heated serving dish, ladle over some of the daube's cooking juices, and serve at the same time as the daube, accompanied by a dish of freshly grated Parmesan.

CALF'S TONGUE POT-AU-FEU
Langue de Veau en Pot-au-feu

Serves 6

1 fresh calf's tongue
Coarse sea salt
*Large bouquet garni (leek greens, celery stalk, savory, bay
     leaf)*
1 head garlic, cut in two crosswise
1 large onion, stuck with 2 cloves
1 cup white wine
Water
12 young carrots, peeled
*1 1/2 pounds leeks, white and light green parts only, cleaned
     and tied in a bundle*
1 1/2 pounds small yellow-fleshed potatoes, peeled
1 pound tender crisp turnips, quartered if large
Thin slices of baguette, partially dried in a low oven
3 cups tomato sauce (page 74)

Rub the tongue with coarse salt and leave it overnight. Rinse it, soak it in cold water for 3 hours, drain it, and lay in a large, deep oval casserole. Surround it with the bouquet garni, the garlic, and the onion stuck with cloves, add a small handful of coarse salt and the white wine, and pour over cold water to cover generously. Bring to a boil, skim off the foam that rises, and adjust the heat to maintain a bare simmer, lid slightly ajar, for about 3 ½ hours in all.

After 2 hours, remove the tongue. When it is cool enough to handle, trim the base of the tongue, removing throat bones and gristly parts, slit the skin to one side, the length of the tongue, and peel it off. Return the peeled tongue to the casserole, bring back to a boil, and adjust to a simmer. An hour later, add the vegetables, turn up the heat to reach a boil, adjust the heat again to a simmer, and cook for 30 minutes longer.

Keep the tongue and the vegetables warm in broth while serving part of the broth at table, poured over the crusts of baguette in soup plates. Slice the tongue thin, on the bias, lay out slices, overlapping, on a heated platter, surround with the vegetables, strings clipped free of the leeks, and accompany with hot tomato sauce.

BLANQUETTE OF BEEF TRIPE
Gras-double en Blanquette

Serves 4

TRIPE IS SOLD cleaned and partially cooked. It is often sold "bleached" for cosmetic purposes. Bleaching, unfortunately, removes the flavor, as well as the grayish color. Shop in ethnic markets to find unbleached tripe. Use a mixture of all four stomachs, if available. The second stomach, or honeycomb, is the most commonly available in the United States; if you can find the lovely, delicate, leafy bible tripe, or third stomach, by all means combine it with honeycomb.

(continued)

199

*1 pig's trotter, split in two, covered with cold water, brought
    to a full boil, drained, and rinsed in cold water*
2 pounds unbleached beef tripe, cut into $^1/_3$ x 3-inch strips
3 medium carrots, peeled and cut into 1-inch lengths
*Bouquet garni (thyme, bay leaf, parsley, celery stalk, leek
    greens)*
2 medium onions, one stuck with 2 cloves
Coarse sea salt
6 cups water

GARNISH
$^1/_2$ pound pickling onions, peeled
$^1/_2$ tablespoon butter
$^1/_2$ teaspoon sugar
Salt
Water
*8 small yellow-fleshed potatoes, boiled in their skins at the
    last minute and peeled while hot*

LIAISON
2 egg yolks
Juice of $^1/_2$ lemon
Pepper
Nutmeg

Place the trotter halves in the bottom of a *daubière* or other heavy pot, preferably earthenware. Scatter over a handful of tripe and some carrots, place the bouquet garni in the center with an onion to either side, and sprinkle with salt. Press the remaining tripe and carrots, intermingled, on top, sprinkle with salt, and pour over water to cover by a good inch. Bring slowly to a boil, the pot separated from direct heat by a heat disperser. Adjust the heat to maintain a bare simmer, covered, for 7 hours. Keep the lid slightly ajar, if necessary, to control the degree of simmer. Scrape the bottom of the pot with a wooden spoon, displacing the trotter halves, a couple of times during this period to make certain that nothing is sticking. Add a little boiling water, if necessary, to keep the tripe barely immersed in liquid. Discard the bouquet and the two onions. Remove the trotters, bone them, cut the flesh into small pieces, and return it to the pot.

Put the garnish onions in a saucepan of a size to just hold them in a single layer, add the butter, sugar, and salt, and pour over enough water to not quite cover the onions. Bring to a boil and cook, covered, at a simmer, shaking the pan occasionally, for about 10 minutes. Remove the lid, raise the heat, and cook at a light boil, shaking the pan regularly, until all the liquid has disappeared and the onions have acquired a light golden glaze. Add the onions and the hot peeled potatoes to the pot and remove it from the heat to cool for a few minutes.

In a small bowl, combine the egg yolks, lemon juice, pepper, and nutmeg and beat lightly with a fork. Stir in 3 or 4 tablespoons of the tripe cooking liquid and pour the mixture, slowly, into the pot, stirring at the same time with a wooden spoon. Return the pot to low heat and stir, slowly but without stopping, until the cooking juices acquire a light, velvety texture—until they coat the spoon. The liquid must not approach a boil. Remove the pot from the heat and continue stirring for 30 seconds or so. Serve with a ladle, directly from the pot, into heated soup plates.

ROAST PORK LOIN WITH SAGE AND ONIONS
Filet de Porc aux Oignons

Serves 8

FOR A LOIN of pork prepared in exactly the same way, Lulu often replaces the little glazed onions with a half pound of black olives.

4 pounds pork loin (including tenderloin), excess fat trimmed from surface, boned, bones broken up and reserved

MARINADE
3 fresh sage leaves
2 cloves, pounded to a powder
Pinch of freshly grated nutmeg
Pepper
Milk

Salt
Fresh sage leaves
1 cup white wine

GARNISH
2 pounds small pickling onions, peeled
1 teaspoon sugar
Salt
1 tablespoon butter
Water

Lay the loin out in a large deep dish with the boned interior facing up, surround it with the bones, press the sage leaves into its surface, sprinkle over the spices, pour over milk to cover, seal the dish with plastic wrap, and hold for several hours or overnight in a cool place, or refrigerate.

Preheat the oven to 450°F.

Remove the loin from the milk and drain. Discard the milk and bones. Pat the meat dry with a cloth or paper towels. Sprinkle the inside surface with salt, lay sage leaves, end to end, the length of the cut, between the loin and the tenderloin, roll the meat into a cylinder, enclosing the tenderloin in the middle, and tie it. Salt the surface of the roast, place it in a heavy, shallow, oval oven dish, and put it in the oven. Ten minutes later, turn the oven down to 325°F. Begin to baste, about every 15 minutes, as soon as the roast has released enough fat. After 45 minutes, remove all the fat from the pan, bring ½ cup white wine to a boil, and add it to the pan. Continue to baste every 10 or 15 minutes, adding small quantities of heated wine when necessary to keep the pan from drying up. Roast for 1 hour and 30 minutes, in all.

Meanwhile, put the onions, sugar, salt, and butter in a pan large enough to hold them in a single layer, if possible. Pour over water to almost immerse the onions, bring to a boil, cover the pan, and simmer for 8 to 10 minutes. Remove the lid, turn up the heat, and shake the pan regularly until all the water has evaporated and the onions acquire a light golden glaze. Fifteen minutes before removing the roast from the oven, degrease the juices as well as possible and add the onions to the pan.

Remove the roast to a carving board, clip and remove the strings, carve into ⅓-inch-thick slices, spread the slices, overlapping, the length of a heated serving platter, surround with the onions, pour over the juices, and serve.

Pork Chops with Juniper
Côtelettes de Porc au Genièvre

Serves 6

PEELED AND CORED APPLES, cut into finger-thick rings, brushed with butter, and cooked, unturned, until golden in a broiler, are a good accompaniment to these chops.

> *1 teaspoon juniper berries (3 or 4 per person)*
> *4 tablespoons butter, softened at room temperature*
> *2 tablespoons olive oil*
> *6 6- to 7-ounce pork chops (2¹/₂ pounds), preferably*
> * neck-end*
> *Salt and pepper*
> *¹/₄ cup white wine*

In a mortar, pound the juniper berries to a powder. Mix thoroughly with the butter.

Heat the olive oil in a large frying pan, season the chops with salt and pepper, and cook over medium heat for about 5 minutes on each side. Remove the chops to a heated platter, empty all fat from the pan, return it to the heat, and add the white wine, stirring and scraping the bottom of the pan with a wooden spoon, until all adherences are dissolved and the wine is reduced by half. Pour a few drops of the deglazing liquid over each chop and smear each with juniper butter. Serve immediately.

STUFFED ROAST SUCKLING PIG
Cochon de Lait Farci

SERVES 12 OR MORE

THE PIG'S STUFFING evolved from the souvenir of a roast suckling pig served to Lulu and Lucien in Sardinia years ago. Suckling pig stuffed with figs numbered on nearly all the family's lists of favorite dishes.

To close the belly opening after the pig is stuffed, pierce the skin to either side of the vent, at 1- to 1½-inch intervals with metal trussing skewers and pull the edges of the skin flaps together by looping the middle of a yard length of kitchen string around the first skewer and lacing back and forth, crisscross, from one skewer to another, as if lacing up a boot. Tie at the last skewer and clip off excess string. If the legs are trussed into a crouching position, the pig takes up less oven space, the presentation is more attractive, and the cooking more even than if left untrussed. You will need a trussing needle at least 10 inches long. Thread it with a 30-inch length of strong kitchen string. Pull the hind legs up to the sides of the body, push the needle through the thickest part of one leg, through the body, and out through the thickest part of the other leg. Fold the trotters under the legs at the heel joints, push the needle back through the trotters and the body, tie the string ends tightly, and clip off the excess. Fold the front legs into place, against and partially beneath the body so that the trotters lie beneath the jawbone. With another length of string, run the needle first through the thickest part of the shanks and the lower throat, then back near the trotters and through the upper throat. Tie and clip. Thus prepared, the pig lies firmly and primly on its belly.

The finished roast pig is much too beautiful not to be presented before carving but, because of the required work surface, it may be more practical to carve it in the kitchen. Presented at table with one half carved, the other half and the head still intact, it is also impressive. From one side, remove the front leg at the shoulder joint and the back leg at the hip joint. Cut them into serving portions. Cut down to the bone the length of the backbone. Slice through the belly flesh from the shoulder cut to the leg cut and remove the entire length of rack and loin, working down from the back and hugging the rib cage with the knife blade. Cut the boneless rack and loin across into serving sections, each with its skin attached. With a small, sharply pointed knife, slit the flesh to either side of each rib; with knife tip and fingertips, lift the ribs loose from the stuffing and twist each free from the backbone, baring the stuffing, either to be spooned out or cut into sections with the carving knife. At mid-service, return the pig to the kitchen, carve the other half, remove the head, and split it with a cleaver, held in place and pounded with a wooden mallet.

1 suckling pig (10 to 12 pounds)
Salt

Stuffing
4 ounces fresh goat cheese
4 ounces brousse or ricotta
2 eggs
4 ounces chopped walnuts
12 ounces fresh figs, coarsely chopped
1 pound chard leaves, green parts only, parboiled for a few
*   seconds, drained, refreshed under cold running water,*
*   squeezed thoroughly, and chopped*
12 ounces 2- or 3-day-old bread, crusts removed, soaked in
*   milk, and squeezed almost dry*
2 cloves, pounded to a powder in a mortar
Pinch of freshly grated nutmeg
Salt and pepper

3 tablespoons olive oil
3 cups (1 bottle) vin rosé

Rub the pig, inside and out, with coarse salt, place it on a tray or large platter, and leave overnight in a cool place. Discard the liquid that has been drawn out by the salt and wipe the animal dry with a cloth or paper towels. Transfer it to a work surface.

Preheat the oven to 350°F. With a fork, mash together the cheeses and eggs in a mixing bowl. Add all the other stuffing ingredients and mix intimately with your hands. Push stuffing into the pig's chest cavity before filling the abdominal cavity. Lace up the belly opening and truss the legs (see above). With a razor blade, score the skin very superficially, never cutting all the way through, once down the back and three or four times to each side, diagonally, taking care that no score mark touches another. Rub the pig all over with olive oil and position it on its belly in a heavy shallow roasting pan. Wrap pieces of aluminum foil around the ears and the tail to prevent their burning and put the pan into the oven. After 30 minutes, if the pig's own fat has not begun to flow, sprinkle with a bit more olive oil. Ten minutes later, bring ½ cup of the wine to a boil and add it to the roasting pan. Baste regularly, about every 15 minutes, adding heated wine in small quantities so that the pan never dries up. Roast for 3 to 3½ hours, or until the skin is an even, rich, glistening mahogany color. If after a couple of hours it seems to be coloring too rapidly, turn the oven down to 325° or 300°F. Turn it up again later, if necessary. A few minutes before removing the pig from the oven, remove the foil from the ears and the tail.

Transfer the pig to a platter or carving board and pull out the skewers from the belly; the lacing string will fall free. Snip the leg trussing strings and pull on each knot to remove the strings. Pour the roasting juices into a bowl of a size to just contain them and leave to settle while carving the pig (see above). Remove as much fat as possible from the surface of the roasting juices, reheat them in a small saucepan, pour them into a heated sauceboat, and serve.

GRILLED LAMB SKEWERS
Brochettes à la Provençale

Serves 6

I HAVE TEASED LULU mercilessly by taking notes on the same recipes over and over again. Often I receive quite different instructions and ingredients and usually, when I point this out, she will say, "Well, sometimes I do it one way and sometimes another—both are good." The first time we discussed brochettes, she included among the ingredients small tomatoes and red and green peppers. The next time around, she said, "Vegetables are very pretty on brochettes, but I don't like them. They never want to stay in place, they're never cooked, and they keep the meats from cooking properly—you'd better get rid of them."

Lulu's bay leaves come straight from the tree. If only dried bay leaves are available, they will break up when you try to thread them on skewers—discard them after they have served in the marinade or, if you like, instead of marinating with whole bay leaves, reduce a few leaves to a powder in a blender and add a small pinch to the marinade. If only dried sage is available, eliminate it; dried sage always has a musty flavor.

Pale beige lamb's kidneys with a rose cast are delicate in flavor. Those that are a dark reddish-brown are always strong tasting. If you cannot find light-colored lamb's kidneys, substitute 2 calf's kidneys for the 8 lamb's kidneys, thin membrane removed, split lengthwise through the core, fat cut away, each half cut crosswise into 7 or 8 wedges. If lamb's liver is not available, substitute calf's liver. Finally, if one of these meats is not to your taste, substitute lamb's loin with fat removed. Twelve-inch disposable bamboo skewers are practical.

Large pinch (mounded teaspoon) of coarse sea salt
Pepper

3 garlic cloves, lightly crushed and peeled

3 tablespoons olive oil

*4 lamb's hearts, trimmed of fat and gristly tubes at the
    entrance, split lengthwise into 4 sections, each section
    cut across in two*

*8 light-colored lamb's kidneys, fine membrane peeled off, cut,
    fanlike, from the core, into 3 wedges each*

*½ pound lamb's liver, cut into 18 cubes (approximately ½-
    ounce pieces)*

*½ pound lean, streaky salt bacon, cut into 24 wedges,
    covered with cold water, brought to a boil, drained,
    rinsed in cold water, and dried in paper towels, or slab
    bacon, unsmoked*

1 medium-small onion, finely chopped

*9 fresh bay leaves, cut in two crosswise, or 4 dried bay leaves
    or a pinch of powdered bay leaf*

4 fresh sage leaves

In a marble mortar, pound the salt, pepper, and garlic cloves to a
paste with a wooden pestle. Stir in the olive oil with the pestle. If
the mortar is not large enough to hold all the meats, spoon the contents into a mixing bowl, wipe the mortar and pestle clean with
some of the meats, and add them to the mixing bowl along with all
the other ingredients. Turn and toss repeatedly with your hands
and leave to marinate for an hour or two.

Discard the sage leaves. Thread the meats and bay leaves (if they
are fresh) onto skewers, loosely but touching, beginning and end-
ing with a piece of heart, which, because its flesh is firmer than the
others, will serve to hold the others in place. Count as you go: for
each skewer, you will have 5 pieces of heart (6 on two of the skewers), 4 wedges of kidney, 3 of liver, 4 of bacon, and 3 half bay
leaves. Lay the skewers, side by side, on a long platter or tray as

they are finished and pour over the left-behind marinade. Hold them, if you like, for an hour or two before grilling.

Preheat an iron grill over a solid bed of wood embers and grill the brochettes, at about 4-inch distance from the coals, for 10 minutes in all, turning them every 2 or 3 minutes. Serve, at the same time, a pilaf with tomatoes (page 302).

GRILLED LAMB CHOPS
Côtelettes d'Agneau sur la Braise

Serves 6

FRENCH BUTCHERS have a bad habit of hacking the bone of a rib chop with a cleaver, just beneath the loin, and folding the broken rib back upon itself. Lulu insists, "Above all, don't let your butcher chop into the rib!" She likes to serve a potato and sorrel gratin (page 283) with these chops.

> *12 single rib lamb chops, rib bone unbroken, outer layer of*
> *   fat removed*
> *Pepper*
> *Small pinch of cayenne*
> *3 tablespoons olive oil*
> *3 bay leaves, cut or broken into small fragments*
> *Bouquet of fresh savory sprigs*
> *Salt*

Lay the chops out on a platter. Grind pepper over both sides. Mix the cayenne into the olive oil and dribble it over the chops, turning them around and over until evenly coated. Press bay and savory to all the surfaces, cover, and macerate at room temperature for a couple of hours.

Heat the grill over very hot wood embers. Salt the chops and grill them, 6 inches from the coals, for about 3 minutes on each side.

STRING-TURNED ROAST LEG OF LAMB
Gigot à la Ficelle

Serves 8 to 10

GIGOT À LA FICELLE is a leg of lamb hung by a string, which slowly winds and unwinds, before the flames in a fireplace. It is the most primitive and most satisfying method of roasting a leg of lamb. A hook is affixed beneath the fireplace mantle, one end of a length of strong kitchen or butcher's string is tied tightly to the shank bone of a leg of lamb, just above the heel, and the string is tied to the mantle hook so as to suspend the leg about 5 inches above a pan placed on the hearth floor. The fire should be prepared in advance so that a solid heart of incandescent coals has built up, and it should be fed regularly with small logs to maintain a steady flame. Fruit woods are good—François, who is the master of open-fire cookery, uses uprooted vinestock and oak. To set the leg in motion, it is only necessary to give the heel a light twist in the direction in which the leg has begun to turn. The heavier the object, the longer the revolutions will persist. A 6-pound leg of lamb will turn slowly, then progressively more slowly, for up to an hour, winding up and pausing for a couple of seconds each time before beginning to unwind and rewind again in the opposite direction. From time to time, the heel of the leg can be given a light twist, in the direction in which the leg is turning, to maintain the regularity of the revolution.

(continued)

*1 leg of lamb (about 6 pounds), pelvic bone removed, leg
    bone intact, including heel*
2 tablespoons olive oil
4 garlic cloves, crushed and peeled
Several bay leaves and sprigs of fresh thyme and savory

BASTING MIXTURE
Salt
Pepper
Cayenne
Juice of ¹/₂ lemon
4 tablespoons olive oil
*Several large branches of fresh thyme, tied together to form a
    brush*

In a large oval dish, rub the surfaces of the leg of lamb with 2 table-spoons olive oil and crushed garlic. Press the garlic and herbs into the surfaces, cover with foil, and hold in a cool place for several hours or overnight. If refrigerated, remove from the refrigerator 2 or 3 hours before roasting.

Prepare the fire. Discard the garlic and the herbs from the mari-nade and add any oil in the dish to the basting mixture. Tie the string to the shank bone and tie the other end so that the leg hangs directly in front of the heart of the fire (see above). Place a pan be-neath to collect the drippings. The leg will begin to turn; give the heel a twist in the direction in which it is turning.

After about 15 minutes, begin to baste regularly, dipping the bundle of thyme into the basting mixture and brushing all the sur-faces of the leg as it revolves. Survey the movement and give the heel a light twist whenever necessary. Feed the fire at an angle from both sides, pushing the wood to the center as it is consumed, so as to hold the flames mostly at the heart; after an hour and a half's time, stop feeding, permitting the flames to slowly subside so that, finally, the roast receives only the heat radiated by the embers. Count about 2 hours in all. Remove the leg to a heated platter. Discard the drippings from the pan.

Carve at the table. With a folded napkin, hold the leg by the heel, at an angle, with the butt end resting on the platter. Slice away from yourself, at a sharp bias, with the knife blade almost parallel to the bone, removing slices first from the thick, rounded fleshy section of the leg, then, turning the leg over, from the leaner muscle to the other side, and finally, holding the knife at a slight angle upward, remove small slices from the shank. Serve a slice of each cut onto each plate, tip the platter, and spoon carving juices over each serving.

LEG OF LAMB ON A BED OF THYME
Gigot sur Lit de Thym

Serves 8 to 10

LEG OF LAMB on a bed of thyme was high on the list of the Peyraud family's preferred dishes. Lulu says, "The thyme branches should contain quite a lot of wood so that, when the leg is placed on them, it doesn't touch the bottom of the pan. After roasting, the thyme and the fat in the pan are discarded."

The Provençal hillsides are covered with gnarled and woody plants of wild thyme. If only fragile garden thyme is available, use a roasting rack and scatter over an abundance of thyme sprigs before placing the leg on top. Sometimes, Lulu mixes sprigs of winter savory with the thyme. In late spring and summer, when garlic is fresh, she often surrounds a leg of lamb, with or without thyme, with whole heads of garlic—1 per person—before putting it to

Peppers on the grill.

roast. At table, guests pull the heads apart, pressing the cloves with the tines of a fork to force the purée from the skins before spreading it on the meat or on pieces of bread.

> *2 large handfuls of fresh thyme branches*
> *1 6-pound leg of lamb, at room temperature, pelvic bone and*
>   *superficial fat removed*
> *1 tablespoon olive oil*
> *Salt and pepper*
> *8 to 10 fresh heads of garlic (optional)*

Preheat the oven to 450°F.

Prepare a bed of thyme branches in the bottom of a heavy shallow roasting dish or large oval gratin dish. Rub the leg of lamb with the olive oil, season with salt and pepper, place it on the bed of thyme, and surround with garlic. Roast for about 1 hour, lowering the temperature after 10 minutes to 350°F and, 20 minutes later, to 275°F. Transfer the leg to a heated platter and hold it for 20 minutes in the turned-off oven or other warm place before carving.

POT-ROASTED LEG OF LAMB
WITH BLACK OLIVES
Gigot en Cocotte Aux Olives Noires

Serves 8

WITH THIS quintessentially Provençal preparation, Lulu serves a zucchini gratin (page 303). You may need slightly more or less white wine. The important thing is to add it, a little at a time, throughout the cooking process. There should never be an abundance of liquid nor, once liquid is added, should it be permitted to completely evaporate.

(continued)

4 tablespoons olive oil
1 6-pound leg of lamb, pelvic bone removed, shank bone
   sawed at the heel, and superficial fat removed
Salt and freshly ground pepper
1 large sweet onion, coarsely chopped
2 heads fresh, crisp garlic, cloves separated, lightly crushed,
   and peeled
2 tomatoes, peeled, seeded, and quartered
Large branch of fresh thyme, or several sprigs, tied together
1 cup dry white wine
5 ounces Provençal black olives, prepared in salt, or Greek-
   style black olives
2 salt anchovies, rinsed, filleted, and cut up, or 4 fillets

In a large heavy oval pot, warm the olive oil over medium-low heat. Season the leg of lamb with salt and pepper and color it lightly on all sides, turning it regularly over a period of about 30 minutes. Add the chopped onion and stir it regularly with a wooden spoon, scraping the bottom of the pot and turning the leg a couple of times, until the onion begins to turn golden. Add the garlic, tomatoes, thyme, and 2 or 3 tablespoons white wine, cover the pot, and cook over low to very low heat for about 2 hours. Survey the cooking carefully, adding small quantities of white wine every 15 minutes or so and turning the leg from time to time. After an hour's cooking, add the black olives. A few minutes before removing the pot from the heat, add the anchovies so that they melt into the sauce. Discard the thyme.

Carve the leg in the kitchen, arrange the slices on a heated serving platter, scatter over some of the garnish, and pour the remaining garnish and sauce into a heated sauceboat.

LAMB STEW WITH TOMATOES AND POTATOES
Ragoût de Mouton, Tomates, et Pommes de Terre

Serves 4

LULU USES a variety of potato called *ratte,* small, twisted, and elongated, with firm, moist, nonstarchy flesh.

*1 lamb shoulder (3 ¹/₂ to 4 pounds), surface fat removed,
    boned, and cut into 1 ¹/₂- to 2-inch cubes*
Salt
Flour
3 tablespoons olive oil
1 large onion, coarsely chopped
4 garlic cloves, crushed and peeled
¹/₂ cup white wine
Bouquet garni (bay leaf, savory, thyme)
*1 pound tomatoes, peeled, seeded, coarsely chopped, salted,
    and drained in a colander for at least ¹/₂ hour*
¹/₂ cup tomato sauce (page 74)
1 pound small yellow-fleshed potatoes

Salt the pieces of meat and dredge them in flour. Choose a heavy sauté pan of a size to just hold them without crowding. Heat the olive oil, brown the pieces of meat on all sides over medium heat, add the onion and garlic, turn the heat down, and shuffle the contents of the pan around until the onions are softened and lightly colored. Turn the heat up again and deglaze with the white wine, stirring and scraping the bottom and sides of the pan with a wooden spatula or spoon, until all frying adherences are loosened and dissolved. Add the bouquet garni, the tomatoes, and the tomato sauce, bring to a boil, adjust the heat to maintain a gentle simmer, covered, for 1 ¹/₂ hours in all.

(continued)

After 45 minutes, put the potatoes to cook in boiling salted water. Cook until just done, about 20 minutes; drain and peel them while hot, holding them in a kitchen towel to protect your hands. Add them to the stew and continue to cook gently until the time is up and the lamb is tender.

BRAISED SHOULDER OF LAMB WITH EGGPLANT AND TOMATO CONFIT
Epaule d'Agneau, Confit d'Aubergines et Tomates

Serves 4

*1 lamb shoulder (3 ½ to 4 pounds), boned, trimmed of
    superficial fat*
3 garlic cloves, peeled and cut lengthwise into slivers
Pepper
*2 bay leaves, sprigs of thyme and savory, or a pinch of dried,
    crumbled, mixed thyme and savory*
1 tablespoon olive oil
⅔ cup white wine
Salt
Bouquet garni (bay, thyme, savory)
1 recipe Eggplant and Tomato Confit (page 273)

Lay out the boned shoulder, skin side down. With a small, sharply pointed knife, pierce the flesh at regular intervals and tuck a sliver of garlic into each vent. Grind over pepper. Press herbs into both sides (or sprinkle with dried herbs), place the shoulder in a round deep dish, dribble over half the olive oil, pour over the white wine, turn the shoulder over and around several times, and marinate, covered, for 3 or 4 hours, turning it a couple of times.

Preheat the oven to 450°F.

Remove the shoulder from the marinade, discard bay leaves and herb sprigs, drain the shoulder, dry it with paper towels, lay it out, skin side down, and sprinkle the surface lightly with salt. The shape is that of an irregular square. Pull up two opposite corners to meet. With a trussing needle and kitchen string, tack them together, tie, and clip the string. Repeat with the two other corners. Turn the shoulder over, rounded, skin surface up, loop string around horizontally, tie and clip, then loop string around vertically several times, twisting and tying, to form a melon shape. Rub the surface with olive oil, sprinkle with salt, place in a small heavy pan, and roast for 30 minutes.

Transfer the shoulder to a heavy saucepan of a size to just hold it at ease, tuck in the bouquet garni, pour off the fat from the roasting pan, and deglaze it with the marinade. Pour the boiling marinade over the shoulder, cover, and cook over very low heat for 1 hour, basting from time to time.

Remove the shoulder to a plate. Pour the braising juices into a small saucepan. Return the shoulder to its saucepan, surround it with the simmering eggplant and tomato mixture, and return the saucepan, covered, to very low heat. Bring the braising juices to a boil, pull the pan half off the heat, keeping a light boil to one side, skim until no more fat rises to the surface, place the saucepan fully over heat, and reduce the juices to a light syrupy consistence. Pour them over the shoulder, cover, and leave to braise gently for 20 to 30 minutes.

To serve, remove the shoulder to a carving board, clip and remove the strings, and slice it. Spread the contents of the saucepan onto a heated serving platter and place the slices of shoulder, overlapping, on top.

RAGOUT OF LAMB SHOULDER AND FLAGEOLETS
Epaule de Mouton en Ragoût aux Flageolets

Serves 4

IF FRESH FLAGEOLET shell beans are not available, substitute white "coco" shell beans. If neither are available, substitute 12 ounces dried flageolets, first soaked overnight, drained, covered with cold water, brought to a full boil, drained, covered with boiling water, and simmered until half-cooked—about 40 minutes. Drain them, reserving their cooking water, and add them to the stew after it has been cooking for 30 minutes. Add some of their water, if necessary, to completely immerse them.

1 shoulder of lamb (3 ½ to 4 pounds), unboned, cut across the bone (by butcher) into approximately 1-inch slices
Salt and pepper
Flour
4 tablespoons olive oil
1 large onion, coarsely chopped
3 garlic cloves, crushed and peeled
2 medium tomatoes (about 12 ounces), peeled, seeded, and coarsely chopped
Branch of fresh savory, or a large pinch of dried, crumbled savory
1 cup white wine, brought to a boil
Boiling water
2 pounds fresh flageolet shell beans, shelled

Season the pieces of lamb with salt and pepper and dredge them in flour. In a large heavy sauté pan, heat 3 tablespoons olive oil and sauté the pieces of meat over medium heat until browned on all sides. Adjust the heat to low. Remove the meat to a plate. If the pan is dry, add a little more oil and add the onion to the pan. Stir often with a wooden spoon until the onion softens and begins to color, add the garlic, turn up the heat, add the tomatoes, and sprinkle with coarse salt. Stir and shake the pan until the tomatoes begin to disintegrate. Put the meat back into the pan, pour in any juices that have accumulated, tuck in the herbs, add the boiling wine, and pour over enough boiling water to completely immerse the pieces of meat. Cook, covered, at a simmer, separating the pan from the heat source with a heat disperser, if necessary, to keep the heat sufficiently low. Thirty minutes later, turn the pieces of meat over and add the flageolets, taking care that they are completely immersed— if necessary, add a little more boiling water. Return to a boil, adjust to a simmer, and cook, covered, for another 45 to 50 minutes, or until meat and beans are tender. Remove and discard the herbs. Taste for salt and serve directly from the sauté pan.

Leg of Lamb Stuffed with Tapenade
Gigot Farci à la Tapenade

Serves 8

LULU ASKS her butcher to bone the leg for her. The heel is sawn off from the tip of the shank, but the shank bone is left in place. The section of pelvic bone is removed. On the inside surface of the leg (the side that will be facing down when positioned in the roasting pan), the flesh is slit to the bone from the hip joint to the knee joint and the thigh bone is removed. After being stuffed, the leg is sewn up the length of the cut and across the top end. A loop stitch (the trussing needle passed through the loose loop of each stitch before the string is pulled tight) at approximately 1½-inch intervals is the most effective method. Care should be taken when stitching to pierce the skinlike membrane, or bark, of the leg a good half inch in from either side of the cut edge.

> *1 leg of lamb (about 6 pounds), boned by butcher (see above)*
> *1 recipe Tapenade (page 79)*
> *2 teaspoons olive oil*
> *Salt and pepper*

Preheat the oven to 450°F.

Open out the boned leg of lamb on a work surface, spread the tapenade the length of the area from which the thigh bone has been removed, close the leg up into its original form, and sew it up (see above).

Rub the surface with olive oil, season with salt and pepper, place the roast on a rack in a shallow roasting pan, and roast for about 1 hour, reducing the heat to 350°F after 10 minutes and, 20 minutes later, to 275°F. Remove the roast to a heated platter and hold it for 20 minutes in the turned-off oven or other warm place. Clip and remove the strings. Carve in the kitchen on a board, cutting across into slices, each with a black center. Place the uncarved section of leg at one end of the platter and arrange the slices, overlapping. Pour over any carving juices and serve.

STUFFED BREAST OF LAMB
Poitrine d'Agneau Farcie

Serves 6

LULU ALWAYS serves stuffed breast of lamb cold "because, then, the meat and the stuffing both become very firm and can be cut into neat clean slices, which are very beautiful, accompanied by a green salad."

STUFFING
1 tablespoon olive oil
2 lamb kidneys (about 2 ounces each), cut into ⅓-inch dice
1 medium onion, finely chopped
2 garlic cloves, crushed, peeled, and finely chopped
1 cup long-grain rice
Pinch of coarse sea salt
⅛ teaspoon powdered saffron
Pinch of cayenne
1½ cups boiling water

*1 breast of lamb (about 3 pounds), boned and opened up by
   the butcher to create a pocket ready for stuffing*
Salt and pepper
1 teaspoon olive oil
1 cup white wine

In a *poêlon* or heavy saucepan, heat the olive oil over medium heat, add the diced kidneys, and stir with a wooden spoon until gray or lightly colored. Add the chopped onion and garlic, turn the heat low, and stir occasionally until the onion is translucent but uncolored. Add the rice, salt, saffron, and cayenne, stir regularly until the rice is evenly coated with oil, colored with saffron, and has turned opaque. Pour over the boiling water, stir once, cover tightly, and cook for 15 to 18 minutes, or until the rice is dry.

Preheat the oven to 450°F.

Season the inside of the breast pocket with salt and pepper. Stuff the lamb breast, without packing. With a trussing needle threaded with kitchen string, sew up the opening, using a loop stitch for the neatest result. Salt and pepper the exterior and rub with olive oil, place the roast in a shallow heavy pan of a size to just hold it, and put it into the oven. Ten minutes later, reduce the oven temperature to 350°F. Begin to baste after 20 or 30 minutes. After 45 minutes, remove all fat from the roasting pan, bring $\frac{1}{2}$ cup white wine to a boil, add it to the pan, and continue to baste at 10 to 15 minute intervals, adding more heated wine when necessary. Count 1 $\frac{1}{2}$ hours cooking time in all. Leave to cool in the roasting pan, cover loosely with foil, and refrigerate overnight.

Transfer the roast to a carving board (remove all of the congealed fat from the jellied juices and save them to enrich an eventual stew). Slice it into $\frac{1}{3}$-inch-thick slices, spread them out, slightly overlapping, on a platter, and serve, accompanied by one of Lulu's garlicky green salads (page 290).

LAMB CROQUETTES
Croquettes de Viande

Serves 4

"ABOUT A POUND of meat," said Lulu. I innocently asked, "What kind of meat?" She answered, "Well, lamb, of course!" Lulu deep-fries these croquettes in olive oil. For reasons of economy, I have suggested vegetable oil in the recipe. You may, however, obtain perfect results by heating $\frac{1}{3}$ inch olive oil in a large frying pan, adding the croquettes, and gently shaking the pan with a back-and-forth jerking movement to turn them around and over, flipping any that fail to turn with the tines of a fork, until they are golden and crisp on all sides.

> *1 tablespoon plus $\frac{1}{2}$ teaspoon olive oil*
> *1 onion, finely chopped*
> *2 garlic cloves, lightly crushed, peeled, and finely chopped*
> *1 pound ground shoulder of lamb*
> *2 to 3 cups cold, leftover mashed potatoes*
> *Salt and pepper*

Pinch of fresh savory leaves, finely chopped, or a pinch of
    dried, finely crumbled savory
3 eggs
¹/₂ cup flour
3 cups semidry bread crumbs, prepared in a food processor
2 quarts corn or peanut oil (for deep-frying)
2 cups tomato sauce (page 74)

Warm 1 tablespoon olive oil in a small pan, add the chopped onion, and cook over low heat, stirring occasionally with a wooden spoon, until soft but not colored. Add the garlic and cook a minute longer. Add the onion and garlic to a mixing bowl containing the lamb, potatoes, salt, pepper, savory, and 1 egg. Mix thoroughly with your hands. Form the mixture into walnut-size balls by rolling a spoonful between the palms of your hands, keeping your hands moistened to prevent sticking. Line the balls up, not touching, on a tray.

Put the flour into a soup plate. In another soup plate, beat 2 eggs and a dash of olive oil with a fork. Lay out a couple of thicknesses of wide wax paper and spread crumbs thickly at the center. One by one, roll the balls in flour, toss lightly in your hand to rid each of excess flour, roll in egg, rotating the plate until evenly coated, transfer to the crumbs, pile crumbs on top, and roll around until evenly coated in crumbs. As each is ready, transfer to a tray lightly coated with crumbs.

Spread out several thicknesses of newspaper and spread paper towels on top. Line a platter with a large napkin. In a deep-fryer or a metal pot of at least twice the capacity of the oil, heat the oil to between 350 and 375°F, or until a cube of bread dropped in browns in less than a minute. One at a time, drop the balls into the hot oil, releasing each just above the oil's surface to avoid splashing. Don't crowd them. Fry until golden and crisp; with a spider or a slotted spoon, remove them to the paper towels to drain. Add more balls to the hot oil and transfer the first batch from the paper towels to the platter, folding the napkin over to keep them warm. When all are fried, drained, and transferred to the platter, serve, accompanied by hot tomato sauce.

LEG OF VENISON IN RED WINE
Gigue de Chevreuil au Vin Rouge

Serves 8

AFTER FIRST SEIZING the leg in a hot oven, Lulu often finishes cooking it on top of the stove, over low heat, in a large covered casserole, moistening it regularly with small quantities of heated marinade. Because she always has an abundant stock of bottled Domaine Tempier *vin de presse* with which to cook, she is not constrained to economize. When I asked what she did with the red wine in which the pears were poached, she answered, "I don't do anything with it. Of course, if you want, you can add sugar to it and poach pears in it for a dessert."

1 5-pound leg of venison
3 garlic cloves, peeled and cut lengthwise into slivers

MARINADE
1 large strip of dried orange peel
Several branches of fresh thyme and savory
4 bay leaves
1 large onion, finely sliced
Pepper
1 tablespoon olive oil
3 cups (1 bottle) young, deeply colored, tannic red wine
1 tablespoon olive oil

1 sheet of pork fatback (barde), sliced ¹/₁₆ inch thick
Salt

Accompaniment
8 firm (slightly under-ripe) eating pears, peeled whole, stem
    attached
1 strip of dried orange peel
1 bay leaf
About 15 peppercorns, coarsely crushed
Red wine (same as above) to cover

With a small, sharply pointed knife, pierce the surface of the leg at regular intervals, on the bias, to a depth of about 1 inch and tuck a sliver of garlic into each slit. Place the leg in a large deep dish, arrange the orange peel, herbs, and sliced onion all around, grind over pepper, sprinkle with olive oil, pour over the wine, and marinate, covered with a sheet of foil, for about 5 hours, turning the leg over and around several times in its marinade.

Preheat the oven to 450°F.

Remove the leg from its marinade and drain well. Strain the marinade and discard the solid elements. Wipe the leg dry with a cloth or paper towels, rub it with olive oil, press the sheet of fatback over the rounded, fleshy surface of the leg, and tie three lengths of string around the leg to hold the fatback in place. Put the leg, fat side up, in a heavy shallow roasting pan of a size and shape to hold it without wasted space and roast for about 20 minutes. Season with salt.

Bring 1 cup of the marinade to a boil, add it to the roasting pan, turn the oven down to 350°F, and baste regularly for 1 hour, adding more heated marinade when necessary to keep the pan from drying up. After 50 minutes, clip the strings and remove them and the fatback.

Meanwhile, arrange the pears, standing up side by side, in a saucepan of a size to just hold them, slip the orange peel and the bay leaf into empty spaces, scatter over the pepper, pour over wine to cover, bring to a boil, and adjust the heat to a simmer, lid ajar, for 15 minutes. Hold the pears in their cooking liquid until the leg is ready.

Transfer the leg to a heated serving platter. Pour the basting juices into a very small saucepan or low-sided sauté pan. If there are caramelized adherences remaining in the roasting pan, deglaze it over heat with a bit of the marinade or, if none is left, with some of the pear poaching liquid, scraping the bottom and the sides of the pan with a wooden spoon. Add the deglazing liquid to the juices, bring to a boil, pull the pan halfway off the heat, and adjust to maintain a light boil to one side of the liquid's surface. As a fatty skin forms on the still side, pull it, with the edge of a tablespoon, to the side of the pan and remove it. When no more fat rises, pour the juices over the roast. Remove the pears from their poaching liquid and arrange them, stems up, in a glass bowl. Carve the leg at table, exactly as for a leg of lamb. The carving juices will intermingle with the basting juices. Spoon juices over the meat as it is served out and place a pear on each plate.

RABBIT STEW
Civet de Lapin

Serves 4

CIVET OF RABBIT or hare (*lièvre*) is one of the mythic dishes of Provence, adored by everyone, and everyone agrees that it must be accompanied by a fine, old Provençal red wine. A few years ago, Jean-Marie regularly chose Domaine Tempier vintages from the 1960s to accompany Lulu's civets. Now, a 1972 is a typical choice.

If you are unable—or disinclined—to finish the sauce with blood, don't worry. With or without the blood liaison, the ragout is delicious. American cottontails, which are usually shot by farmers and left to die in the fields, are wonderful prepared in this way.

Physically, the blood acts in a red wine sauce in the same way as egg yolks in a blanquette, reinforcing the sauce's body and lending it a sensuous, velvety texture; like a sauce finished with egg yolks, a civet must not approach a boil after the blood has been added lest the sauce break and become grainy.

The blood is always collected and stirred in a bowl containing a tablespoon of wine vinegar, which prevents it from coagulating. The blood of a wild rabbit or hare, which has been shot, collects in the chest cavity, behind the diaphragm, a membrane that separates the chest cavity from the abdomen. After the animal has been skinned and gutted, the liver removed, and the gall bladder carefully cut away and discarded, the diaphragm is slit open and the blood poured into the bowl containing vinegar. A hutch rabbit, sacrificed with a civet in mind, is killed by rupturing the spinal column at the base of the skull. The jugular vein is then slashed and the blood collected in the bowl containing vinegar before the rabbit is skinned.

To cut up a rabbit for a sauté, use a large heavy knife. The forelegs are attached to the body only by flesh and connective tissue. Slice beneath the shoulder blade with the knife blade held flat against the body to remove each foreleg. Cut across the body at the point where the hind legs join the saddle; separate the legs by cutting to the side of the tail end of the spinal column. Cut the saddle across into 2 or 3 sections, depending on the size of the animal, leaving the kidneys attached. Fold one belly flap over a kidney or the underside of the saddle section, wrap the other flap over the first and partly around the body, fixing it to the flesh with a toothpick to form a neat package. The rib cage can be left whole or split in two. Split the head in two, holding the knife in place and giving it a firm smack with a wooden mallet. The head will add flavor to the sauce and those who are not offended at the sight of a head will find the cheeks, tongue, and brain to be delectable morsels.

Lulu mixes the puréed rabbit's liver into the blood to thicken her civets and she likes to serve a creamy purée of sweet potatoes (page 296) as an accompaniment; at other times, the civet is simply accompanied by boiled potatoes or macaroni. A civet, above all, for Lulu, must be prepared with "lots of thyme."

If you do not intend to finish your ragout with blood, sprinkle an extra tablespoon of flour over the pieces of rabbit as they are browning, before being moistened with marinade.

1 3-pound rabbit (or 2 cottontails), cut up as for a sauté, blood stirred with 1 tablespoon red wine vinegar, and liver reserved (see above)

MARINADE
1 large onion, finely sliced
6 garlic cloves, crushed
3 thyme branches
2 bay leaves
2 cloves
Pepper
1 tablespoon olive oil
3 cups (1 bottle) young, deeply colored, tannic red wine

Salt
Flour
4 tablespoons olive oil
1 head garlic, cloves separated, superficial chaff removed, but uncrushed and unpeeled
Bouquet garni ("lots of thyme," bay leaf, strip of dried orange peel)
Pepper

In a large mixing bowl, mingle the rabbit pieces with all the dry ingredients of the marinade, sprinkle over the olive oil, and pour over red wine to cover. Marinate for several hours or overnight, covered, turning the rabbit pieces around in the marinade two or three times.

Empty the bowl into a colander, collecting the marinade in another bowl. Drain well, remove the rabbit pieces (discard the residue in the colander), and dry them in paper towels. Salt them and dredge them in flour. In a large heavy sauté pan, heat the olive oil, arrange the rabbit pieces in the pan, side by side, tuck in the garlic cloves where space permits, and cook over medium heat, turning rabbit and garlic over and around until the rabbit is golden on all sides. In a saucepan, bring the marinade to a boil, pour it over, scrape the bottom and sides of the pan with a wooden spoon to dissolve any caramelized adherences, tuck in the bouquet garni, and adjust the heat to maintain a bare simmer, lid slightly ajar. Turn the rabbit pieces over in the sauce after 30 minutes and simmer for 15 minutes longer (for a young rabbit), or until a thigh, when pricked with a knife tip or trussing needle, is tender. Remove the pan from the heat.

Purée the rabbit's liver, either in a blender or by crushing it in a sieve and working it through with a wooden pestle. Stir the purée into the blood, stir in a ladle of the rabbit's sauce, grind over pepper, and pour the mixture into the sauté pan, stirring and moving around the contents. Return the pan to low heat and rotate it, slowly swirling to keep everything moving, until the sauce has noticeably thickened and its color has turned from red to rich chocolate. Remove from the heat and serve, directly from the sauté pan, onto heated plates.

Rabbit Stuffed with Prunes
Lapereau Bourré de Pruneaux

Serves 6

LULU ROASTS the rabbit on a turnspit before the flames of a fireplace. To adapt the preparation to an oven, preheat the oven to 450°F, place the prepared rabbit in a shallow roasting pan, roast for 30 minutes, pour red wine into the pan, turn the oven down to 350°F, and baste regularly, adding more red wine if necessary to keep the pan from drying up. Remove the fatback after about 1 hour and continue to baste. The rabbit should be beautifully colored and tender after 1 hour and 15 minutes. If the rabbit is from your hutch, leave the head attached.

18 prunes
2 cups deep-colored, tannic young red wine
1 small can (about 4 ounces) foie gras
1 3½-pound rabbit, cleaned
Salt and pepper
Fresh thyme leaves, or crumbled dried thyme flowers and
　　leaves
1 tablespoon olive oil
1 thin sheet of pork fatback (barde), about 4 x 8 inches

BASTING LIQUID
Red wine drained from the prunes (plus more if necessary)
1 tablespoon olive oil
Salt and pepper
Crumbled thyme

Several branches of thyme, tied together into a basting brush

Soak the prunes overnight in the red wine, drain, reserving the wine, slit each halfway to remove the pit, tuck a half teaspoon of foie gras into each, and close it up.

Dice the rabbit's liver. Sprinkle the rabbit's abdominal cavity with salt, pepper, and a bit of thyme and stuff the chest and abdominal cavities with the stuffed prunes, mingled with the diced rabbit's liver. Skewer the abdominal flaps and lace up with kitchen string. Rub the rabbit all over with olive oil, sprinkle with salt, pepper, and thyme, place the fatback the length of the back and fix it in place with three lengths of kitchen string, tied around the rabbit's body. Run the spit through the body, tie the ends of the hind legs together, and tie them to the spit.

Prepare a fire with a solid heart of embers, fed regularly from each side with semi-small hardwood. Place the dripping pan beneath the turnspit, protected from the heat of the embers by a low wall of bricks. Combine the basting ingredients in a bowl.

For about 1 hour, turn the rabbit on the spit before lively flames, dipping the brush of thyme repeatedly into the basting liquid and brushing the animal as it turns. Continue basting but stop feeding the fire, so that, for the next 45 minutes, the flames diminish and die, the embers alone furnishing heat.

The service is not so easy—better carve in the kitchen: Remove the legs, cut the hind legs in two, empty out the stuffing, and cut across the body to produce regular sections. Arrange the pieces and the stuffed prunes on a heated platter, pour over the roasting juices, and serve.

RABBIT WITH MUSTARD
Lapin à la Moutarde

Serves 4

RESERVE THE rabbit's liver for another preparation.

1 rabbit, cut up as for a sauté
6 tablespoons Dijon mustard
Salt and pepper
3 tablespoons olive oil

Preheat the broiler.

Smear the rabbit pieces all over with mustard and place them on a rack resting on the edges of a shallow baking pan. Season the top surfaces of the rabbit with salt and pepper and dribble over a bit of olive oil. Broil for 20 to 25 minutes, turn the pieces over, season the other sides, add a bit more oil, and cook for about 20 minutes longer, or until a thigh is tender when pierced with a trussing needle.

RABBIT AND CARROTS IN ASPIC
Lapin aux Carottes en Gelée

Serves 10

LULU HAS SOMETIMES prepared her jellied rabbit in large molds but, because it is difficult to cut neat serving slices from a large mold of aspic, she prefers to prepare it in individual molds. She uses the traditional French breakfast coffee bowls, each containing, when filled to the brim, the equivalent of an American 8-ounce measuring cup. She fills each about two-thirds full with garnish and aspic. She serves the rabbit either as a first course or as a main

course, always accompanied by a green salad, usually lambs' lettuce or a mixture of lambs' lettuce and curly chicory, scattered with
chopped tarragon.

2 rabbits, cut up as for a sauté, livers reserved

MARINADE
1 onion, finely sliced
4 garlic cloves, crushed
2 bay leaves and branches of thyme
Pepper
1 tablespoon olive oil
3 cups (1 bottle) dry, slightly acidic white wine

*1 pig's foot, split in two, covered with cold water, brought to
    a boil, drained, and rinsed in cold water*

TO COOK THE FOOT
1 onion, stuck with 2 cloves
1 bay leaf and branch of thyme
4 garlic cloves, crushed
1 cup white wine
Water
Salt
1 pound young carrots, peeled, whole

Salt
6 tablespoons olive oil
2 onions, coarsely chopped
4 garlic cloves, crushed
Bouquet garni (thyme, bay leaves, stalk of celery)
2 egg whites plus the crushed, crumbled eggshells
Lettuce leaves (for presentation)

(continued)

In a large bowl, mingle together the rabbit pieces, sliced onion, garlic, and herbs, grind over pepper, sprinkle over olive oil, pour over the wine, and marinate, covered, for 4 or 5 hours or overnight, turning the rabbit around in the marinade two or three times.

In a saucepan, assemble the pig's foot, onion stuck with cloves, herbs, and garlic, pour over the white wine, and add enough water to cover the sections of trotter by about 2 inches. Salt lightly, bring to a boil, and adjust to a simmer, lid held slightly ajar. Cook for about 4½ hours, checking to make certain the pig's foot remains always well immersed in liquid; add small amounts of boiling water, if necessary. Remove and discard the onion stuck with cloves, the herbs, and the garlic. Add the carrots, return to a boil, and continue to simmer for 30 minutes, or until the carrots are tender but still slightly firm. Remove from the heat, strain off and reserve the cooking liquid, remove the carrots to a plate, and hold in reserve. Bone the trotter, discard the bones, cut the flesh into small pieces, and reserve it.

Remove the rabbit pieces from their marinade, drain well in a colander placed over a bowl, and dry them in towels. Strain the marinade into the bowl over which the rabbit has drained and discard the debris. Salt the rabbit pieces. Heat 3 tablespoons olive oil in each of two large heavy pans, add the rabbit pieces, brown lightly on one side, turn them over, and add the chopped onions and crushed garlic cloves. Move the contents of the pans around to prevent the onions from overbrowning. When the rabbit pieces are nicely colored on all sides, transfer everything to a large deep casserole, bury the bouquet garni at the center, and arrange the rabbit pieces so that no space is wasted. If there is any loose fat in the sauté pans, drain it off. Deglaze each pan with half the reserved marinade and pour the boiling marinade over the rabbit. Bring the trotter's cooking liquid to a boil and pour it over. Bring the contents of the casserole to the boiling point and adjust the heat to maintain a gentle simmer, lid slightly ajar, for 45 minutes, or until the rabbit is tender. Ten minutes before removing from heat, add the livers.

Transfer the rabbit pieces to a platter and leave to cool. Strain the cooking liquid through a fine-meshed sieve. Discard the bouquet garni and the onion-garlic debris. Pour a tablespoon of the liquid into a saucer and refrigerate until set to test its gelatinous content. If it does not set firmly, reduce at a light boil, with the saucepan partially off the heat, periodically removing the fatty skin that forms on the still surface. Test again. Taste for salt, remembering that cold dishes need to be more highly seasoned than hot dishes.

Line a large sieve with several layers of dampened, wrung-out cheesecloth. Pour the warm cooking liquid into a saucepan large enough to be less than half-filled by all of the liquid. Beat the egg whites with a pinch of salt until they form soft peaks. Add them, along with the crushed egg shells, to the saucepan and whisk the liquid and the egg whites together over high heat, until the liquid boils and the egg whites rise in a foam to the pan's brim, threatening to overflow. Remove the pan from the heat for 10 minutes; return the pan to the heat but do not whisk this time; when the foam again rises to the brim, remove and cool again; repeat once more. Pour the contents of the saucepan into the cheesecloth-lined sieve, held over a bowl; the clarified liquid will now be a transparent amber.

With your fingers, remove the rabbits' flesh from the bones, scraping here and there with a small knife tip. Cut the larger pieces of flesh, from the thighs and backs, into ½-inch cubes. Cut the livers into strips. In a bowl, mix together the cubes, shreds, and smaller pieces of rabbit meat and liver with the pieces of boned pig's foot. Slice the carrots into ⅛-inch-thick rounds. Line the bowls (or other rounded or slant-sided molds) about halfway up the sides with the carrot slices and partially fill each bowl, loosely, with the equivalent of an American half-cup measure of the mixed meats, taking care not to displace the carrot rounds. Ladle over clarified cooking liquid to cover, cool to room temperature, and refrigerate, uncovered, overnight.

To serve, line a large platter with lettuce leaves and arrange the unmolded aspics on top; with a small knife tip, loosen the aspic from the sides of each bowl, very superficially, to separate the jelly at its contact with the bowl; unmold onto the palm of your hand. If it resists unmolding, a shake or, sometimes, a nudge with fingertips at one edge of the aspic's surface is all that is necessary to loosen it.

GARLIC RABBIT
Lapin à l'Ail

Serves 4

RESERVE THE rabbit's liver for another preparation.

Large pinch of coarse sea salt
Pepper
3 garlic cloves, peeled
Large pinch of crumbled thyme leaves
3 tablespoons olive oil
1 rabbit, cut up as for a sauté
1/4 cup white wine

Preheat the oven to 375°F.

In a mortar, pound the salt, pepper, and garlic to a paste with a wooden pestle. Stir in the thyme and olive oil. Put the rabbit pieces in a large bowl, spoon over the garlic mixture, and rub all the rabbit pieces in your hands to thoroughly coat them. Arrange them side by side in a shallow baking dish and put it in the oven. After 20 minutes, turn the pieces over, bring the white wine to a boil, add it to the baking dish, and baste two or three times during the next 20 minutes. Bake for about 40 minutes in all, or until the thigh is tender when pierced with a trussing needle.

GRILLED CHICKEN
Poulet à la Crapaudine

Serves 8

LULU'S MARRIAGES between meats and garnishes are often quite surprising; they are thoughtfully conceived and always successful. With the ginger and tarragon–flavored chicken, she likes to serve a squash purée (page 299).

Guinea fowl can be prepared in the same way but it lends itself better to herbs more rustic in flavor than tarragon—savory, thyme, or oregano, alone or in combination. Pigeon squabs prepared in this way require only 15 minutes grilling in all.

It is important when grilling birds to watch the skin sides carefully—the skin chars easily and in no time; most of the cooking must be done with the split surface facing the coals.

To prepare the chickens, self-trussed, for grilling, cut away and discard the oil gland above the tail of each chicken. Cut off the wing tips at the second joint. With poultry shears, beginning at the tail, cut through the center of the tail and the backbone to the middle of the back, then cut to one side of the backbone and the neck. Cut back down the other side of the neck to remove it and the upper part of the backbone. Open the carcass out, turn it skin side up, and press firmly on the breastbone to rupture it. It will break at the point where it joins the collarbones, folding over to one side. Push it toward the other side and press firmly again. Turn the chicken over and pull out the breastbone, first cutting it free from the collarbones with the tip of a small knife if the rupture is not complete. Turn the chicken skin side up again and, with the tip of a small knife, pierce the abdominal skin and thin layer of flesh between each leg and the lower part of the breast, pull the drumstick gently up toward the breast, folding it at the thigh joint, and force the tip of the drumstick through the knife slit in the abdominal skin. Pull the chicken into shape, flattening it, so that the knees, or drumstick-thigh joints, meet with the lower part of the breast, facing each other.

> *2 broiling chickens, 2½ to 3 pounds each, opened out and*
> *   self-trussed (see above)*
> *Pepper*
> *1 tablespoon grated fresh ginger*
> *2 tablespoons olive oil*
> *1 tablespoon red wine vinegar*
> *1 bouquet of fresh tarragon*
> *Salt*

Grind pepper over all the chickens' surfaces, smear with grated ginger, rub with olive oil, sprinkle over vinegar, press sprigs of tarragon onto all the surfaces, lay the chickens out on a large platter, cover with plastic wrap, and marinate for 1 hour at room temperature.

Prepare a bed of wood coals of good depth until beginning to die down, with a film of ash masking the incandescence. Preheat the grill and raise it to about 8 inches above the coals. Discard the tarragon, salt the chickens on both sides, and grill them for 30 to 35 minutes in all, beginning skin side down and checking often to make certain the skin doesn't begin to char. After 7 or 8 minutes, when the skin is nicely colored with golden-brown grill marks, turn

the chickens over and grill the split-open surfaces for about 20 minutes, turning the chickens around on the grill from time to time. As
the intensity of the coals' heat progressively diminishes, turn the
chickens back over, skin side down, giving them a quarter of a turn
so that the bars of the grill cross the original grill marks. Remove
about 10 minutes later, checking the while to make certain the skin
does not color too much. If necessary, finish grilling on the split
side.

Present the chickens on a large platter with a carving board to
the side. To carve, remove one to the carving board, split it down
the middle, at the crest of the missing breastbone, slit the skin
around the contour of each drumstick and thigh, and cut through
the fragment of backbone to which the thigh is joined; the chicken
falls apart into quarters. To serve both white and dark meat to each
person, cut through the drumstick-thigh joint and cut across the
breast, on a bias, from beneath the wing to the upper extremity of
the breast.

ROAST CHICKEN WITH GINGER,
MACARONI WITH ROASTING JUICES
Poulet Rôti au Gingembre, Coudes au Jus

Serves 4

IF POSSIBLE, use a 6-month-old farm chicken that has had space in which to run and a natural diet of grains, green stuff, worms, and kitchen leftovers.

1 3$^{1}/_{2}$-pound roasting chicken
Salt and pepper
1 tablespoon grated fresh ginger
3 tablespoons olive oil
Juice of 1 lemon
$^{1}/_{2}$ cup white wine, at a simmer
12 ounces elbow macaroni
2 garlic cloves, crushed and chopped
1 pound tomatoes, peeled, seeded, coarsely chopped, salted,
  and spread in a colander for 1 hour
Handful of freshly torn-up basil leaves

Preheat the oven to 450°F.

Season the chicken's body cavity with salt and pepper, smear the inside with grated ginger, and truss (or not). Smear the outside with olive oil, season with salt and pepper, and place the chicken on its side in an oval oven dish. Put it in the oven, turn to the other side when the first is lightly colored, then turn onto its back. After 20 minutes, turn the oven down to 350°F, remove excess fat from the dish, and begin to baste with lemon juice; when there is no more, pour some boiling white wine into the dish and continue basting. Roast for about 45 minutes, or until the juice runs clear when the thigh is pricked above the drumstick joint with the tip of a trussing needle.

Boil the macaroni in abundant salted water according to the package instructions (about 12 minutes). Meanwhile, add the garlic to 2 tablespoons olive oil in a large heavy frying pan over high heat. As soon as the garlic begins to sizzle, add the tomatoes. Shake the pan constantly, tossing the tomatoes repeatedly for a minute or so, until they are nearly dry and give off a caramelized scent. Add the basil, toss again, and remove from the heat. Drain the macaroni, empty it into a wide, deep, heated serving dish, add the tomatoes and the chicken's roasting juices, and toss well with a fork and a spoon.

Carve the chicken at table and serve, accompanied by the macaroni.

SAUTÉED CHICKEN WITH APPLES AND CALVADOS
Poulet aux Pommes de Reinette Flambé au Calvados

Serves 4

LULU ASSOCIATES this dish with the years during which the family was growing up and with precious moments of silent communions with the sea in her little sailboat. She says, "Of course it's not Provençal cuisine, but the children loved it; all I had to do was to prepare and assemble the apples and chicken, set the oven to go off half an hour later, and I was free to go sailing. When I returned, I was relaxed, the chicken was cooked, and it was still hot." She insists on the importance of russet apples (*reinettes*); the apples should be, in any case, neither mealy nor excessively acid and should hold their shape during cooking.

(continued)

1 frying chicken, about 3 pounds, cut up
Salt and pepper
4 tablespoons butter
2 pounds russet apples, quartered, cored, peeled, each
     quarter sliced into 2 or 3 wedges
Cinnamon
4 tablespoons Calvados

Preheat the oven to 375°F.

Season the chicken pieces on all sides with salt and pepper. In a heavy sauté pan of a size to just contain the chicken pieces, placed side by side, heat half the butter until it begins to bubble. Arrange the chicken in the pan and sauté over moderate heat, turning the pieces regularly, until lightly colored on all sides—about 15 minutes.

Meanwhile, melt the remaining butter in a large frying pan, add the apples, and toss regularly over medium heat until they are softened and lightly caramelized on all sides. Sprinkle discreetly with cinnamon and toss again.

Layer half the apples in a deep oven dish, place the chicken pieces on top, and spread the remaining apples over the chicken. Discard the fat from the sauté pan, pour in the Calvados, place over high heat, and deglaze the pan, scraping the bottom repeatedly with a wooden spatula or spoon, until all caramelized adherences are dissolved. If the Calvados has not begun to flame, set it alight and pour it regularly over the surface of the apples. Place the oven dish over medium heat for a few minutes, or until the characteristic scent of caramel fills the air, cover the dish, and bake for 30 minutes. Turn off the oven and serve 15 minutes later—or more.

ROAST GUINEA FOWL
Pintade Rôtie

Serves 6

LULU FIGURES that guinea fowl is about the only flesh she knows that is flattered by the aggressive presence of smoked bacon. "The sausage is not meant to be a stuffing," she says, "I just put it there to add flavor." She specified that the bird should be spit-roasted before an open fire. If I have transformed it into an oven roast, it is simply because I know that most readers would do so in any case. To spit-roast it in front of a fireplace, add 10 to 15 minutes to the roasting time. There should be a solid heart of incandescent coals and a sheet of flames, which can be permitted to die down after 20 minutes. With the guinea fowl, Lulu serves a sweet potato purée (page 296).

> *3 tablespoons olive oil*
> *1 large onion, finely chopped*
> *4 ounces sausage meat*
> *2 young guinea fowl, $2^{1}/_{2}$ to 3 pounds each*
> *Salt and pepper*
> *Sprigs of savory*
> *12 thin strips smoked bacon*

Preheat the oven to 450°F.

Warm 1 tablespoon olive oil in a small pan, add the onion, and cook over low heat, stirring occasionally with a wooden spoon, until lightly colored, but not browned. Mix it with the sausage meat.

Give the breastbones of the guinea fowl a blow with the heel of your hand or with a wooden mallet, to rupture them and make more compact shapes of the birds. Season the insides of the birds with salt and pepper, tuck half the onion-sausage mixture into each, along with a few sprigs of savory, and truss them. Rub each with olive oil, season with salt and pepper, and press strips of bacon the length of the breast, to cover. Tie two lengths of kitchen string around the birds to hold the bacon in place. Place them on their sides in a shallow roasting pan, put them in the oven, and 10 minutes later, turn them to the other side. Ten minutes later, turn them breast up, lower the oven setting to 325°F, and roast for a further 20 to 25 minutes, or until the juice from the thigh runs clear when pierced with a trussing needle. Clip and remove the strings. Remove the bacon strips and carve at table.

DUCK WITH OLIVES
Canard aux Olives

Serves 4

THE FLESH OF A DUCK is lean. Except for loose fat in the abdomen and at the throat, which can easily be pulled out, the fat is an integral part of the skin structure. To lose as much fat as possible during the initial roasting, the skin is pricked superficially with a sharp trussing needle, but not so deep as to pass all the way through the skin and touch the flesh.

To truss the duck, cut off the wing tips at the second joint. Use two lengths of string. Thread the trussing needle with one, push the needle through the wings, near the shoulder joint, and the back, pinning the flap of neck skin to the back at the same time; push the needle back through the drumsticks, near the thigh joints, tie the loose ends of string together tightly, and clip off the excess. Run the other length of string through the lower ends of the wing joints and the back and back through the lower ends of the drumsticks, pinning the flesh of the abdomen in between; tie and clip.

> *1 5-pound duck, cleaned, loose fat removed, skin pricked*
>   *superficially*
> *Salt and pepper*
> *¹/₂ pound Greek-style black olives, pitted*
> *1 teaspoon grated fresh ginger*
> *1 teaspoon olive oil*
> *2 cups young, deeply colored, tannic red wine*

Preheat the oven to 450°F.

Season the inside of the duck with salt and pepper. Mix together the pitted olives and the grated ginger. Stuff the duck with the mixture and truss it (see above). Rub the surface with a little olive oil and a sprinkling of salt, place the duck in a heavy, shallow, oval oven dish of a size to just hold it, wrap the extremities of the drumsticks with fragments of aluminum foil to keep them from charring, and roast for 30 minutes. As soon as fat begins to collect in the bottom of the dish, baste the duck with the hot fat at 8 to 10 minute intervals to help draw out more fat.

Discard all the fat from the roasting dish, bring ¹/₂ cup red wine to a boil in a small saucepan, pour it over the duck, turn the oven setting down to 375°F, and cook for about 1 hour, basting regularly and adding more heated wine to maintain about the same level of liquid in the dish. After 30 minutes, remove the foil from the drumstick tips. When done, transfer the duck to a heated platter, clip the trussing strings, and pull on the knots to remove them. Degrease the cooking juices and pour them into a heated sauceboat. Carve at table.

STUFFED DUCKLING WITH TURNIPS
Canette Farcie aux Navets

Serves 4

STUFFING

2 tablespoons olive oil

The duck's gizzard (fleshy lobes cut free from gristly skin), liver, and heart, cut into small pieces

1 medium onion, finely chopped

3 garlic cloves, finely chopped

½ cup diced raw ham (prosciutto)

4 ounces semidry bread, crusts removed, soaked in milk, and squeezed almost dry

½ pound green salad leaves (escarole, for instance), parboiled for a few seconds, refreshed under cold running water, squeezed thoroughly, and chopped (about 1 cup)

1 teaspoon grated fresh ginger

1 egg

Salt and pepper

1 4-pound duckling, cleaned, loose fat removed, and pricked superficially with a trussing needle

1 teaspoon olive oil

Salt

2 pounds crisp young turnips, peeled and thinly sliced

Boiling broth

Preheat the oven to 450°F.

In a small frying pan, heat enough olive oil to coat the bottom. Add the giblets and stir around with a wooden spoon for a few seconds, or until just seized. Empty into a mixing bowl.

In a larger pan, warm 1 tablespoon olive oil over low heat, add the onion and garlic, and cook gently, stirring occasionally, until the onion is softened but not colored. Add the onion and garlic, along with all the other stuffing ingredients, to the mixing bowl and mix together thoroughly with your hands. Stuff the duck without packing. With a trussing needle and kitchen string, sew up the abdominal opening and truss the duck, as in the preceding recipe. Rub the surface with a little olive oil, then with salt, and put the duck in a heavy, shallow oval oven dish. Roast for about 35 minutes, basting regularly as soon as the duck begins to release its fat.

Transfer the duck to a deep, heavy oval casserole. Discard the fat. Pack the turnips all around the duck, pour over enough boiling broth to barely immerse the turnips, bring to a boil on top of the stove, and simmer, covered, over very low heat, for 1 hour. Transfer the duck to a heated platter, clip, and remove the strings. Strain the turnips, collecting the cooking juices. Hold the turnips in a heated serving dish. Degrease and reduce the juices and pour over the turnips. Carve at table.

PIGEON SQUABS WITH PEAS
Innocents aux Petits Pois

Serves 4

"FRANÇOIS KILLS THEM for me," says Lulu. "He takes them from the nest as they are learning to fly and smothers them—they are not bled. They are called *innocents*." Commercial squabs in America will be bled and probably less innocent than François's—never mind. A squab is easily trussed by running a trussing needle, threaded with a length of kitchen string, through the wings and the back, returning it through the drumsticks and the abdomen, tying the two ends of string and clipping the surplus.

(continued)

1 small head tender lettuce
4 small sweet onions
4 pounds (in pods) little peas, freshly picked and shelled
Salt
1 teaspoon sugar
4 tablespoons olive oil
4 pigeon squabs, trussed
Pepper
4 thin sheets of pork fatback (bardes), about 3 x 4 inches
    each
1 ⅓-inch-thick slice lean, streaky salt bacon, diced

Remove the outer leaves from the lettuce; wash both the heart and the loose leaves, leaving the water clinging. Place the heart of lettuce and the onions in a heavy saucepan, add the peas, sprinkle with salt, the teaspoon of sugar, and 2 tablespoons of olive oil. Press the loose leaves of lettuce on top, cover tightly, and sweat over very low heat for about 30 minutes.

Meanwhile, rub the pigeon squabs with olive oil, season with salt and pepper, press a sheet of fatback over the breast of each, and tie two lengths of string around each bird to hold the *bardes* in place. In a heavy saucepan of a size to easily hold the squabs, side by side, heat enough olive oil to just coat the bottom, add the squabs and the diced salt bacon, cover, and cook over medium-low heat for about 15 minutes, turning the squabs regularly to color them on all sides. They should remain slightly pink to be moist and succulent.

Remove the squabs from their pan, remove and discard the outer strings and the *bardes*, clip the trussing strings and pull them out by the knots, and return the birds to their pan. Remove and discard the leaves and the heart of lettuce from the peas and empty the peas, the onions, and their juices into the pigeons' pot. Cover and hold over medium heat for 5 minutes for flavors to intermingle. Remove the pigeon squabs to a plate, empty the contents of the pot into a heated, wide, deep serving dish, place the squabs on top, and serve.

GRILLED FLATTENED QUAILS
Cailles à la Crapaudine

Serves 8

8 quails
Pepper
1 teaspoon fresh savory leaves, finely chopped, or a pinch of
*   crumbled dried savory*
3 tablespoons olive oil

SAUCE
Pinch of coarse salt
1 garlic clove, crushed and peeled
4 salt anchovies, rinsed and filleted, or 8 fillets
1/2 pound black olives, pitted
2 tablespoons olive oil

Salt

With poultry shears, split the quails the length of the back, from tail to neck. Open them out, skin side up, on a work surface and press firmly on each with the heel of your hand to rupture the bones of the breast and the rib cage. Sprinkle with pepper and savory, rub with olive oil, arrange them, side by side, on a platter, cover with plastic wrap, and leave for 4 or 5 hours.

In a mortar, pound the salt, garlic, and anchovies to a paste. In a food processor, add the paste to the olives and reduce to a coarse purée, adding enough olive oil to render the purée supple, but not liquid.

Salt the quails. On a preheated grill, about 6 inches distant from incandescent embers, grill the quails for about 10 minutes in all, first on the skin sides for 3 or 4 minutes (check to be certain that the grill marks are golden brown and not black), then on the opened-out insides. Serve, accompanied by the olive sauce.

Mortars, earthenware poêlons, *gratin dishes, pot-au-feu, and daubière.*

Vegetables, Salads, Grains, Pasta

Country of sun, of light, and of little water, our vegetables arrive freshly picked with concentrated flavor.

Pays de soleil, de lumière, et de manque d'eau, nos légumes arrivent en primeur et ont une saveur très concentrée.

Lulu

PROVENÇAL SUMMERS are famously dry. From mid-June until mid-August, rainfall is a rarity and, in many years, nonexistent. In difficult years, water is rationed. The quality of summer vegetables profits from this parsimony.

Provençal traditions and personal fantasy are allied in Lulu's vegetable preparations to create a rich tapestry of dishes, many of which stand admirably alone as a first course or, in a simple menu, as a main course. In no other culinary area is the Provençal wit and genius so evident as in its treatment of vegetables.

Opposite: Artichokes.

ARTICHOKES
Artichauts

FOR ALL ARTICHOKE preparations, Lulu specifies "tender, young, violet artichokes without chokes." These instructions are easy to respect in Provence, where artichokes are picked to be eaten raw, the leaves and hearts dipped in a vinaigrette prepared at table. To be chokeless, they must be picked before attaining their mature size. In any case, buy them as young and fresh-looking as possible—chokes will probably have begun to develop. When the artichoke is trimmed and cooked whole, it is easy enough for each guest to remove the choke; if it is to be cut into sections or sliced, the choke can first be cut away from the split halves or quarters.

Size is not necessarily an indication of youth or tenderness. Depending on the variety, a fully formed artichoke can be the size and shape of a small hen's egg or the size and shape of a large grapefruit. Good artichokes develop at the summit of a tall stalk. If most or part of the stalk is left when the artichoke is picked, small, inferior artichokes will sprout from the leaf joints. The best superficial indications of tenderness are: clean colored (clear green or green and violet, depending on the variety), crisp-looking outside leaves; a cleanly defined, curving contour (egg-shaped or spherical, depending on the variety), without undulations; a stalk that is proportionally thick in relation to the artichoke (a maturing artichoke continues to grow on a stalk of unchanging size—the diameter, at its widest part, of a chokeless artichoke is only twice that of its stalk).

Artichokes blacken in contact with carbon knives and, when cut into, in contact with air. Blackened artichoke is not only unsightly, but the purity of its flavor is marred by an acrid edge. Use only stainless steel knives (one large, one small) to pare, or "turn," the artichokes. Most cooks rub or toss cut artichokes with lemon juice

to keep them white. Lulu doesn't like the imposition of lemon flavor and prefers to coat the sectioned or sliced artichokes with olive
oil to keep them from contact with air.

To turn an artichoke, break off the stem end (with very tender artichokes, Lulu peels the stems, leaving a 2- or 3-inch length of the
heart of the stem attached to the bottom), break off the outer
leaves, bending each backward, then down, until the tender flesh at
the base snaps free, remaining attached to the bottom. Cut off the
tough extremities of the leaves, slicing across the artichoke—about
one quarter for very young artichokes to as much as half or two
thirds for more advanced specimens. Hold the artichoke upside-
down and trim, spiraling, from the bottom to the base of the leaves,
removing dark green surfaces. Trim the extremities of the cut outer
leaves, if necessary. If using artichokes whole, add each, as it is
turned, to a bowl containing a tablespoon of olive oil and turn it
around to coat all surfaces. To remove the chokes, split each artichoke into halves or quarters, cut out the chokes with the tip of a
small knife, and toss the artichoke sections in the olive oil.

SAUTÉED ARTICHOKES AND POTATOES
Artichauts Sautés aux Rattes

Serves 6

EARTHENWARE is the ideal material in which to cook artichokes.
The *poêlon* or casserole should be large enough to pretty much
hold the artichokes and potatoes in a single layer. If you have none
large enough, the potatoes can be cooked in another casserole or
pan (which need not be earthenware) and mingled with the artichokes just before adding the persillade. Lulu uses the small,
twisted, elongated potatoes called *rattes*, whose flesh is exception-

ally firm and resistant to falling apart. Instead of a yellow-fleshed potato, walnut-size new potatoes with nearly undeveloped skins can be rubbed in water, then in a towel, and used, unpeeled.

In May, Lulu eliminates the persillade (and sometimes the potatoes) and sweats little freshly picked and shelled peas separately, which she swirls into the artichokes just before serving (4 pounds unshelled peas, a handful of small white spring onions, 4 tablespoons cold, diced butter, salt, large pinch of sugar, a lettuce heart, a tablespoon of water, assembled in a *poêlon* or heavy saucepan, tightly covered, sweated over low heat for about 30 minutes—the lettuce is removed before the peas are added to the artichokes).

> *2 tablespoons butter*
> *1 pound small, firm yellow-fleshed potatoes, peeled, and rubbed dry in a towel*
> *1 pound tender artichokes, turned, left whole if very small, quartered, chokes removed if larger, and tossed in a little olive oil to coat them*
> *Salt and pepper*
> *Persillade (1 chopped garlic clove, 2 tablespoons chopped flat-leaf parsley, mixed and chopped again, together)*

Melt the butter in a large *poêlon* or other low, wide earthenware casserole. Add the potatoes and the artichokes, season with salt, cover tightly, and cook gently over low heat. From time to time, lift the lid without tilting, move it away, and wipe the underside free of condensation. Shake the *poêlon* to and fro regularly. Count from 30 to 40 minutes, or until both the potatoes and the artichokes offer little resistance to a knife tip or skewer. Grind over pepper, add the persillade, shake and toss for less than a minute, and serve.

BRAISED ARTICHOKES
Artichauts à la Barigoule

Serves 4

4 tablespoons olive oil
1 pound sweet onions, finely sliced
4 garlic cloves, crushed and peeled
12 to 16 tender young artichokes the size of hens' eggs,
*   pared and coated with olive oil*
Salt
1 tablespoon flat-leaf parsley, finely chopped
2 to 3 sprigs of fresh winter savory, or a large pinch of
*   crumbled dried savory*
½ cup white wine
½ cup boiling water

In a large earthenware *poêlon*, warm 2 tablespoons olive oil, add the onions, cover, and cook over very low heat, stirring occasionally with a wooden spoon, until melting but uncolored—about 30 minutes. Stir in the crushed garlic and push the artichokes, bottoms down, into the bed of onions. Sprinkle with salt and parsley, tuck the sprigs of savory into the onions, and dribble olive oil over the artichokes to anoint the inner leaves and hearts. Cover and sweat for about 10 minutes.

Heat the white wine, pour it over, and add enough boiling water to partially immerse the artichokes. Cook, covered, at a gentle simmer for about 40 minutes, turning the artichokes around and over a couple of times. Toward the end, turn the artichokes bottoms down again and spoon onions and liquid over them. When done, the artichoke bottoms should offer no resistance to a knife tip and the liquid should be reduced to form a thick, textured sauce with the onions. If there is too much liquid, remove the lid and raise the heat slightly for 5 to 10 minutes. Serve hot, tepid, or cold, directly from the *poêlon*. The flavors come through best if served tepid, the *poêlon* kept covered for half an hour after removal from the heat.

ASPARAGUS VINAIGRETTE
Asperges à la Vinaigrette

Serves 6

IN PROVENCE, asparagus is green or purple-tipped. To the north of the line beyond which olive trees are no longer cultivated, white asparagus is usually preferred. Green, purple, or white, it is cut well beneath the surface of the earth. The skin on the lower part of the stalk is tough and, often, the lower extremity of the stalk is tough. In America, asparagus is often cut above the earth's surface and all, or nearly all, of the skin is tender. In any case, each stalk should be tested with a knife, the bottoms cut off, if tough, and the stalks peeled from the bottom to the point at which the skin becomes tender, so that the entire remaining stalk is edible. The best cultivated asparagus is quite thick, the stalks about ¾ inch in diameter and 8 to 9 inches long, regularly shaped with crisp stalks and smooth, tight, unwrinkled skin. The purple-tipped Niçois asparagus is as thick but the stalks are shorter, about 6 inches long.

Small quantities of asparagus can be cooked loose and drained with a lid held ajar against the tipped saucepan, but large quantities need to be tied in bundles, both for correct cooking and for an acceptable presentation. The following quantity will have to be tied into two or three bundles, depending on the capacity of your hand. Separate the peeled asparagus stalks so that each bundle will be composed of stalks of approximately the same length. Arrange the stalks on the palm of your hand, tips above the thumb. The stalks will fall into place, like stacked logs, each turned until it finds its place. When your curved hand can contain no more, press a length of kitchen string between your thumb and the asparagus bunch, wrap string in a downward spiral four or five times around the bundle, and wrap it back up, clipping it with a generous amount left over. Pull together the two ends of string, tie tightly, and clip off the excess.

The asparagus is served hot or warm, with salt, pepper, vinegar, and olive oil at table. Asparagus plates, with a well to one side in which to prepare the vinaigrette, are useful; otherwise, each guest tips a plate, propped from behind with a knife or a fork, and prepares a vinaigrette with salt and pepper, first stirred with vinegar before adding olive oil. The asparagus is held at the stem end and twirled in the vinaigrette before each bite.

4 pounds asparagus, peeled and tied into bundles (see above)
Large handful of coarse sea salt
Boiling water
(Salt, pepper, vinegar, and olive oil at table)

Choose a pot large enough to hold the asparagus bundles at their ease, fit them in, add the salt, place the pot over high heat, pour over boiling water to cover generously, and when the water returns to a boil, adjust the heat to maintain a light boil, lid well ajar, turning the bundles over in the water after 5 minutes, until the stalks can be easily pierced with a knife tip—about 8 minutes.

While the asparagus is cooking, line a large platter with a napkin. Slip a prong of a kitchen fork beneath the strings of a bundle of asparagus, lift the bundle above the water for a few seconds to drain, and place it on the napkin to one end of the platter. Clip the strings, remove them, and spread out the asparagus to either side. Repeat with the other bundle (or bundles), placing the bundle halfway down the length of the first. Fold over the towel edges and serve immediately or while still warm.

CARDOONS IN ANCHOVY SAUCE
Cardons à l'Anchois

Serves 6

LULU PREPARES cardoons in anchovy sauce each year for the Christmas Eve supper.

2 tablespoons vinegar
Cold water
4 pounds cardoons

BLANC
1 teaspoon lemon juice
2 quarts water
2 tablespoons flour
1 tablespoon olive oil
Coarse salt

SAUCE
2 tablespoons butter
2 tablespoons flour
3 cups milk
2 garlic cloves, crushed and peeled
Pinch of coarse salt
4 salt anchovies, rinsed and filleted, or 8 fillets
Pepper

Add the vinegar to a mixing bowl half-filled with cold water. Pull off and discard the tough outer stalks of the cardoons. Break the inner stalks off at the base, one by one. With a stainless steel knife, cut the stalks into 3-inch lengths, pulling out the strings between thumb and knife blade, as for celery. Split each length in two and throw into the bowl of acidulated water. Trim the base, cut off and discard all leafy parts from the heart, split the heart and base into quarters, and add to the acidulated water.

To prepare the *blanc:* In a large saucepan, add the lemon juice to the water. In a small bowl, make a slurry with the flour, adding water at a trickle and stirring until the mixture is liquid and smooth. Stir it into the saucepan, add the olive oil and coarse salt, and bring to a boil, taking care not to let the liquid boil over. Drain the cardoon sections, add them to the *blanc,* and adjust the heat to maintain a light boil for 30 to 45 minutes, or until the sections are tender.

Preheat the oven to 375°F.

In a heavy saucepan over low heat, melt the butter, add the flour, and stir with a wooden spoon for a minute or so without browning. Pour in the cold milk, all at once, whisking at the same time with a wire whisk. Turn up the heat and continue whisking until the sauce comes to a boil. Adjust the heat to a simmer and cook for 20 minutes, stirring regularly with a wooden spoon.

In a mortar, pound the garlic cloves and salt to a paste, add the anchovy fillets, and pound to a paste. Stir the paste into the white sauce, taste for salt, and grind in pepper.

Drain the cardoon sections, spread them in a gratin dish, pour over the sauce, and bake for 20 minutes. Serve hot.

TART OF MIXED GREENS
Tarte aux Herbes

Serves 6 to 8

"THIS IS EXACTLY the same recipe as the squash tart," says Lulu, "except that chard needs lots and lots of garlic."

(continued)

4 tablespoons olive oil

1 large sweet onion, finely sliced

*1 head garlic, cloves separated, crushed, peeled, and coarsely
    chopped*

*½ pound young sorrel leaves, stemmed and shredded or
    chopped*

*1½ pounds chard greens (without ribs), parboiled for a few
    seconds, refreshed under cold running water, squeezed,
    and chopped*

*½ pound spinach, stemmed, parboiled, refreshed, squeezed,
    and chopped*

Salt

1 recipe short crust pastry (see Pissaladière, page 87)

4 eggs

2 cups heavy cream

Pepper

¼ cup freshly grated Parmesan cheese

Warm the olive oil in a large *poêlon* or heavy sauté pan, add the
onion and garlic, and sweat, covered, over very low heat, stirring
occasionally with a wooden spoon, until melting but uncolored,
about 15 minutes. Add the sorrel, stir until it turns gray, add the
chard and spinach, season with salt, adjust the heat to medium-
low, and cook, stirring often, for about 10 minutes. Leave to cool
partially.

Preheat the oven to 350°F.

Roll out the pastry and line a 10-inch pie tin or tart mold. Roll
the edges under and crimp them. In a mixing bowl, whisk together
the eggs, cream, and pepper. Stir in the greens, taste for salt, and
pour the mixture into the pastry. Smooth the surface, sprinkle with
Parmesan, and bake for 40 minutes. Serve hot or tepid as a first
course.

STUFFED CABBAGE LEAVES
Feuilles de Chou Farcies

Serves 4

THE POT-AU-FEU broth can be replaced by chicken broth or any other meat and/or vegetable broth. If you have no homemade broth at hand and are pressed for time, use water in preference to a commercial product.

1 large green cabbage, blemished outside, leaves discarded
2 tablespoons olive oil
1 medium onion, finely chopped
3 garlic cloves, crushed, peeled, and finely chopped
1/2 pound sausage meat
1/2 cup rice, parboiled for 15 minutes, refreshed in a sieve
    beneath cold running water, and well drained
2 cloves, pounded to a powder in a mortar
Salt and pepper
1 egg
Pot-au-feu broth (see above)
1/4 cup grated Parmesan

Cut a cone out of the bottom of the cabbage to remove the core. Detach the leaves, one by one, until they are no longer large enough to stuff. Cut up the heart of the cabbage, parboil it for 4 minutes, drain and refresh under cold running water, squeeze in both hands, and chop it. Layer the large leaves in a large pot, pour over boiling water to cover, bring to a boil, and empty the pot into a large colander, gently, so as not to damage the leaves. Refresh beneath cold running water. From the back or outside surface of each leaf, pare the thick rib to the thickness of the leaf, without cutting through the leaf. Lay the leaves out on towels to drain.

Preheat the oven to 350°F.

(continued)

In a *poêlon* or heavy pan, warm the olive oil, add the onion, and cook, stirring with a wooden spoon, until softened but not colored. Add the garlic and cook, stirring, until the onion begins to turn golden. In a mixing bowl, combine the onion and garlic with the chopped heart of cabbage, the sausage meat, rice, seasoning, and egg; mix thoroughly. Place a heaped tablespoon of stuffing at the base of the inside surface of each cabbage leaf, begin to roll it up, fold the sides of the leaf over the top, finish rolling up, and place the packages, seam sides down, side by side, in a deep gratin dish, with no space wasted. Pour over broth to just cover, sprinkle with cheese, cover with a lid or with foil, and bake for 1 hour, removing the cover after 45 minutes. Serve immediately.

CHARD GRATIN
Gratin de Blettes

Serves 4

VARIATIONS ON THIS comforting homely gratin are common in Provençal families, but visitors will never find it on a restaurant menu. Lulu serves it often with roast meats, but also as a base on which to bake a boneless 2- to 3-inch-thick section of white-fleshed fish, such as cod, anglerfish, grouper, or halibut, bread crumbs and olive oil sprinkled over the fish as well as the chard's surface, counting 20 to 30 minutes in the oven, depending on the thickness of the fish. As with all her baked fish, a slice of butter is placed on top to melt upon removing it from the oven. Lulu often adds a handful of stemmed, shredded raw sorrel leaves to the sauté pan at the same time as the chopped chard.

2 pounds Swiss chard
3 tablespoons olive oil
2 tablespoons butter

1 head garlic, cloves separated, crushed, and peeled
Salt and freshly ground pepper
2 teaspoons flour
1 cup milk
Coarsely grated dry bread crumbs
Handful of small croutons, cut from crustless slices of
  semifresh bread, fried in olive oil until golden and crisp

Separate the green leafy parts of the chard from the thick ribs. Wash and drain them separately. Trim the ribs and cut them into large dice. Cook the ribs in a large pot of salted, boiling water for 10 minutes, then add the greens and stir with a wooden spoon until the water returns to a boil. As soon as the greens are completely limp—a few seconds after the boil is reached—empty the pot into a colander and refresh the chard beneath cold running water. Squeeze the mass of chard repeatedly in both hands to form a firm ball. Chop it, slicing thin, give the ball a quarter of a turn, and slice thin again.

In a heavy sauté pan over medium-low heat, warm 2 tablespoons olive oil and most of the butter. Add the crushed garlic and, when the air is filled with its scent but before it begins to color, add the chard, salt, and pepper. Stir regularly with a wooden spoon for 10 minutes, or until the chard has lost all superficial moisture. Sprinkle over the flour, stir well, and begin to add the milk, a little at a time, over a period of some 20 minutes, stirring and waiting until the chard absorbs each addition before adding more milk.

Preheat the oven to 375°F.

Process the mixture rapidly to form a coarse purée. Pour it into a buttered gratin dish, grate over dry bread, dribble over olive oil, crisscross fashion, and bake for 30 minutes, or until golden. Scatter croutons over the surface before serving hot or tepid—or serve without croutons at room temperature.

HOT CHICK-PEA SALAD
Salade de Pois-chiches

Serves 6

PERFECT CHICK-PEAS should be absolutely intact when cooked but, when one is pressed between the tongue and the roof of the mouth, it should collapse into a smooth purée with no hard or granular edges. As for any dried legume, it is important to use chick-peas from the most recent harvest. They are especially sensitive to the water in which they are soaked and cooked. A high calcium content prevents them from cooking correctly, imposing much too long a cooking period, during which they begin to fall apart without ever becoming tender. Even under perfect conditions, it is difficult to gauge the cooking time unless you are using chick-peas whose origin is familiar to you. The best require no more than 1 hour to, at the most, 1 ½ hours after soaking. Provençal cookbooks from the last century often recommend soaking chick-peas in leftover spinach cooking water and cooking them in rainwater. Modern cookbooks recommend adding baking soda to the soaking water and, sometimes, even to the cooking water. Lulu does not take these heresises lightly. She says, "I certainly do not want my chick-peas to taste either like spinach or like bicarbonate of soda! I used to use rainwater both for soaking and cooking but, in recent years, so much has been said and written about air pollution that I now use bottled mineral water with perfect results."

In Provence, chick-pea cooking water is used as a substitute for stock in any number of preparations. It is a wonderful soup base. Lulu sometimes holds back a portion of the cooked chick-peas to pass through a vegetable mill into the stock for a supper soup, accompanied by little croutons fried in olive oil. Instead of the vinaigrette presented here, she sometimes prepares a sauce with salt, pepper, cayenne, finely chopped garlic and parsley, and a bit of lemon juice; this salad she calls "Pois-chiches à l'Orientale."

1 pound chick-peas
3 to 4 liters Volvic or other noncalcareous bottled water
Bouquet containing 1 bay leaf and 2 or 3 sprigs of winter
*   savory*
1 whole peeled onion
Salt

VINAIGRETTE
Salt and pepper
3 garlic cloves, lightly crushed, peeled, and finely chopped
1 small sweet onion, finely chopped
2 tablespoons fine wine vinegar
6 tablespoons olive oil

Rinse the chick-peas, put them in a large bowl, and pour over bottled water to about 2 inches above their level. Soak overnight. Drain them, empty them into a large earthenware *poêlon*, cover generously with bottled water, bring slowly to a boil, boil for 3 or 4 minutes, and drain them. Return the chick-peas to the *poêlon*, pour over boiling bottled water to about 2 inches above their level, add the bouquet and the onion, return to a boil, and adjust the heat to a simmer, lid slightly ajar. Add salt after about 45 minutes. Continue simmering until a chick-pea, crushed against the side of the *poêlon* (or in your mouth), collapses into a purée. Drain the chick-peas, discard the onion and the bouquet (reserve the cooking liquid for a soup base or to replace meat stock), and in a large bowl, toss them with all the elements of the vinaigrette. Serve immediately.

BRAISED ENDIVES
Endives Braisées

Serves 8

LULU SERVES this as a garnish to roast leg of lamb or roast beef, or, with a bit of cream added at the last minute, as a first course.

4 tablespoons butter, softened at room temperature
8 Belgian endives, imperfect outer leaves removed, stem ends
     trimmed, not washed
Salt
¼ cup white wine
½ lemon
Pepper

Choose a large *poêlon* or other low, wide earthenware casserole (preferably) or a heavy sauté pan of a size to just hold the endives, placed side by side. Smear about half the butter in the bottom and the sides, fit in the endives, spread the remaining butter on their surfaces, season with salt, cover tightly, and sweat over low heat in the butter and the liquid released by the endives, turning them over when golden on one side. When no more liquid remains in the casserole, add a couple of tablespoons of white wine. Count 45 to 50 minutes in all, adding a bit of wine from time to time to keep the bottom of the vessel moist. When the endives are golden brown on all sides, meltingly tender but still intact, squeeze over a few drops of lemon juice, grind over pepper, turn them around in their juices, and serve directly from their cooking vessel.

GRILLED EGGPLANT WITH GARLIC CREAM
Aubergines Grillées, Crème d'Ail

Serves 8

LULU SERVES this as a garnish to roast meats. It is especially good with lamb.

4 heads garlic, cloves separated and peeled
Salt and freshly ground pepper
About ¹/₂ cup olive oil
8 small, elongated eggplants (about 4 pounds)

Cook the garlic cloves in salted water at a light boil for 12 to 15 minutes, or until purée-tender. Drain them and push them through a fine sieve. Taste for salt, season with pepper, and stir in enough olive oil to loosen the purée to a thin spreading consistency.

Meanwhile, cut off the stem ends from the eggplants and split each in two. With a small, sharply pointed knife, make crisscross incisions on the cut surfaces. Dribble olive oil over the cut surfaces, smear it evenly around, season with salt and pepper, and grill the eggplant halves on a preheated grill, split surfaces first until golden brown, then finish grilling, skin side down, until a knife tip meets no resistance near the stem end. Alternatively, broil the eggplant halves, split surfaces facing up until golden brown, then finish grilling skin side up. Spread the crisscross surfaces with the warm garlic cream and serve.

GRATIN OF EGGPLANT AND TOMATOES
Gratin d'Aubergines aux Tomates

Serves 4

1 cup olive oil
2 pounds firm, young elongated eggplant without seeds, stem
ends and flower ends sliced off, cut lengthwise into ½-
inch slices
Salt and pepper
2 cups hot tomato sauce (page 74)
Coarsely grated bread crumbs

In a large frying pan, heat about ¼ inch olive oil. Fry the eggplant slices in batches, turning the heat up and down as necessary, turning the slices and adding more oil as necessary, until they are golden brown on both sides and tender to the fork at the stem ends. Drain on paper towels.

Preheat the oven to 350°F.

Press a layer of eggplant slices into the bottom of a large gratin dish, salt and pepper lightly, spread over tomato sauce, add another layer of eggplant, season, and cover with tomato sauce. Sprinkle over crumbs, dribble over olive oil, and bake for 30 minutes, or until the crumbs are golden. Serve hot or tepid.

EGGPLANT AND TOMATO CONFIT
Confit d'Aubergines aux Tomates

Serves 4

4 tablespoons olive oil
1 large onion, finely chopped
3 garlic cloves, crushed and peeled
2 pounds eggplant, unpeeled, cut into ⅔-inch cubes
Salt
1½ pounds tomatoes, peeled, seeded, and coarsely chopped
Bouquet garni (bay leaf, thyme, savory)

Warm the olive oil in a large *poêlon* or heavy sauté pan, add the onion, cook over low heat, stirring occasionally with a wooden spoon, until softened. Add the garlic and the eggplant. Season with salt. Stir regularly until the eggplant begins to soften. Add the tomatoes, turn up the heat, and stir until the tomatoes are boiling and beginning to disintegrate. Add the bouquet garni. Adjust the heat to maintain a simmer, or light boil, uncovered, stirring regularly, for about 1 hour, or until the stew is no longer liquid. Taste for salt. Serve hot, tepid, or at room temperature.

FENNEL À LA GRECQUE
Fenouil à la Grecque

Serves 6

*2 pounds fennel bulbs, outer stalks removed, stems and root
bases trimmed, strings pulled out of visible inner stalks,
quartered vertically, parboiled in salted water for 10
minutes, and drained*

1 onion, thinly sliced

6 garlic cloves, crushed and peeled

1/2 teaspoon coriander seeds

1/2 teaspoon peppercorns

Juice of 1 lemon

Coarse sea salt

1/2 cup white wine

Boiling water

In a saucepan, assemble the parboiled fennel and all the other ingredients except the water. Pour over boiling water to just cover
and cook, covered, at a light boil until the fennel is tender, but still
slightly firm. Remove the lid, turn up the heat, and reduce the liquid by about two thirds. Transfer to a serving dish, cool, uncovered, and refrigerate, covered. Remove from the refrigerator 1 hour
before serving as an hors d'oeuvre.

FENNEL BAKED WITH WHITE WINE
Fenouil au Four

Serves 6

4 tablespoons butter
2 pounds fennel bulbs, outer stalks removed, trimmed, split
*   in two, parboiled in salted water for 10 minutes, and*
*   drained*
Salt
1 medium onion, chopped
1 cup white wine

Preheat the oven to 400°F.

Melt the butter in a large, heavy sauté pan, place the parboiled fennel halves in the pan, split sides down, salt lightly, and cook over low heat until the cut surfaces are an even golden brown. Turn them over, add the chopped onion, and cook until the rounded surfaces of the fennel are lightly colored. Shuffle the contents of the pan around with a wooden spoon to make certain that no fragments of onion become too darkly colored. Transfer the pan's contents to a gratin dish, split fennel surfaces down. Over high heat, deglaze the sauté pan with the white wine, scraping sides and bottom with a wooden spoon. Pour the boiling wine over the fennel and onion and bake for 15 minutes, or until the wine is reduced to a near syrup.

GRATIN OF FENNEL IN TOMATO SAUCE
Fenouil au Coulis de Tomates

Serves 6

2 cups tomato sauce (page 74)
2 pounds fennel bulbs, outer stalks removed, trimmed, split
  in two, parboiled in salted water for 10 minutes, and
  drained
Pepper
Coarsely grated dried bread crumbs
2 tablespoons olive oil

Preheat the oven to 350°F.

Spread a thin layer of tomato sauce in the bottom of a large gratin dish, and arrange the fennel halves on top, split sides down. Grind over pepper, cover evenly with tomato sauce, sprinkle generously with the bread crumbs, dribble a thread of olive oil back and forth across the surface, and bake for 40 minutes, or until the crumbs are golden.

LENTIL SALAD
Salade de Lentilles

Serves 4

SMALL LENTIL-SIZED grains of gravel are occasionally found in lentils. The lentils should be picked over carefully. To do so, spread them, a handful at a time, onto a plate and push them, little by little, over the edge into a bowl, watching for the possible grain of gravel—there may be none. Lulu does not want her lentils to be flavored with anything but garlic and she is precise about the composition of the vinaigrette: "It should contain no onion or herb, only salt, pepper, vinegar, and olive oil." The lentil cooking liquid is a precious soup base.

*1 ¾ cups small French lentils, called lentilles du Puy or
    lentilles vertes, picked over and soaked in cold water for
    2 or 3 hours*
1 head garlic, cloves separated, crushed, and peeled
Salt

VINAIGRETTE
Salt and pepper
1 tablespoon fine red wine vinegar
4 to 5 tablespoons olive oil

Drain the lentils, put them into an earthenware *poêlon,* cover generously with cold water, bring to a full boil, drain, return them to the *poêlon,* and cover by about 1 ½ inches with boiling water. Add the garlic and cook, covered, at a light simmer. Add salt after 45 minutes. The lentils should be tender after 1 hour to 1 hour, 10 minutes. If not (if the lentils are older than they should be), cook until soft but intact. Drain the lentils, return them to the *poêlon,* toss with salt, pepper, vinegar, and olive oil, and serve hot.

SAUTÉED WILD MUSHROOMS
Champignons Sauvages Sautés

Serves 4

THE COMMONEST autumn mushrooms in the region around Bandol are saffron milkcaps (Lactarius deliciosus), called *safranés* or, often, because they grow beneath pine trees, *champignons des pins*. Chanterelles or girolles (Cantharellus cibarious), and most other small, edible mushrooms, including cultivated button mushrooms, are prepared in the same way. Larger cultivated mushrooms and cèpes (Boletus edulis) should be first sliced or cut into pieces. (Morels and Caesar's mushrooms are too delicate to support the garlic treatment.) Saffron milkcaps and chanterelles are best when no more than ¾ to 1 inch in diameter and absolutely dry in appearance. The stem ends may have to be trimmed, but the mushrooms should not be washed; clean them by brushing lightly, blowing on them, and rubbing with the tip of a slightly damp cloth.

3 tablespoons olive oil
1 pound mushrooms, cleaned
Salt and pepper
Persillade (handful of chopped flat-leaf parsley, chopped
*   again with 2 finely chopped garlic cloves)*

In a large heavy frying pan, heat the olive oil, add the mushrooms, season with salt and pepper, and sauté over high heat, tossing the mushrooms repeatedly, until they are dry and lightly colored, about 5 minutes. Add the persillade and sauté for another minute, or until the scent of frying persillade fills the room. Serve directly from the frying pan onto heated plates, or scatter the mushrooms over any grilled meat or poultry.

Wild mushrooms.

STUFFED BAKED ONIONS
Oignons Farcis à la Marseillaise

Serves 6

MY ORIGINAL NOTES for this stuffing called only for the chopped insides of the onions, garlic, anchovy, and seasoning. I figured it needed some body so I asked Lulu to go over it again. She began by saying, "I always make stuffed onions when I have leftover roast lamb at hand . . . lamb and onions are delicious together . . . and of course, it needs some garlic . . . " I said, "The last time, you called for anchovies but no meat." "Oh, did I? Well, of course, they're very good with anchovies—but you can use both anchovies and lamb if you want to." "Do you ever add bread—or rice?" "Obviously. You have to! I add bread." "Egg?" "Well, naturally!" "Do you add liquid to the gratin dish?" ". . . you need white wine."

> 6 large sweet onions, at least ½ pound each, root tips and
>   stem tips cut off, outer parchment skins peeled off,
>   parboiled for 20 minutes, refreshed in cold water, and
>   drained
> Large pinch of coarse sea salt
> Pepper
> 2 garlic cloves, peeled
> 2 salt anchovies, rinsed and filleted, or 4 fillets
> Large pinch of fresh savory leaves, finely chopped, or finely
>   crumbled dried savory
> 4 tablespoons olive oil
> 1 cup fresh bread crumbs (prepared without crusts in a food
>   processor)
> ½ pound leftover roast lamb, all fat removed, hand chopped
>   (about 1 cup)

1 egg
½ cup white wine
Coarsely grated dried bread crumbs

Preheat the oven to 350°F.

Cut a slice from the top of each onion. With a teaspoon, carefully scoop out the centers, leaving the outer three or four sheaths intact. Remove and discard the outermost sheath, or skin. Cut free the tender inside flesh from the top slices and chop it along with the flesh that has been removed from the insides. Transfer the chopped onion to a mixing bowl.

In a marble mortar, with a wooden pestle, pound the salt, pepper, garlic, anchovies, and savory to a paste. Stir in about a tablespoon of olive oil to loosen it, add half the bread crumbs, mix, and transfer to the mixing bowl. Wipe out the mortar with the remaining crumbs and add to the mixing bowl. Add the chopped lamb and the egg and mix thoroughly, squishing the mixture repeatedly between your fingers. If it seems stiff, mix in a dribble of olive oil or white wine.

Choose a gratin dish of a size to just hold the onions, placed side by side, touching but not packed. With a teaspoon, stuff each, packing the stuffing gently into place with the back of the spoon and mounding it over the top, molding the surface with the overturned spoon. Arrange the onions in the gratin dish, pour white wine into the bottom to a depth of about ¼ inch, sprinkle the surfaces of the onions generously with dried bread crumbs, dribble olive oil over each, and bake for 45 to 50 minutes, or until the surfaces are golden and crisp and the onions meltingly tender. Keep an eye on the bottom of the dish, adding a bit of white wine, if necessary, to prevent its drying up. Serve hot.

GRATIN OF CELERIAC AND POTATOES
Gratin de Céleri-rave et Pommes de Terre

Serves 8

2 pounds celeriac, thickly peeled, and cut into large cubes
Salt
2 pounds potatoes, peeled and quartered
10 tablespoons cold butter
Freshly ground pepper

Boil the celeriac in a generous amount of salted water for 10 minutes, add the potatoes, and cook until both are tender, about 40 minutes in all.

Preheat the oven to 375°F.

Drain the vegetables, saving the water. Push the vegetables, preferably, through a large sieve with a wooden pestle, or purée them in a vegetable mill, adding a little cooking liquid, if necessary, to help them through.

Dice 6 tablespoons of the butter, stir it into the purée with a wooden spoon, without beating, and stir in enough of the cooking liquid to form a loose, not quite pourable, purée. Season with pepper and taste for salt. Spread the purée into a buttered gratin dish, ripple the surface lightly with the edge of the wooden spoon or with the tines of a fork, distribute thin shavings of butter over the surface, and bake for about 20 minutes, or until the surface is lightly golden.

POTATO AND SORREL GRATIN
Gratin de Pommes de Terre à l'Oseille

Serves 6

3 tablespoons butter
10 ounces young sorrel leaves, stems pulled off, washed,
    drained, and chopped
Salt
3 pounds large potatoes, peeled, thinly sliced lengthwise
    (a mandoline will produce almost paper-thin slices),
    unrinsed
1 large sweet onion, finely sliced
1 cup heavy cream

Preheat the oven to 375°F.

In a frying pan, melt 2 tablespoons butter over medium heat, add the chopped sorrel and salt, and cook for a few minutes, stirring with a wooden spoon, until the sorrel has turned gray and begun to fall into a purée. Remove from the heat.

Thickly butter a large gratin dish. Combine the sliced potatoes and onions in a saucepan and add a large pinch of coarse sea salt and just enough water to almost cover. Bring to a boil, stirring and scraping the bottom of the saucepan with a wooden spoon to prevent the potatoes from sticking. Spread half the potato and onion mixture in the bottom of the gratin dish, spread the stewed sorrel on top, and finish with the remaining potatoes and onions and enough (or all) of their cooking liquid to almost cover. Spread the cream over the surface and bake for 1 hour, until the surface is richly browned and the liquid completely absorbed. Serve hot.

POTATO SALAD
Salade de Pommes de Terre

Serves 4

UNADORNED, this is a delicious opener to a meal. It is, also, a wonderful base upon which to improvise, by the addition, alone or in combination, of rinsed and filleted salt anchovies, chopped hard-boiled eggs, smoked herring fillets, grilled, peeled, and slivered peppers, mussels or clams opened in white wine, or strips of cold pot-au-feu meat ("I like it most of all with boiled beef," says Lulu, "then, I add capers.") Or, prepared in the bottom of a salad bowl (with or without a choice of the above ingredients or others), with a variety of leafy salads placed atop to be tossed at the last minute.

The onions should be sweet and abundant—sliced green onions or freshly dug spring shallots, finely sliced rings from midsummer white onions or elongated violet Florence onions, autumn dark, purple-red, finger-staining onions, pale, yellow-skinned winter onions. . . . The potatoes must be hot—a cold, boiled potato will resist all attempts to imbue it with flavor.

1 pound firm, yellow-fleshed potatoes, unpeeled
Salt and pepper
3 tablespoons aged red wine vinegar
1/2 cup olive oil
1 medium-large sweet onion (4 to 5 ounces), finely sliced into
*   rings, or a handful of finely sliced green onions or green*
*   shallots*
1 tablespoon finely chopped flat-leaf parsley

Boil the potatoes in salted water until just done—25 minutes, more or less, depending on their size.

While the potatoes are cooking, combine the salt, pepper, and vinegar in a mixing bowl, swirl in the olive oil, and add the onions.

As soon as the potatoes are done, drain them and peel them: holding a potato in a doubly folded kitchen towel, slit the skin the length of the potato with the blade point of a small knife and pull it off between thumb and knife blade. Slice the potato against the folded towel, letting the slices fall into the bowl. After slicing each potato, move the slices around to make certain that none are sticking together and that all are coated in vinaigrette. Add most of the parsley and toss lightly with a spoon and a fork, taking care to break up the potatoes as little as possible. Turn them out onto a serving dish, sprinkle with the remaining parsley, and serve while still warm.

SCALLOPED POTATOES WITH OLIVES
Pommes de Terre aux Olives

Serve 6

3 pounds large potatoes
3 tablespoons olive oil
Salt
4 ounces black olives, pitted
3 or 4 small fresh savory sprigs, or a pinch of dried,
*   crumbled savory*
2 cups white wine

Preheat the oven to 375°F.

Boil the potatoes in their skins for about 15 minutes, or until half-cooked but still very firm. Peel them and slice them, lengthwise, as thin as possible. Oil a large gratin dish lightly, layer half the potatoes in the bottom, season with salt, scatter over the olives and savory, and layer the remaining potatoes on top. Bring white wine to a boil and pour over enough to not quite immerse the potatoes, sprinkle with salt, dribble a thread of olive oil, crisscross, over the surface, and bake for about 45 minutes. Serve hot.

POTATO SOUFFLÉ
Soufflé de Pommes de Terre

Serves 4

1 1/2 pounds potatoes, peeled and quartered
Salt
6 tablespoons butter
1 cup milk, heated
Pepper and nutmeg
1/2 cup freshly grated Parmesan
3 eggs, separated
1 egg yolk, beaten with a fork

Preheat the oven to 400°F.

Boil the potatoes in salted water until just done, about 30 minutes. Drain them and push them through a sieve with a wooden pestle, stir in 5 tablespoons butter, cut into small pieces, and enough hot milk to make a fairly loose purée. Taste for salt. Grind over pepper, scrape over nutmeg, and stir in the cheese.

Beat the 3 egg yolks with a fork and stir them in. Whisk the egg whites with a pinch of salt until they form soft peaks and fold them in, gently, with a wooden spoon. Empty the mixture into a generously buttered gratin dish and, with a pastry brush, paint the surface loosely with the other beaten egg yolk, spreading here and there with a knife blade. Bake for 20 to 25 minutes, or until golden and evenly swelled. Serve immediately.

RATATOUILLE
Ratatouille

Serves 6

THE SMOKY NOTE from the peppers grilled over wood embers is unique to Lulu's ratatouille. The vegetables are precooked, separately, each in a different way, before being assembled, simmered together, and reduced to a melting perfection in which some are dispersed and absorbed into the whole while others retain their identity. Ratatouille can be served hot as an accompaniment to roast or grilled meats and it is delicious incorporated into scrambled eggs. Lulu usually serves it at room temperature as a vegetable course on its own. As a variation, she recommends stirring in, at the last minute, a handful of pitted black olives and the diced crisp heart of a head of celery.

About ⅔ cup olive oil
1 pound large sweet onions, split in two and finely sliced
Salt
6 garlic cloves, lightly crushed, peeled, and finely sliced
1 pound zucchini, quartered lengthwise and cut into ¾-inch
*   sections*
1 pound firm young eggplant, unpeeled, cut into ¾-inch
*   cubes*
1 pound tomatoes, peeled, seeded, and quartered
3 large sweet peppers (1 red, 1 yellow, 1 green) grilled,
*   peeled, seeded, and cut lengthwise into narrow strips*
*   (see following recipe), juices reserved*
Bouquet garni containing 2 bay leaves and 2 or 3 thyme
*   sprigs*
Pepper

(continued)

Warm 3 tablespoons olive oil in a wide, heavy 8 to 10-quart pot, add the onions, and cook, covered, over very low heat, stirring occasionally with a wooden spoon, for at least 30 minutes, or until they are melting and simmering in their own juices but uncolored. Remove the lid, raise the heat slightly, and cook, stirring regularly, until they are uniformly light golden brown. Add the salt, garlic, and zucchini and continue to stir regularly.

Meanwhile, heat 4 tablespoons olive oil in a large frying pan and add the eggplant and salt. Sauté, tossing and turning until the pieces are softened. Add them to the pot with the onions and zucchini, reserving any remaining oil in the frying pan.

Add more oil to the frying pan if it is nearly dry. Over high heat, add the tomatoes and salt; sauté, shaking the pan and tossing constantly until their liquid has evaporated. Remove them from the heat before they begin to disintegrate and empty the frying pan into the pot. Add the peppers and their juices to the pot, immerse the bouquet garni, and adjust the heat to maintain a simmer, pot uncovered, for about 2 hours. Displace the vegetables gently, scraping the bottom and sides of the pot with the wooden spoon from time to time and lowering the heat as the liquid reduces, until all excess liquid has evaporated and the vegetables are coated in a syrupy sauce. Remove from the heat, grind over pepper, and taste for salt. If prepared ahead, transfer to a dish and leave to cool before covering and refrigerating—the flavors will ripen over a day or two. If meant to be served at room temperature (too cold, the flavors are paralyzed), remove the ratatouille from the refrigerator an hour or so before serving and stir in a couple of tablespoons of olive oil at the last minute.

GRILLED PEPPERS
Piments Doux au Gril

Serves 6

LULU SCORNS the barbaric habit of turning peppers over a gas flame to blister the skins and holding them beneath running water to rub the skins off. "First of all," she says, "the purpose of grilling them is not only to loosen the skins—the peppers must be cooked, the flesh tender. As they cook, a delicious juice is collected inside the peppers that must be saved. When they are grilled over a bed of wood embers, they acquire a lovely, delicate smoky taste." Lacking a bed of coals, a professional electric grill, sometimes called a salamander, does a good job—or they can be grilled in an oven broiler. If grilling in a salamander or a broiler, it is practical to place the peppers on a baking tray lined with a sheet of aluminum foil to protect the tray from escaping juices that burn to an unremovable crisp.

Grilled peppers are often served in a vinaigrette. Lulu likes to serve them cut lengthwise into narrow strips, unseasoned, with their sweet juices poured over and dribbled with a film of olive oil. Salt, pepper grinders, and cruets of vinegar and olive oil are at table for those who wish to season them.

6 large, fleshy sweet peppers (2 each red, yellow, and green)
Olive oil

Arrange the peppers, not touching, on a grill, preheated over wood coals, or on a foil-lined baking tray. Grill, turning the peppers at regular intervals, until the skins are unevenly charred and blistered on all surfaces—20 minutes, more or less, depending on your method of grilling. Transfer the peppers to a platter and enclose it in a large plastic bag, tucking in the opening beneath the platter to prevent the escape of steam. Leave until the peppers are cool enough to handle—the steam trapped in the plastic bag will have loosened the skins so that they can easily be slipped free. Pull off and discard the skins. Pull out and discard the stem and core. Pull the peppers apart, lengthwise, into halves or large sections, collecting the juices in the platter. Remove and discard all clinging seeds and stack the pepper sections on a plate. Pass the juices through a sieve into a bowl to remove seeds. On a flat surface, slice the pepper sections, lengthwise, into narrow strips, arrange them decoratively on a platter, pour over their juices, and dribble olive oil over the surface.

GREEN LEAFY SALADS
Salades Vertes

A MENU WITHOUT a green leafy salad is a rarity at the Domaine. The vinaigrette is prepared at the last minute, salt and pepper stirred or swirled in a salad bowl with aged red wine vinegar, olive oil stirred in. Garlic vinaigrette is made by first pounding coarse sea salt, pepper, and garlic to a paste in a mortar, stirring in the vinegar, then the oil. The proportions are approximately one part of vinegar to three of oil, a bit less vinegar for delicate, sweet garden lettuces, a bit more for slightly bitter or peppery leaves—and quite a lot more for distinctly bitter salads like dandelions, which can also support a heavy dose of garlic. Often, instead of preparing a garlic vinaigrette, Lulu adds a handful of *chapons* (slices of day-old bread, partially dried out in a slow oven, rubbed well on both sides with garlic cloves, and cut into cubes) to a salad with plain vinaigrette (she has even been known to add *chapons* to salads in garlic vinaigrette). The salad leaves must be absolutely dry before being tossed with a vinaigrette. A salad spinner is a practical first step, but the leaves should then be spread out on kitchen towels and rolled up tightly before being added to the salad bowl and tossed at table.

A garlicky salad of mixed lambs' lettuce, radicchio, and curly chicory, sometimes wild chicory, rocket, and cress, is often served with cold (i.e., tepid or room temperature) roasts. Lulu said, "Walnuts are wonderful with Roquefort. When Roquefort is on the cheese platter, I serve at the same time a salad of Belgian endive with peeled and cored thinly sliced apple and a handful of walnuts." Then, in a sudden avalanche of words, she said, "I often add hard-boiled eggs and anchovies to the garlicky salads and throw a handful of diced Gruyère into the endive, apple, and walnut salad." "To accompany roasts and cheeses . . . ?" "No, of course not—then, they are first courses . . . I always serve dandelions as a first course because I always add garlic and anchovies."

Lulu's autumn menu diary often indicates *salade des champs*—field salad, which, in Provence, is collected not in fields but on the hillsides. When I asked what she meant by *salade des champs*, she said, "Coustelline, of course." In Provence, everyone eats garlicky coustelline salad with roast game birds; in Paris, no one has ever heard of coustelline. The plant dies back to the root with the heat and drought of summer. After the autumn rains, in November, tender tufts of delicate, deeply indentate, grayish-green leaves push out from the gnarled black roots and stark stalks. Then, coustelline is at its best. By winter and early spring, when it bears small dandelion-like flowers on tall, frail stems, the leaves are no longer tender. Coustelline is less bitter than dandelion and less peppery than rocket or watercress. Young dandelion is probably the best replacement.

RAW ARTICHOKE AND PEPPER SALAD
Salade d'Artichauts Crus aux Poivrons

Serves 8

BEFORE COMPLETING the vinaigrette, the sliced artichokes are added to the olive oil to prevent their blackening in contact with air. Serve as a first course.

¹/₂ cup olive oil
2 pounds tender young artichokes
2 garlic cloves, peeled
Large pinch of coarse sea salt
Pepper
3 tablespoons red wine vinegar
1 medium sweet onion, sliced into thin rings, or a bundle of
  spring onions, cleaned and finely sliced
4 elongated light green, sweet salad peppers, split, seeded,
  and cut lengthwise into narrow strips
12 salt anchovies, rinsed, and filleted, or 24 fillets
Pinch of flat-leaf parsley, finely chopped

Pour the olive oil into a bowl. Break off the stems of the artichokes, pull the outermost leaves back and downward and break them off from the flesh at the bases. With a large, sharp, stainless steel knife, cut off the top third of the leaves from an artichoke. With a small, sharp, stainless steel knife, trim the bottom of the artichoke and the tops of the outer leaves, removing dark green from the bottom and tough parts from the leaves. If you are certain that chokes have not begun to form, hold each artichoke on its side against the chopping board and, with the large knife, thinly slice from top to bottom, adding the slices immediately to the olive oil and turning them around to coat them. Or, split each artichoke in two vertically, cut out the choke with the tip of the small knife, place each half cut surface down, and, with the large knife, thinly slice from top to bottom, tossing the slices, as each half is finished, in the olive oil.

In a marble mortar, pound the garlic, salt, and pepper to a purée. Stir in the vinegar and transfer the mixture to a wide salad bowl. Add the artichokes and the olive oil, toss well, scatter over the onion slices, the pepper strips, and the anchovy fillets, sprinkle with parsley, and toss again thoroughly at table.

CABBAGE SALAD
Salade de Chou

Serves 8

LULU: "You can do the same thing with the hearts of fennel bulbs, split and sliced paper-thin. Two or three crushed cloves of garlic are tossed with the fennel and the olive oil—with cabbage, I don't use garlic."

> *1 white cabbage, blemished outer leaves removed, quartered vertically, cores removed, visible thick ribs removed, and shredded as for slaw or sauerkraut*
> Salt
> *½ cup red wine vinegar*
> *½ cup olive oil*

In a large mixing bowl, press layers of shredded cabbage, sprinkling each generously with salt and vinegar. After an hour, press with your hands and turn the cabbage around so that it is immersed in liquid. An hour later, empty it into a colander, rinse thoroughly under cold running water, squeeze well between both hands, and toss in a salad bowl with the olive oil.

PROVENÇAL SALAD
Salade d'Oeufs Durs

Serves 6

THIS IS ANOTHER of Lulu's childhood memories, a salad that opened the family lunch several times weekly. It sounds like nothing at all, but it is delicious and much the best for being assembled, imperfectly mixed, and seasoned at the last minute at table—the flavors remain separate and vibrant. Much, naturally, depends on the quality of the olive oil and the vinegar.

> *9 eggs*
> *20 salt anchovies, rinsed and filleted (or 40 fillets), gathered together in 3 bundles and finely sliced crosswise*
> *2 sweet onions (or a large handful of scallions), finely chopped*
> *Large bouquet of flat-leaf parsley, finely chopped*
> *6 fresh, crisp garlic cloves, lightly crushed, peeled, and finely chopped*
> *Olive oil, vinegar, salt, and pepper grinders (at table)*

Cover the eggs with cold water, bring to a boil, and hold at a simmer for 8 to 10 minutes, depending on the size of the eggs. Shell them (if they are very fresh, they are often difficult to shell—cut into them shallowly, break them in two, and scoop the halves from the shells with a teaspoon). Separate the whites from the yolks. Finely slice the whites, then chop across the slices. Finely slice the yolks—they will crumble. Mix the whites and yolks together, loosely, so as not to crush the crumbled yolks.

Make a neat pile of the chopped eggs at one end of a large platter and arrange separate piles of anchovies, chopped onion, parsley, and garlic all around. At table, each person chooses proportions to taste and seasons to taste with salt, pepper, olive oil, and vinegar.

GREEN BEAN AND
FRESH SHELL BEAN SALAD
Salade de Haricots Verts et Egrenés

Serves 6

LULU SERVES this summer salad as a first course. She insists on the quality of the vinegar and suggests scattering over hyssop flowers after the salad has been tossed.

3 pounds fresh white shell beans (cocos) or fresh cranberry
    beans, shelled
1 branch of thyme
1 bay leaf
1 onion, stuck with 2 cloves
Salt

VINAIGRETTE
3 salt anchovies, rinsed and filleted, or 6 fillets
Pepper
3 tablespoons old wine vinegar
½ cup olive oil

1 pound small, freshly picked green beans, topped and tailed
3 tablespoons persillade (flat-leaf parsley and 3 garlic cloves,
    first chopped separately, then finely chopped together)

Add the shell beans, thyme, bay leaf, and onion stuck with cloves to salted boiling water and cook at a light boil, lid ajar, for about 40 minutes, or until a bean, pressed with a wooden spoon against the side of the pan, offers no resistance to being crushed. Hold the beans in their cooking liquid.

In the bottom of a large salad bowl, crush the anchovies and pepper with a wooden pestle, adding the vinegar slowly. Stir in the olive oil.

(continued)

Put the green beans in a large saucepan, add a handful of coarse sea salt, place over high heat, and pour over boiling water to cover by at least 2 inches. Boil until just done—2 to 8 minutes, depending on the quality of the beans. Drain.

Drain the shell beans, discard the herbs and onion stuck with cloves (save the liquid for a soup or stock), and empty the beans into the salad bowl. Add the green beans and the persillade, toss repeatedly, and serve warm.

PURÉE OF SWEET POTATOES
Purée de Patates Douces

Serves 4

LULU RESERVES this purée as an accompaniment to game dishes. She says, "For a more consistent purée, you can bake a starchy potato and purée it with the sweet potatoes, but I like it better without."

2 pounds sweet potatoes
Salt and pepper
¹/₂ cup heavy cream

Preheat the oven to 375°F.

Bake the sweet potatoes for about 45 minutes, or until purée-tender when pierced with a small knife tip. Split them, scoop out the flesh, and with a wooden pestle, push it through a sieve into a saucepan. Season generously with salt and pepper, stir in a little cream, and reheat over medium heat, stirring constantly with a wooden spoon. Stir in as much more cream as the purée can absorb without becoming runny. Turn out into a heated serving dish.

SQUASH GRATIN
Gratin de Courge

Serves 6

6 tablespoons butter
1 large sweet onion, chopped
2 pounds squash (Hubbard, pumpkin, etc.), peeled, seeded,
  and cut into ¹/₃-inch cubes
Salt and freshly ground pepper
¹/₄ teaspoon coriander seeds, crushed in a mortar
2 teaspoons flour
1 cup milk
2 tablespoons heavy cream
1 tablespoon chopped fresh mint leaves
¹/₄ cup freshly grated Parmesan or Gruyère cheese
Dried bread crumbs

Over very low heat, melt 4 tablespoons butter in a large earthen-ware *poêlon* or heavy sauté pan. Add the onion, squash, salt, pepper, and coriander and sweat, covered, for about 45 minutes, stirring occasionally with a wooden spoon and shaking the *poêlon* from time to time.

Preheat the oven to 375°F.

Sprinkle the squash with the flour, stir, adjust the heat to medium, and add milk, a little at a time, stirring, until the squash is bound in a thin sauce. Turn the heat very low again and leave to simmer gently, uncovered, for about 15 minutes, stirring from time to time. Stir in the cream and mint, empty the mixture into a buttered gratin dish, smooth the surface, sprinkle with cheese, grate over bread crumbs, scatter the surface with shavings of butter, and bake for 30 minutes, or until the surface is golden.

SQUASH TART
Tarte à la Courge

Serves 6

4 tablespoons olive oil
1 large sweet onion, finely sliced
2 pounds pumpkin, Hubbard, or other orange or red-fleshed
  squash, peeled, seeded, and diced
Salt
1 recipe short crust pastry (see Pissaladière, page 87)
4 eggs
2 cups heavy cream
Pepper and nutmeg
1/4 cup freshly grated Parmesan cheese

Warm the olive oil in a large *poêlon* or heavy sauté pan, add the onion, and sweat over low heat, stirring occasionally with a wooden spoon, until the onion is melting but uncolored. Add the squash and salt and continue to cook over low heat, stirring regularly, until it has disintegrated into a coarse purée, about 40 minutes. Leave to partially cool.

Preheat the oven to 350°F.

Roll out the pastry and line a 10-inch large pie tin or tart mold. Put the eggs and cream in a mixing bowl, grind over pepper, and with a small knife blade, scrape in some nutmeg. Whisk together, stir in the squash, taste for salt, and pour into the pastry. Smooth the surface, sprinkle over Parmesan cheese, and bake for 40 minutes. Serve hot or warm.

SQUASH PURÉE
Purée de Courge

Serves 8

MANY DIFFERENT varieties of what we call "winter squash" (not because it ripens in the winter but because, thanks to a hard flesh and a hard, tough, protective skin, it can be stored and used throughout the winter), red, orange, and yellow-fleshed, for the most part shaped like a flattened sphere with deep vertical ridges, appear on the Provençal market. Except for pumpkin (*potiron*), they are all called *courge;* the merchants know no other name and the farmers, who save their *courge* seeds from one year to another, know no other name. They are all used in the same way in the kitchen.

Lulu often prepares this purée in advance and reheats it at the last moment.

> *4 tablespoons butter*
> *1 large sweet onion, chopped*
> *3 pounds winter squash (pumpkin, Hubbard, etc.), peeled, seeded, and diced*
> *Salt*
> *Pepper and nutmeg*
> *1 cup heavy cream*

In a large *poêlon* or heavy sauté pan, melt the butter, add the onion, and stew gently, stirring from time to time with a wooden spoon, until soft but not colored. Add the squash and salt and continue to cook, covered, over very low heat, stirring occasionally, for about 45 minutes, or until the squash is falling into a purée. Grind over pepper, scrape over nutmeg, and purée it in a food processor (Lulu uses her hand blender). Stir in cream to create a loose but not quite pourable consistency, taste for salt, and just before serving, reheat over medium heat, stirring constantly with a wooden spoon.

TOMATOES À LA PROVENÇALE
Tomates à la Provençale

Serves 8

AFTER MONTHS of note-taking sessions with Lulu, I was struck by the absence, in my notes, of Tomatoes à la Provençale. I asked her if there was a reason. She said, "But *everyone* knows how to make *tomates à la provençale*—I never thought to mention it." As usual, everyone does not make them quite like Lulu: "The tomatoes should be cut in two crosswise, the seed pockets loosened slightly with a fingertip, each half held cut side down and given a shake—but only lightly, without squeezing, to rid it of enough loose seeds to make some space in the pockets. Above all, you don't want to lose all the seeds—or the jelly surrounding them, which is delicious when reduced. It is the excess water contained in the flesh that must first be drawn out, by salt and heat, for the tomatoes to cook correctly."

The bread crumbs should be quite dry, but slightly coarse and crumbly; if the bread used for making them is too dry, it will be reduced to a powder in the food processor or, if underprocessed, it will form a mixture of too coarse and too fine. The best tomatoes are sweet and richly flavored with a good balance of acidity; when cut into, the scent should cause one's saliva to flow abundantly. Modern varieties are often sweet but bland-tasting and lacking in acidity.

> 8 medium-sized (about 3 pounds), regular-shaped, firm, garden-ripe tomatoes, stem pulled off but uncored, rinsed and dried
> Salt
> 6 garlic cloves, lightly crushed and peeled
> Large handful of freshly picked, flat-leaf parsley leaves
> 1 cup semidry bread crumbs, prepared in a food processor

Pepper
About 5 tablespoons olive oil

Preheat the oven to 450°F.

Cut the tomatoes in two, horizontally, to expose cross sections of the seed pockets. Loosen the seeds superficially with a fingertip and give each half a gentle, upside-down shake to rid it of loose seeds. Place the halves, cut sides up, on an oven tray, sprinkle the cut surfaces liberally with salt, and put the tray into the oven for 10 minutes, or until the tomato halves are visibly filled with liquid. They are already fragile at this point—carefully remove each half with a spatula and place it, cut side down, on a wire rack to drain while preparing the persillade mixture.

Finely chop the garlic cloves. Finely chop the parsley, then chop the two together. Add the mixture to a mixing bowl with the bread crumbs, salt lightly, and grind over pepper generously. Mix with a fork, first tossing repeatedly, then stirring, to keep it light and airy.

Rub a large gratin dish with a few drops of olive oil—enough to form a film on the bottom and the sides. Arrange the tomato halves, cut sides up, barely touching, in the dish and, with a teaspoon, sprinkle the persillade-crumb mixture over each, at first gently pushing it with fingertips into the seed-pocket crevices, then mounding it lightly, without pressure, so that none of the cut surfaces remain visible. Dribble olive oil in a fine thread, back and forth and crisscross, over the crumbs and bake in the oven for 30 minutes. Serve hot or tepid, alone or with a roast. Served tepid, the tomatoes can only improve by being held in the cooling oven for half an hour.

PILAF WITH TOMATOES
Riz à la Tomate

Serves 6

THIS PILAF is specifically intended to accompany grilled lamb skewers (page 208), but it is delicious as an accompaniment to almost any grilled or pan-fried meat or poultry. Served by itself, a handful of torn-up fresh basil leaves sautéed with the tomatoes will do wonders. A pinch of saffron can be added to the rice before it is moistened.

3 tablespoons olive oil
1 onion, finely chopped
2 cups long-grain rice
Large pinch of coarse sea salt
4 cups boiling water
2 garlic cloves, lightly crushed, peeled, and finely chopped
*1 pound tomatoes, peeled, seeded, coarsely chopped, layered
    and salted in a colander, and left to drain for 1 hour*
4 tablespoons cold butter, diced

Warm 1 tablespoon olive oil in an earthenware *poêlon* or casserole, protected from direct heat by a heat disperser. Add the onion, and sweat, covered, over low heat until soft but not colored; add the rice and the salt. Stir regularly with a wooden spoon for a couple of minutes, or until the rice turns milky and is well coated with oil. Pour in the boiling water, stir once, and leave, tightly covered, to barely simmer for 20 minutes.

Heat 2 tablespoons olive oil in a large frying pan, add the chopped garlic, and as soon as it begins to sizzle, add the tomatoes and toss repeatedly over high heat for a couple of minutes, or until their liquid has evaporated but before they begin to fall apart from cooking. Add the tomatoes and the diced butter to the rice and toss lightly together with two forks. Serve immediately.

ZUCCHINI GRATIN
Gratin de Courgettes

Serves 4 to 6

6 tablespoons butter
1 large sweet onion, cut in two from top to bottom, each half
 finely sliced
2 pounds small, firm zucchini, quartered lengthwise and cut
 into 1/2-inch lengths
Salt
1 tablespoon flour
1 cup milk
Freshly ground pepper
1/4 cup freshly grated Parmesan or Gruyère cheese
Handful of coarsely grated dry bread crumbs

Over low heat, warm half the butter in a large earthenware *poêlon* or heavy casserole, add the onions, and sweat, covered, stirring occasionally with a wooden spoon, for about 30 minutes, or until melting but uncolored. Add the zucchini and salt and cook, first covered, then uncovered, until tender but not falling apart.

Preheat the oven to 400°F.

Sprinkle the onion and zucchini with flour and stir gently. Raise the heat somewhat and add the milk, a few spoonfuls at a time, stirring until the sauce boils before adding more. Simmer gently for 10 minutes before seasoning with pepper, tasting for salt, and pouring the mixture into a buttered gratin dish. Mix together the cheese and bread crumbs, sprinkle over the surface, distribute shavings of butter on top, and bake for 20 minutes, or until golden. Serve hot or tepid.

Zucchini blossoms.

STUFFED ZUCCHINI FLOWERS
Tian Niçois

Serves 8

LULU SERVES this as a garnish to roast lamb or beef. It can hold its own admirably as a first course.

> 4 tablespoons olive oil
> 1 onion, finely chopped
> 1 small zucchini, finely diced
> 1 pinch of coarse sea salt
> Pepper
> 1 garlic clove, peeled
> 2 salt anchovies, rinsed and filleted, or 4 fillets
> 1 large handful of fresh bread crumbs
> Small handful of finely chopped flat-leaf parsley
> 1 egg
> 24 freshly picked zucchini flowers, stems cut off at flower
>   base
> 1/4 cup white wine
> Coarsely grated dried bread crumbs

Warm 2 tablespoons olive oil in a *poêlon* or heavy sauté pan, add the onion, and cook, covered, stirring occasionally, until soft but uncolored. Add the diced zucchini and continue to cook over low heat, stirring regularly, for about 20 minutes, or until it is meltingly tender and most of its liquid has evaporated. Empty the pan into a mixing bowl.

In a marble mortar, pound the salt, pepper, and garlic to a paste. Add the anchovy fillets and pound to a paste. Add the bread crumbs and chopped parsley and mix until the bread has absorbed the paste. Empty into the mixing bowl, add the egg, and mix thoroughly.

(continued)

Preheat the oven to 400°F.

Oil a gratin dish of a size to hold the stuffed flowers in a single layer with no wasted space. With a teaspoon, forcing with a finger-tip, stuff each zucchini flower about three-quarters full, fold the pointed petal tips over the stuffing, and arrange the stuffed flowers, side by side, in the gratin dish. Pour the wine into the bottom, sprinkle the surface of the flowers with bread crumbs, dribble over olive oil, and bake for 20 minutes, or until the surface is golden. Serve hot, tepid, or at room temperature.

STUFFED ZUCCHINI AND TOMATOES
Courgettes et Tomates Farcies au Maigre

Serves 6

ZUCCHINI SHELLS are usually parboiled in preparation to being stuffed. Lulu deep-fries them in olive oil. I asked her if that was not unusual. She answered, "That's the way my mother always did it so that's the way I do it . . . I know that most people add chopped meats to the stuffing, but I don't think that meat makes any sense in stuffed vegetables."

6 medium tomatoes (about 3 pounds)
Salt
6 zucchini (2 to 3 pounds)
2 quarts vegetable oil (for deep-frying)
2 tablespoons olive oil
1 large onion, finely chopped
4 thick slices of semifresh bread, crusts removed, soaked in
*   milk, and squeezed nearly dry*

3 tablespoons chopped flat-leaf parsley, chopped again with
*   3 finely chopped garlic cloves*
1 egg
Pepper
Coarsely grated dried bread crumbs
4 tablespoons butter

Slice off the top quarter of each tomato. Scrape the flesh from the skins of the tops, coarsely chop, and reserve it. Loosen the seeds in the bottoms with your little finger and shake them out. With a small knife and a teaspoon, remove the flesh from the centers, leaving bottoms and walls intact. Chop the flesh and add it to that from the tops. Sprinkle salt inside the emptied tomatoes and place them upside-down on a wire rack to drain.

Cut off the stem and a sliver at the flower end of each zucchini. Split each in two and empty the halves with a melon baller, leaving walls ¼ to ⅓ inch thick. Chop and reserve the insides. In a deep-fryer or large pot, heat the oil to 375°F and fry the zucchini halves, in batches, until lightly colored and barely tender. Drain them upside down on paper towels.

Preheat the oven to 375°F.

Warm the olive oil in a frying pan, add the onion, and stew gently over low heat, stirring with a wooden spoon until it begins to soften. Add the chopped zucchini flesh, season with salt, and stew over low heat until it releases its liquid; turn the heat up and stir or toss regularly until the mixture is nearly dry. Add the reserved chopped tomato and stir or toss until its liquid has evaporated. Empty the pan into a mixing bowl with the soaked bread, chopped parsley and garlic, egg, and pepper. Mix thoroughly, first with a fork, then with your hands. Taste for salt.

Oil a gratin dish for the tomatoes and arrange the tomato shells in it. Arrange the fried zucchini halves in another dish or on an oven tray. With a teaspoon, fill the tomatoes and the zucchini halves, mounding the stuffing slightly. Sprinkle with dried bread crumbs, distribute shavings of butter over the surfaces, and put both dishes in the oven. Remove the zucchini after 25 minutes and the tomatoes 15 minutes later. With a spatula, transfer the tomatoes and the zucchini to a large platter and serve warm, either as a first course or to accompany a roast.

PASTA WITH BASIL AND ANCHOVY
Pâtes au Pistou à l'Anchois

Serves 6

PASTA IS an integral part of the Provençal diet, though nearly all the pastas on the market in France are imported from Italy. Fresh pasta is prepared in the same way as in Italy, with the same variations.

For this dish, Lulu uses one of the short, macaroni-like pastas—rigatoni, tortiglioni, penne rigate, etc. Cooking times, usually around 12 minutes, are printed on the packages.

Coarse salt
Pepper
3 garlic cloves, crushed and peeled
6 salt anchovies, rinsed and filleted, or 12 fillets
2 large handfuls of fresh basil leaves and flower buds
⅔ cup olive oil
1 pound commercial pasta (see above)
Freshly grated Parmesan cheese

In a marble mortar with a wooden pestle, pound a pinch of coarse salt with the pepper, garlic, and anchovy fillets to a smooth paste.

Add the basil and pound until the mixture is reduced to a coarse, liquid purée. Add the oil slowly, stirring vigorously with the pestle.

Add the pasta to a large pot of rapidly boiling salted water, stir with a wooden fork, and when the water returns to a boil, adjust the heat to prevent the water's boiling over. Drain, empty into a wide, low, heated serving bowl, add the sauce, toss well, and serve, accompanied by a dish of Parmesan.

FRESH PASTA
Pâtes Fraîches

About 1 pound, serving 4

LULU MAKES her own pasta for the recipes that follow—in these, fresh pasta is preferable to dried, commercial pasta and, of course, ravioli can only be made with fresh pasta.

2 1/2 cups flour
Salt
3 eggs
1 tablespoon olive oil

Put 1 1/2 cups flour and a good pinch of salt in a mixing bowl. Stir with a fork, leaving a well in the center. Add the eggs and the olive oil to the well and stir with the fork, working outward from the center, mashing and stirring, until all the flour is absorbed. Sprinkle over a little more flour. Continue working and sprinkling lightly with flour until you have a supple, cohesive dough. Clean off the fork and knead the dough with your knuckles, folding it repeatedly and sprinkling with a little flour, if necessary, until it is silken and resilient. Form the dough into a ball, cover with a folded towel, and leave to rest for a least 1 hour.

(continued)

If rolling out by hand, flatten the ball of dough with the heel of your hand on a well-floured board. Sprinkle flour over the flattened dough and roll it out until thin, giving it a quarter turn a couple of times and turning it over once.

To make noodles, sprinkle the rolled-out dough with more flour and fold it, from either side, into very loose rolls meeting at the center of the circle. Slice across the rolls to form noodles. Slip the flat of the knife blade beneath the noodles with the noncutting edge at the center, between the rolls, and lift up the knife so that the noodles unroll to either side of the blade. Slip them back onto a floured surface, sprinkle with flour, and toss them loosely with fingertips to prevent their sticking to each other.

If rolling out by machine, separate the ball of dough into two or three sections on a floured surface, flatten a section with the heel of your hand, and pass it slowly between the rollers, positioned at the widest, or kneading, setting. Dust the strip of dough with flour, fold it in three, and pass it again at the widest setting. It should be passed through the kneading rollers no more than necessary to pull it together. Fold it double and pass it once more, if necessary. The more often it is folded and passed, the more it will resemble commercial pasta. Pass it, without folding, through two or three intermediate settings before passing it a last time at the next-to-finest setting. Repeat with the other sections. Hang the strips of dough over a broomstick, propped between two chair backs, until no longer tacky before passing them through the noodle-cutting rollers. On a floured surface, sprinkle the noodles lightly with flour and toss them loosely with fingertips.

The fresh noodles may be held—not for too long—15 to 30 minutes. Toss them loosely in your hands, fingers splayed, to shake them free of superficial flour, and plunge them into salted boiling water, stirring with a wooden fork to prevent them from sticking together. They need no more than 2 or 3 minutes cooking.

FRESH PASTA WITH SPRING VEGETABLES
Pâtes Printanières

Serves 4

TO BE WONDERFUL after being cooked, garden peas should be sweet and succulent eaten raw, with no hint of hardness or starchiness. In Provence, May is the end of the season for asparagus and fava beans, but it is the only month in which peas answer to this description. Bundles of *cébettes*—freshly dug sweet white onions, varying in size from a walnut to a golf ball—are in every shop.

1 pound little peas, freshly picked, freshly shelled
1 cup sweet, white spring onions, quartered
6 tablespoons butter
Salt
Several leaves of tender leaf lettuce, washed, water left
　　clinging, rolled up, and finely shredded
1 pound young fava beans, shelled, each bean peeled
Large fresh savory sprig
3 tablespoons olive oil
1 cup small asparagus tips
1 pound fresh pasta, cut into noodles (page 309)
Pepper

In an earthenware *poêlon*, mix together the peas, onions, and 2 tablespoons cold butter, diced. Season with salt and scatter the lettuce chiffonade over the surface. Cover tightly, place the *poêlon* over high heat for 30 seconds to warm it up, adjust the heat to very low, and sweat for about 30 minutes, shaking the *poêlon* gently from time to time.

Add the fava beans and savory to a saucepan of salted boiling water, boil for about 3 minutes, drain, discard the savory, and add the fava beans to the peas. At the same time, add a dash of olive oil to a large pot of salted boiling water, add the asparagus tips and the noodles, and boil for about 3 minutes, stirring with a wooden fork to separate the noodles. Adjust the heat to prevent the water's boiling over. Drain and add to the peas and fava beans. Grind over pepper, add 2 tablespoons olive oil, toss the contents of the *poêlon* with a fork and spoon, and scatter shavings of butter over the surface. Toss again when serving.

FRESH PASTA WITH SEAFOOD
Pâtes Fraîches aux Fruits de Mer

Serves 4

FOR THIS DISH, Lulu uses *palourdes*, or carpet shells, the same bivalves that are named *vongole* in Italy and are translated into English as clams.

> *2 pounds littleneck or cherrystone clams*
> *Sections of wild fennel stalk, or summits of dried stalk, or 1*
> *   teaspoon fennel seeds*
> *1/2 cup dry white wine*
> *4 tablespoons olive oil*
> *Salt*
> *1 pound fresh pasta, cut into noodles (page 309)*
> *3 tablespoons butter*
> *Persillade (2 chopped garlic cloves, chopped again with a*
> *   handful of chopped flat-leaf parsley)*
> *Pepper*

Put the clams, fennel, and white wine into a large pot with a tight-fitting lid, place over high heat, and shake the pot from time to time until all the clams are open—3 or 4 minutes. Empty the pot into a colander placed over a large bowl. Strain the cooking liquid through a cheesecloth-lined sieve into a small saucepan and reduce it over high heat by about half. Remove the clams from their shells and discard the shells.

Add a teaspoon of olive oil and a handful of coarse sea salt to a large pot of boiling water, add the noodles, stir with a wooden fork to make certain that none stick together, and boil for about 2 minutes, or until just done, adjusting the heat to prevent the water's boiling over.

While the noodles are cooking, heat 1 tablespoon butter and 2 tablespoons olive oil in a *poêlon* or heavy sauté pan, add the clams, and sauté briefly. Bring the reduced cooking liquid back to a boil, add it to the clams, and stir in the persillade. Drain the noodles, add them to the clams, and toss with a fork and a tablespoon. Remove from the heat, grind over pepper, add 2 tablespoons butter, cut into small pieces, and the remaining olive oil. Toss again and serve directly into heated soup plates.

RAVIOLI
Raviolis à la Daube

Serves 4

FORMULAS FOR RAVIOLI stuffing made from leftover daube usually include chard or spinach, bread, egg, and grated Parmesan, sometimes chopped raw ham or a lamb's brain. The meats are often pounded to a paste or the whole lot reduced to a purée in a processor. Lulu is categorical: the meats must be separated from their juices while still warm and chilled to firm them up before being chopped by hand, above all, not puréed. I asked if she ever added chard or grated cheese. She said, "Never!" My first notes resulted in two ingredients: leftover daube meat and parboiled salt bacon. We returned to ravioli stuffing a couple of months later. Lulu said, "I just chop the meat—that's all." I asked why she parboiled the bacon. She said, "But, I never add bacon to my stuffing! Of course, salt bacon is cooked in the daube—that must be what I meant." "And, do you ever add bread . . . or egg?" "Oh, of course, a pile of things like that." "How would you define 'a pile of things like that'?" "You're always backing me into a corner! Let's forget the 'pile of things'—I chop the meat and that's that. The rich liquid, with its scent of dried orange peel, does the rest."

The ravioli can be prepared an hour or two before cooking; they are easier to handle if slightly dried first on a floured cloth.

> *About 12 ounces daube meats (page 196), separated while*
> *still warm from their cooking juices and refrigerated,*
> *covered, overnight*
> *1 pound fresh pasta dough (page 309)*
> *About 2½ cups daube juices, heated*
> *Freshly grated Parmesan cheese*

Chop the meats fine enough so that, when gathered together, they form a coherent mass, about 1½ cups. Transfer to a bowl. If the mixture is too crumbly, stir in a tablespoon of the jellied cooking juices with a fork.

Divide the dough into two equal parts (or four, if space is limited). Roll each out to a rectangle ¹⁄₁₆ inch thick. On one sheet, place small teaspoon dabs of chopped meat at 2-inch intervals, beginning a good inch in from the sides. With a pastry brush, moisten bands of dough in both directions between the rows of stuffing. Place another sheet of dough on top and press firmly, with the side of your hand or with fingertips, to seal the two sheets of dough between the rows of stuffing. With a serrated pastry wheel, cut down the middle of the sealed bands to form squares, each enclosing a dab of stuffing. Transfer the ravioli, not touching, to trays lined with towels and sprinkled with flour.

Preheat the oven to 325°F.

Bring a large pot of salted water to a rolling boil. Cook the ravioli, about a dozen at a time, adjusting the heat each time the water returns to a boil to maintain a light boil, while moving the ravioli around gently with a wooden spoon to prevent their sticking together. Remove them after 5 minutes with a large, flat wire skimmer (spider), hold for a few seconds over the pot to drain, and slip them into a large heated gratin dish or other wide ovenproof serving dish. Pour over some simmering daube liquid and hold in the oven while finishing the other batches, adding each, in its turn, to the dish and moistening with more daube liquid. Serve directly, accompanied by a dish of freshly grated Parmesan.

CHEESES AND DESSERTS

It is said that a meal without cheese resembles a belle who is missing an eye. Here the belle has beautiful eyes! And she also has a voluptuous smile for in the wake of the cheeses will appear lovely sweet delicacies. . . .

On dit qu'un repas sans fromage ressemble à une "belle" à la quelle il manque un oeil. Ici la "belle" a de beaux yeax! Et elle a aussi un sourire gourmand car à la suite des fromages vous trouverez d'exquises friandises. . . .

Lulu

DESSERTS, at the Tempier table, are often composed of the cheese platter and a choice of seasonal fresh fruits. If apples or pears are among the fruits, they and the cheeses may be served at the same time. At other times, Lulu serves a salad with the cheeses, or the cheese platter is presented alone, followed by fruits or a sweet confection. She says, "You know, I am not really very 'dessert.'" Jean-Marie chooses a series of three or four vintages of Tempier red wine for the menu, the most venerable of which—fifteen or twenty years old—he decants at cellar temperature to accompany the cheeses. A choice of local fresh or semifresh goat cheeses, Comté or Beaufort (French Gruyères), Roquefort and Reblochon fermier are usually present, supplemented often by little disks of runny sheeps' milk

---

Opposite: Cheese platter.

cheese, Tomme de Savoie, Saint-Nectaire, or Vacherin. Strong, stinky cheeses are absent in deference to the wine.

In May, the table is furnished by the avenue of cherry trees that leads up to the house. In late spring and early summer, fresh fruit salads and strawberries are frequent desserts. None of Lulu's desserts are extraordinarily sweet. All can be perfectly accompanied by dessert wines; the Domaine's *vin cuit* is regularly uncorked for that purpose.

FRUIT MACÉDOINE
Salade de Fruits

Serves 8

IN LATE SPRING and early summer, a salad of local fruits is the dessert that most often appears at Lulu's table. She uses either white or yellow peaches—or both. If a peach resists being skinned, dunk it for a second into boiling water and drain immediately—the skin will slip off effortlessly. Lulu uses the orange-fleshed, smooth, green-skinned Charentais or Cavaillon melons. Muskmelon, muscatelle, or honeydew can be substituted. The strawberries are small, intensely flavored, and as red inside as out (a great glass bowl of strawberries is often served alone, with sugar and stiff cream to the side—many guests prefer to add them to their red wine).

Green almonds, which look exactly like green apricots, are picked just after the almond's structure has altered from a sticky jelly to firm, sweet, crunchy but tender white meat. The shells are only semiformed at this stage and can be cut through with a knife; the almonds' soft skins, which later turn to brown husks, are easily peeled off. There are many varieties of almonds. In the south of France, those that have white blossoms are eaten in the green stage because their shells are tender and easily cut into; pink-blossomed trees give hard-shelled almonds, even when green, which must be cracked open—the green almonds inside are just as good. If green almonds are not available, substitute shelled ripe almonds; to peel them, plunge them into boiling water for a few seconds, drain them, and rub them briskly between two towels.

1 pound peaches, skinned and sliced
1/2 pound apricots, pitted and sliced
1 pound small strawberries, rapidly rinsed and husked
*1 small melon, halved, seeded, cut into wedges, peeled, and
    cut into large dice*
*1 handful of green almonds, peeled, or ripe almonds, peeled
    and slivered (see above)*
1/2 cup sugar
1/2 cup kirsch

Toss the fruits and the almonds together in a large glass bowl, sprinkle over the sugar, and leave for an hour to permit the juices to be drawn out. Sprinkle over the kirsch, toss the fruits lightly together, cover with plastic wrap, and macerate, refrigerated, for 2 or 3 hours before serving.

319

BURST VANILLA APPLES
Pommes Eclatées à la Vanille

Serves 6

LULU CALLS THIS dish *pommes éclatées*—burst apples—because the apple quarters swell and begin to collapse, as if exploded by some inner force. For all of her apple desserts, she insists on russet (*reinette*) apples. They are sweet, spicy, not especially crisp, and only moderately acidic; they do not fall apart in cooking. They are common on the French market and uncommon in America. The backyard Jonathans, with which I grew up, would certainly be an honorable substitute—or look for greenings, pippins, or Granny Smiths. With few exceptions, apples known in America as "eating apples" are better for cooking than those known as "cooking apples."

> *4 apples, quartered, cored, and peeled*
> *1 2-inch length vanilla pod, split in two*
> *¼ cup sugar*
> *2 tablespoons water*
> *3 tablespoons dark rum*

Put the apple quarters in a saucepan or sauté pan of a size to just hold them in a single layer, tuck in the vanilla sections, sprinkle over sugar, and pour over the water and the rum. Cook, covered, over low heat, shaking the pan gently from time to time, for about 20 minutes, or until the quarters are soft and on the verge of collapse. Transfer the quarters to a glass serving dish, pour over their juices (the vanilla pod can be dried and reused), and serve tepid.

CARAMELIZED APPLES
Gâteau de Pommes Caramelisé

Serves 8

THE IDEAL MOLD for this "cake" is a *moule à tarte tatin,* heavy tinned copper, 10 to 11 inches in diameter, 2 inches high, with slightly slanting sides. Lacking that, use a round cake tin, a skillet, or any round, preferably slant-sided oven dish that corresponds approximately to these dimensions.

> *4 tablespoons butter, softened at room temperature*
> *1 cup sugar*
> *4 pounds apples, quartered, cored, and peeled*
> *1 teaspoon ground cinnamon*
> *2 tablespoons cold butter*

Preheat the oven to 350°F.

Smear the softened butter thickly on the bottom and the sides of the mold, sprinkle ¾ cup sugar evenly over the bottom, place the mold over very low heat, and as the sugar melts, move it around over the heat, rotating the mold slowly, until the syrup is a golden caramel color. Don't let it brown. Remove from the heat.

Place a tight layer of apple quarters in the bottom of the mold, rounded sides down, to create an attractive design, pack in the rest of the apples, sprinkling layers with cinnamon and slicing some of the quarters, if necessary, to pack tightly. Sprinkle the surface with the remaining sugar, scatter over shavings of cold butter, and bake for 45 minutes to 1 hour, or until the apples are meltingly tender when pierced with a skewer and the surface is lightly caramelized. Leave to settle for 30 minutes before unmolding onto a serving plate. Serve tepid or at room temperature.

CRÊPES WITH APPLES
Crêpes aux Pommes

Serves 6 to 8

FOR THESE CRÊPES, a small crêpe pan (5-inch bottom diameter, 6½-inch rim diameter) is best. A small ¼-cup ladle, half-filled, is practical for spreading the batter in the pan. The stuffed crêpes can be prepared 2 or 3 hours in advance, arranged in the buttered gratin dish, and kept, covered with plastic wrap, to be finished in the oven at the last minute. They are especially good when accompanied by a dessert wine—*vin cuit,* Sauternes, late-harvest Jurançon, Vouvray, or Gewurztraminer, etc.

CRÊPES
⅓ cup flour
Small pinch of salt
2 eggs
About 1 cup milk
2 tablespoons Calvados (or marc *or other brandy)*
4 tablespoons butter, melted in the crêpe pan

8 tablespoons butter
2 pounds apples, quartered, cored, peeled, and thinly sliced
Grated zest of 1 lemon
Sugar

Sift the flour and salt into a mixing bowl, add the eggs, and whisk, working from the center out and adding a little milk, until smooth. Whisk in about half the milk, add the Calvados and melted butter, and with the whisk, stir in enough additional milk to bring the batter to a thin, creamy consistency. Cover with a plate and leave to rest for 30 minutes or so.

Put the ladle in the bowl of batter. Have in readiness a small spatula with an elongated blade or a round-tipped table knife for turning the crêpes and a plate on which to stack them. With a cloth or paper towel, wipe the crêpe pan, leaving only a film of butter. Heat the pan over medium to medium-low heat (you may have to adjust the heat up or down several times while preparing the crêpes— if the pan is insufficiently heated, the first crêpe will be less successful than those to follow). Stir the batter with the ladle, lift the pan off the heat and rotate it while pouring batter from the ladle (it should sizzle on contact), until the bottom and the lower edges of the pan's sides are thinly and evenly coated. Return the pan to the heat until the surface of the batter is dry and the edges of the crêpe turn golden and curl free from the sides of the pan. Gently slip the spatula or knife blade beneath the crêpe and flip it over. The other side requires only a few seconds. Lift the pan off the heat and, pulling gently with fingertips, slip the crêpe from the pan onto the plate. The pan will now be hot enough to receive more batter without being reheated. It should not be rebuttered between crêpes. The batter should be given a brief stir with the ladle each time before pouring. Stack the crêpes, one on top of the other, as they are ready. If preparing them several hours in advance of stuffing them, cover the stack with plastic wrap until ready for use (but don't refrigerate them unless you are prepared to reheat the stack in a slow oven— their butter content makes them stick together when chilled).

In a large heavy frying pan, melt 6 tablespoons butter. Add the apples and the grated lemon zest and sauté over high heat, jerking the pan back and forth and tossing the apples repeatedly in the air (stirring causes them to break up), until they are caramelized and nearly tender, without being mushy (the extent to which they will hold their shape depends on the variety of apple).

Preheat the oven to 450°F.

Butter a large gratin dish. Hold a crêpe, golden brown side (the first side cooked) down on the palm of your hand, spread a heaped tablespoon of sautéed apples down the middle, roll up the crêpe, and place it, seam side down, in the gratin dish. Arrange the stuffed crêpes snugly, touching each other, sprinkle the surfaces lightly with sugar, place a thin strip of butter on each crêpe, and put them into the oven for 10 minutes, or until the sugar is glazed.

BAKED APPLES
Pommes au Four

Serves 6

"I LIFT OUT a carrot from the heart of each apple, but I don't peel them," says Lulu.

¹/₂ cup sugar
8 tablespoons (1 slice) butter, softened at room temperature
6 apples, cored (with an apple corer), but not peeled
3 tablespoons dark rum
Water

Preheat the oven to 350°F.

Mash the sugar and butter together to form a paste and stuff equal parts into the hollows of the apples. Arrange them, standing on end, in a baking dish large enough to just hold them. Dribble ¹/₂ tablespoon rum into the cavity of each apple and over the surface of each, pour water into the bottom of the dish to a depth of about ¹/₈ inch, and bake, basting regularly with a bulb baster after 20 minutes, for about 45 minutes, or until golden. If the syrup in the bottom of the pan threatens to dry up, pour in a little boiling water. Serve tepid with a spoonful of syrup poured over each apple.

APPLE TART
Tarte aux Pommes

Serves 6

ONE DOES NOT want sides to a pastry whose filling is not going to run away; a flat, free-form pastry is practical and permits the most attractive presentation for this and many another rustic tart.

> *1 recipe short crust pastry (see Pissaladière, page 87)*
> *4 apples*
> *2 tablespoons melted butter*
> *1/4 cup sugar*
> *4 tablespoons red currant jelly*

Preheat the oven to 375°F.

On a floured surface, roll out the pastry to an approximate circle and transfer it to a flat baking sheet. Roll up the edges to form a rim and crimp all around, either with the side of your thumb, repeatedly dipped in flour, or with the floured tines of a fork. Prick the pastry's surface at regular intervals with the tines of a fork. Refrigerate while preparing the apples.

Split 3 apples in two from top to bottom, cut out a boat shape from each to remove the core, peel the halves, and slice each, top to bottom, into 1/8-inch thicknesses. Press overlapping slices in a circle against the inside of the pastry rim, then form diminishing, overlapping circles of overlapping slices until the pastry surface is completely covered. If there are not enough slices, split, core, peel, and slice the other apple. With a pastry brush, paint the surface of the apples with melted butter, sprinkle evenly with sugar, and bake for 40 minutes, or until the apples' surface is caramelized and the rims of the crust are golden and crisp. Slide the tart onto a serving platter.

Put the currant jelly in a small bowl and immerse it in hot water until the jelly is melted. With a pastry brush, paint the surface of the apples with the melted jelly. Serve freshly baked, preferably still warm.

APPLE FRITTERS
Beignets de Pommes

Serves 8

LULU SPRINKLES halved apricots with a few drops of kirsch instead of Calvados and prepares them in the same way.

> *2 pounds apples*
> *Sugar*
> *Calvados or other brandy*
> *Oil (olive or vegetable) for frying*
> *1 recipe Fritter Batter (page 105), made with ¼ cup extra*
>   *flour*
> *Confectioners' sugar*

Core the apples with an apple corer. Peel them and cut them into ½-inch-thick rings. Spread the rings out on a tray and sprinkle both sides very lightly with sugar and a few drops of Calvados. Leave to macerate for 1 hour.

Preheat the oven to 300°F and turn it off.

Lay the apple slices on paper towels and place paper towels on top. Before incorporating the beaten egg white into the fritter batter, stir in the sugar and Calvados juices.

Line an oven tray with paper towels. Heat the oil to 375°F, or until a drop of batter sizzles on contact.

Fry the apple slices, a few at a time, first dipping them in batter and transferring each, with a skewer passed through the core hole, from the bowl, held over the oil. Count 4 or 5 minutes, or until golden on both sides, flipping the slices over with the tines of a fork after about 3 minutes. With a spider or a slotted spoon, remove the fritters to the towel-lined tray and hold in the oven while finishing the other batches, adding more paper towels as necessary. Line a platter with a napkin, arrange the fritters on top, sprinkle with confectioners' sugar, and serve hot.

APRICOT PUDDING
Clafoutis aux Abricots

Serves 6

2 tablespoons butter
1 pound apricots, halved and pitted
2 ounces green or ripe almonds, skinned (see Fruit
    Macédoine, page 318)
²/₃ cup sugar
Pinch of salt
3 eggs
¹/₂ cup flour
1¹/₄ cups milk

Preheat the oven to 375°F.

Butter a large shallow oven dish of a size to just hold the apricot halves. Arrange closely, cut surfaces down, in a single layer. Fill spaces with the almonds. In a mixing bowl, whisk together ¹/₂ cup of sugar, the salt, and the eggs. Sift in the flour, whisking at the same time, then whisk in the milk and pour the mixture over the apricots. Sprinkle the remaining sugar over the surface, scatter over shavings of butter, and bake for about 40 minutes, or until a golden crust has formed. Serve tepid.

APRICOT TART
Tarte aux Abricots

Serves 6

BAD APRICOTS are mealy and flat-tasting. Good apricots are quite acidic and require more sugar than most fruits.

> *1 ½ pounds ripe, firm apricots, split and pitted*
> *¾ cup sugar*
> *Handful of peeled green almonds, or peeled, slivered, ripe*
>   *almonds (see Fruit Macédoine, page 318)*
> *1 recipe short crust pastry (see Pissaladière, page 87)*
> *Heavy cream (optional)*

Spread the split apricots on a platter, cut sides up, scatter over the sugar, and leave for 1 hour, or until the sugar has dissolved and drawn a quantity of liquid from the apricots. Transfer to a saucepan or sauté pan and place over low heat, covered, until boiling. Uncover and adjust the heat to maintain a very light boil, stirring gently from time to time, until all loose liquid has disappeared (the time is a function of the reducing surface—the consistency should be that of a loose jam, without the apricots having been reduced to a purée). Cool and stir in the almonds.

Preheat the oven to 375°F.

Prepare a free-form pastry base, as in the Apple Tart (page 325). Spread the apricot and almond mixture over the pastry and bake for 40 minutes, or until the pastry border is golden and crisp and the apricot surface firm and lightly bronzed. Serve tepid with or without heavy cream on the side.

APRICOT COMPOTE WITH VANILLA
Compote d'Abricots à la Vanille

Serves 8

FRUIT COMPOTES nearly always call for a sugar syrup in which to poach the fruits. Lulu simplifies the procedure in the interest of concentrating the fruit's essence. If your apricots lack tang, the juice of half a lemon added at the same time as the sugar will give them a lift.

2 pounds firm, ripe apricots, halved and pitted
1 2-inch length of vanilla pod, split in two lengthwise
3/4 cup sugar

Put the apricots and the vanilla in a mixing bowl, sprinkle over the sugar, and leave to macerate for 1 hour, or until the sugar has melted and drawn juices from the fruit. Empty into a heavy saucepan and place over low heat, covered, for about 15 minutes, or until the apricots are immersed in a simmering syrup. Transfer to a glass compote serving dish, cool to room temperature, remove the vanilla pod, cover, and refrigerate for a couple of hours until chilled.

PEARS IN RED WINE
Poires au Vin Rouge

Serves 6

LULU PREPARES these pears in a deep pot of a size to just contain them, stems uppermost. She uses the same dark, tannic young *vin de presse* that is the base of her black game sauces, and a lot is necessary to cover the pears standing on end. You can economize, to a certain extent, on the wine by laying the pears, carefully fitted together, on their sides in a wide saucepan before pouring over the wine. Cooking times depend partly on the pears, partly on personal taste. Lulu likes the pears only just done; with longer cooking, however, they will hold their shape, for the acid and the tannin of the red wine keep them firm, and the flavor of the wine will penetrate more deeply.

> 6 firm, not quite ripe eating pears, peeled, stems left intact
> 1 2-inch section cinnamon stick
> 3/4 cup sugar
> About 4 cups (to cover) deeply colored, tannic, young red
>   wine

Arrange the pears in a pot or saucepan of a size to just contain them (see above), tuck in the cinnamon, sprinkle over the sugar, pour over red wine to cover, bring to a boil, and adjust the heat to a simmer, lid ajar. Cook for about 20 minutes, or until a skewer encounters little resistance when pierced to the heart of a pear. With a slotted spoon, remove the pears from their liquid and stand them upright, stems in the air, in a glass compote dish. At a light boil, reduce the red wine by from two thirds to three quarters—to the consistency of a light syrup—and pour it over the pears. Serve tepid or cool to room temperature, cover loosely with plastic wrap or foil, refrigerate, and serve chilled.

Sweet Squash Tart
Tarte à la Courge

Serves 6

4 tablespoons butter
1 large sweet onion, finely sliced
2 pounds pumpkin, Hubbard, or other orange or red-fleshed
squash, peeled, seeded, and diced
Salt
1 recipe short crust pastry (see Pissaladière, page 87)
½ cup sugar (or more to taste)
4 eggs
2 cups heavy cream
Freshly grated nutmeg, freshly ground allspice, cinnamon

Warm the butter in a large *poêlon* or heavy sauté pan. Add the onion and sweat over low heat, stirring occasionally with a wooden spoon, until the onion is melting but uncolored. Add the squash and salt, continue to cook over low heat, stirring regularly, until it has disintegrated into a coarse purée, about 40 minutes. Leave to partially cool.

Preheat the oven to 350°F.

Roll out the pastry and line a large pie tin or tart mold. In a mixing bowl, whisk together the sugar and the eggs until the eggs lighten in color. Add the cream and spices, whisk, then stir in the squash. Pour into the pastry and bake for 40 minutes. Serve warm or at room temperature.

DEEP-FRIED PASTRIES
Merveilles

Serves 6

THESE DEEP-FRIED pastries are often named *oreillettes*. In Arles, they are *bugnes,* and in Nice, *ganses.* "In Marseilles," says Lulu, "when I was little, we called them *merveilles.* We lived in a big apartment building and each year, on Mardi Gras, my mother would prepare piles of lacy-edged *merveilles,* cut with a ravioli cutter (serrated pastry wheel) into different shapes—plain ribbons, longer ribbons tied in loose knots, wider ribbons with an inside cut down the middle of each, rectangles and ovals with several parallel cuts inside the borders, and, of course, the scraps (in Florence, they are called *cenci*—rags). She would line a huge basket with a white napkin, heap it high with *merveilles,* and we would go together from floor to floor and from door to door, offering *merveilles* to everyone who lived there."

Lulu fries her *merveilles* in olive oil. To prepare vanilla confectioners' sugar, cut a vanilla pod into short lengths, mix with a pound of confectioners' sugar, and store in a glass preserving jar for a couple of weeks—or as much longer as you like.

2¹/₂ cups flour
Pinch of salt
2 tablespoons sugar
Pinch of ground cinnamon
Freshly grated nutmeg
1 teaspoon each grated orange and lemon zest
2 eggs
2 tablespoons butter, softened
Olive oil or vegetable oil for frying
Vanilla confectioners' sugar

Put 1 1/2 cups flour, the salt, sugar, and spices in a mixing bowl. Stir with a fork, leaving a well in the center. Add the grated orange and lemon zest, eggs, and butter to the well and stir with the fork, working outward from the center, mashing and stirring, until all the flour is absorbed. Continue working and sprinkle lightly with flour until you have a supple, cohesive dough. Clean off the fork and knead the dough with your knuckles, folding it repeatedly and sprinkling with more flour, if necessary, until it is silken and resilient. Form the dough into a ball, cover with a folded towel, and leave to rest for at least 1 hour.

Line trays with kitchen towels and sprinkle lightly with flour. Cut the ball of dough in two. On a floured work surface, coat half the dough well with flour and roll out until thin (1/16 inch). With a serrated pastry wheel, cut it into shapes dictated by your fantasy (simple ribbons, 3/4 x 6 inches; ribbons to be knotted, 3/4 x 8 inches; wider strips, slit through the center, 1 inch x 6 inches; rectangles or ovals, 2 1/2 x 3 1/2 inches). Transfer them, not touching, to the lined tray. Repeat with the other half of the dough.

Heat the oven and turn it off. Heat the oil to 375°F, or until a fragment of dough sizzles on contact.

Fry the *merveilles*, without crowding, in several relays, for about 1 minute on each side, flicking them over in the oil with the tines of a fork when the undersides are golden. Remove with a wire skimmer or a slotted spoon to paper towels, transfer to a napkin-lined platter, and hold in the warm oven until all are finished. Sprinkle generously (from a shaker or through a sieve) with vanilla confectioners' sugar and serve hot.

FLOATING ISLAND
Ile Flottante or *Oeufs à la Neige*

Serves 8

"THIS IS LUCIEN'S favorite dessert because it reminds him of his grandmother's desserts." I was surprised that Lulu adds no sugar to the beaten egg whites but, she says, "That would be too much—the crème anglaise and the caramel are both sweet. It's too complicated to make the crème anglaise from the same milk used for poaching the egg whites—I like to make the crème first and then poach the egg whites. I discard the poaching liquid."

> *2 quarts milk*
> *¹/₂ vanilla pod, split*
> *1¹/₂ cups sugar*
> *8 egg yolks*
> *Small pinch of salt*
> *4 egg whites*
>
> CARAMEL
> *2 tablespoons water*
> *1 cup sugar*

In a saucepan, bring 1 quart of milk and the vanilla slowly to a boil. Remove from the heat and leave for 5 minutes to infuse.

In a bowl, whisk 1 cup of sugar with the egg yolks until the mixture lightens in color. Remove the vanilla from the saucepan and slowly pour the milk over the egg yolks and sugar, whisking at the same time. Pour the mixture into the saucepan, place over low to medium-low heat, and stir constantly with a wooden spoon until the custard thickens enough to coat the spoon. It should not approach a boil. To prevent a skin from forming on the surface of the sauce, partially immerse the saucepan in a basin of ice water and continue to stir until cool.

Line a tray with a damp cloth. Add the salt to the egg whites and whisk them until they form stiff peaks. In a saucepan or other shallow pan, bring ½ cup of sugar and 1 quart of milk to a boil and regulate the heat to maintain a bare simmer. Poach heaped tablespoons of beaten egg white in the milk, three or four at a time, turning them over with a slotted spoon after a couple of minutes. Remove them a couple of minutes later with the slotted spoon and drain on the damp cloth.

Divide the custard sauce among 8 individual serving dishes—deep saucers or shallow coupes. Float one or two "clouds of snow" in each.

For the caramel, put the water in a saucepan, pour in the sugar, and melt over low heat, rotating the pan slowly and moving it around over the heat until the sugar syrup turns a rich amber color—not too dark. Pour it immediately, in a trickle, back and forth over the surfaces of the poached egg whites. Serve chilled.

WALNUT GÂTEAU
Gâteau aux Noix

Serves 8 to 10

DICTIONARIES TRANSLATE *gâteau* as "cake." This is not a cake. Lulu says, "Well, it is really a *galette* of sorts . . ." The dictionaries give excessively vague and various definitions for *galette*. In fact, a *galette* is something round, usually thin and compact, and usually, but not necessarily, baked. This walnut *gâteau* is, in any case, unleavened, dense, moist, and delicious. Lulu likes it thin and, for that reason, uses two round 10-inch cake tins; a single 12-inch diameter tin will do as well. Tempier *vin cuit* usually accompanies it, but a Sauternes or a late-harvest Gewürztraminer will also serve well.

(continued)

8 tablespoons (1 stick) butter, softened at room temperature
    (plus butter for the pan or pans)
1 1/2 cups sugar
Pinch of salt
5 eggs, at room temperature
1/2 pound shelled walnuts, pulverized in a blender (a handful
    at a time) or in a food processor
1/4 cup peeled and finely grated carrot
2/3 cup flour

Preheat the oven to 325°F.

Put the butter in a mixing bowl, add the sugar and salt, and work to a creamy consistency with a wooden spoon (or a rubber spatula). Beat in the eggs, one at a time, stir in the pulverized walnuts and the grated carrot, then gradually sift in the flour, stirring briskly, then beating.

Butter two shallow, round 10-inch diameter cake tins. Butter two circles of parchment paper cut to the size of the tins and press the unbuttered sides to the bottoms of the tins. Pour in the batter and bake for 40 minutes, or until a skewer, pierced at the center of each *gâteau*, comes out clean and dry. Cool in the tins, loosen the *gâteaux* from the sides of the tins with a knife tip, unmold onto plates, and peel off the rounds of parchment paper. Serve tepid or at room temperature.

The dining room at the domaine.

OMAINE TEMPIER
BAN
TION BAND L CONTROL
FRANC
AMIS DE CURNONSKY
MENU
BANDOL

WINE-TASTING NOTES

WORDS CANNOT TOUCH the magic of a wine—its aura, which, like music, can spark strong emotions or draw a tear for the ethereal beauty of the thing. To me, tasting notes minimize a wine's identity. A note for a red Domaine Tempier, read out of context, could as easily apply to a Châteauneuf du Pape, an Hermitage, or a Pomerol of a similar age, all wines with distinct and separate personalities. A wine-tasting note is a personal reaction to a given moment in the constantly evolving career of a wine, which, in the case of a red Domaine Tempier, can easily span thirty years and more, during which time the same bottle never quite presents the same characteristics and, at intervals of several years between tastings, often reveals complexities of scent and flavor that an experienced taster could never have divined to be implicit in the younger wine. It is for good reason that the life of a wine has often been compared to that of a human being, not only in the expected progression from coquettish childhood innocence through exuberant youth to the measured balance of maturity, the serenity of age, and the senility of very old age, but in the surprising turns of unpromising children who blossom into long-lived, gentle philosophers or of a brilliant and boisterous child who discovers, in adulthood, the virtues of discretion.

Nineteen sixty-eight was a difficult year. The rains came early,

Opposite: Old bottles in the tasting room.

gray rot set in, and the grapes had to be picked selectively, to retain only those that were healthy. The young wine was relatively light-bodied and, by comparison to the deep purple of most young Tempiers, light in color. The level of alcohol, 12.8 degrees, although very respectable, was lower than the normal 13 to 13.5 degrees. The wine was clean but discreet; it didn't leap out of the glass to attack the taster. Nineteen sixty-eight was the first year that Lucien separated out a *cuvée speciale* from the *cuvée classique*. I could never tell the difference, but I liked the wine for its delicacy. For years Jean-Marie railed against the "thin little '68" until, one day around 1980, he realized that the object of his ire was filling out, the color was limpid and luminous, the bouquet subtle and many-faceted. Today, the 1968 is a model of sustained, quiet elegance, an intricate, antique lacework with every thread intact. Nineteen seventy-one was a difficult year because the grapes were so concentrated, the sugar readings so high that the fermentations were interminable. The *cuvée speciale* contains 14.3 degrees alcohol and Lucien kept it in the wood for five years before bottling it. It has always been a great showpiece but, to me, it seemed to have too much of everything. Tasted in October 1993, the monster had finally become civilized, the color was still deep but warm, the rich fruit was still present but less violent, punctuated with autumnal scents and flavors, the tannin was discreet and the alcohol unobtrusive, a composition in perfect balance. I didn't recognize it.

I haven't tasted vintages from the 1950s recently—there are none left. The 1960s are rare but all in fine shape. The only 1970s vintage absent from my cellar is 1976; I have no memory of it, but the others need inspire no inquietude. The two great classics, 1970 and 1975, have each reached a plateau of perfection from which they have hardly budged for a decade; '72, '74, '77, and '78 are vigorous and still young; '73 is light and intricate, not unlike the 1968; 1979 was the first year that the single vineyard wines, La Migoua and La

Tourtine, were bottled separately—they are beautiful now but, for those who are patient, they certainly have surprises in store. Cabassaou, from the fifty-year-old, 100 percent Mourvèdre vines on the Tourtine hillside, was first bottled separately in 1987. Lucien had always believed that the intensity of the Mourvèdre grape needed to be tamed by the presence of some Cinsault and Grenache but, after seven vintages, with 1993 the most astonishing of all, everyone is very excited by Cabassaou. Year after year, when the young wines are tasted from the wood, La Migoua is the most forward of the single vineyard *cuvées,* with the most intense wild berry fruit; La Tourtine is more reserved, but more elegant; Cabassaou is a distillation of La Tourtine. The 1980s were blessed with concentrated vintages, in particular '82, '85, '88, and '89. Nineteen hundred eighty-seven stands apart, dominated by the aromas of older wines, game, humus, wild mushrooms, and black truffle. Nineteen ninety is black purple, thick and chewy. Nineteen ninety-one is lighter and already more evolved than the three preceding vintages.

Many people look to tasting notes to tell them when a wine is ready to drink, and wine reviews willingly oblige ("drink up," "drink between 1996 and 2003," etc.). A Tempier rosé is meant to be drunk young, when its fruit is freshest, preferably during the year following its bottling. As far as Domaine Tempier red is concerned, the answer is: it is always ready to drink—and always different, depending on its stage of evolution; drunk young, its fresh fruit will seduce you; if you forget it in a good cellar for twenty years, no harm will come to it and it may take your breath away. Lucien, Jean-Marie, and François agree, in principle, that one should drink the *cuvée classique* in its youth while the *cuvée speciale* and the single vineyard bottlings sort out their complexities in the cellar. This does not mean that the *cuvée classique* will age less well than the others; the sumptuous 1962, '64 and '66 are, after all, *cuvées classiques* and I have often mistaken a 1975 *cuvée classique* for a *cuvée speciale.* Jean-Marie, in the grip of enthusiasm, does not hesitate to bend a principle; I have known him to arrive triumphantly at table with a carafe of cool, year-old Migoua, drawn from the tun, to be drunk with Lulu's octopus and aïoli.

Lucien cleaning a vat, 1967.

Jean-Marie cleaning a vat, 1992.

Sunset in the vineyard.

INDEX

Note: Page numbers in italics refer to photographs.

Lucien raises his glass to the magic of wine and the joy of living, 1968.

The text face is Sabon, designed by Jan Tschichold and first issued in metal by the Stempel Typefoundry, Frankfurt-am-Main in 1964. The headings are set in Charlemagne, designed by Carol Twombly at Adobe Systems Inc. in 1989. The photographs are by Gail Skoff, who also researched and reprinted the photographs from the Peyraud family album. The illustrations, with a few exceptions, are the work of V. Le Campion from *Le Trésor de la Cuisine du Bassin Mediterranéen*, Paris, 1930. The book design is by Patricia Curtan, typeset by the designer with the assistance of Burwell Davis, and printed and bound by the R. R. Donnelley Co.